THE LAST MISSION OF LADY JANE II

LISA A. VANS

THE LAST MISSION OF LADY JANE II

The Life and Death of an
8th Air Force B-17 and Her Crew

Library of Congress Control Number: 2022932872

Designed by Christopher Bower
Cover design by Ashley Millhouse
Type set in Abolition/Adobe Garamond Pro

ISBN: 978-0-7643-6536-2
Printed in India

Published by Schiffer Publishing, Ltd.
4880 Lower Valley Road
Atglen, PA 19310
Phone: (610) 593-1777; Fax: (610) 593-2002
Email: Info@schifferbooks.com
Web: www.schifferbooks.com

DEDICATION

Dedicated to the brave men of the US Army Air Forces.

CONTENTS

ACKNOWLEDGMENTS

Rarely, if ever, is a work penned by a single person; it takes teamwork to produce a volume of non-fiction—in this case, a small army. Several years ago a good friend of mine, Lorraine Williams, told me about the experiences of her dad during World War II. The more Lorraine told me about Rodney Alverson Williams, the more I wanted to learn about him. She gave me great insight into a haunted and quiet man; who, like so many of his generation, rose to accept the call of duty, but in later years would refuse to speak of the horrors he had endured. Without Lorraine's knowledge and encouragement, this book would never have happened.

I would also like to thank our terrific frontline copy editor Judy Burns Lange. She put my nose to the grindstone to make a readable copy of this work to send to our Schiffer editor Bob Biondi. Her expertise in English grammar made me realize how out of practice I had become. Thank you, Judy!

Sioux Center, Iowa, librarian and local historian Wilma Vande Berg put me in touch with the family of 2Lt. David E. Vermeer. The nephews of the *Lady Jane*'s pilot, Jeris Vermeer, Darrell Vermeer, and Dave Vermeer (named for his famous uncle), were all enormously helpful in providing insight into David's character. Apparently, 2Lt. Dave Vermeer never cursed, and the most awful thing this young man could admonish someone with was, "You sausage!" JJ Thompson, the *Lady Jane*'s co-pilot, said Dave was good-natured and was always smiling. Dave must have been a lot of fun to be around.

Also, I would like to thank Martha Stone, grandniece of the *Lady Jane*'s togglier, Ernest J. ("Jim") Butlin, for her generous contributions of photographs and information regarding the uncle she never knew. Additionally, the assistance of 2Lt. John J. Thompson's grandson, Tom Johnson, is greatly appreciated for his plethora of photos and information about his late granddad.

The children of the *Lady Jane*'s navigator, Gene Holley, were additionally helpful. His daughter, Sue Suarez, contributed photographs and information on her dad. His son, Craig Holley, videotaped an interview between Lorraine and his dad in 2013. This interview was extremely insightful and provided many more details about the fateful mission in March 1945.

Sadly, many of the families of the other *Lady Jane* crewmembers had little information about their fathers and uncles. This is presumably because those who survived, like Lorraine's dad, simply did not wish to speak about their experiences.

Other folks of tremendous help were Heinrich Priesterjahn, a native of Uelzen, Germany, who hails from the region where the *Lady Jane II* crashed, and Dr. Dieter Zube, also a native of Uelzen, now living in the United States. Both of these men have been of tremendous value in obtaining information on the circumstances of the crash and its tragic aftermath. Heinrich is the local historian in Uelzen and well acquainted with the *Lady Jane*'s story. Our emails back and forth were tested to the utmost limits of online translation software, as I speak no German and Heinrich knows no English.

Lastly, I wish to thank, from the bottom of my heart, our researcher Robert Jacobs, for his incalculable contributions to this project. Without Bob's help, this book would have been much more difficult. He began this project with initial attempts to find family members of the crew; I was able to locate more, but not all. I was not able to track down the families of Milan Basara, Hal Churchill, or Harold Babcock, despite exhaustive attempts. Hopefully, those families will find this book and get in touch. It was my honest and determined effort to present what little I knew of them to the best of my ability. Please accept my apologies if I related any incorrect information. It was the effort of this work to honor each and every member of this brave crew, leaving none behind.

Unfortunately, Bob, a Vietnam veteran, passed away in August 2017 and never saw this book go to a publisher. Wherever you are Bob, know that *we* did it, the entire group; the *Lady Jane*'s story is told and her crew is honored, something you dearly wanted.

In a word about sources, Gene Holley, JJ Thompson, and John Stiles all wrote down their stories in unpublished memoirs. I was fortunate to have access to these via Gene Holley. As the last surviving crewmember of the *Lady Jane II*, he has provided a wealth of information about the last mission of his aircraft. Thank you, Gene!

Lisa A. Vans

Carson City, Nevada

INTRODUCTION

On Sunday, March 18, 1945, a B-17 with nine souls aboard lifted off from her base in Deenethorpe, England, to bomb a railroad marshalling yard in Berlin. She would never return. She was one of more than 1,250 heavy bombers of the Mighty 8th Air Force sent to pummel Hitler's capital. Accompanying the bombers was an escort of fourteen fighter groups, some 700 long-range piston engine aircraft. This mission should have been a "milk-run"; the Luftwaffe was all but destroyed by this point of the Second World War due to the 8th Air Force's relentless strategic bombing campaign. But there was another element not anticipated by the mission planners.

The use of jet fighters by the Luftwaffe was well known by the Allies in March 1945, with the advanced aircraft having first taken to the air above Germany for defensive operations by mid-1944, but their numbers were always miniscule in comparison with the enormous bombing formations and their formidable fighter escorts employing the magnificent P-51 Mustang. The Allies also knew that the jets had limited air time due to the insufficient metallurgical technology of the day; several passes at a bombing formation were usually the extent of the threat. This day would see the largest deployment of fighter jets of the war. Of the thirty-six jets sent to confront the 8th Air Force, six would be equipped with new high-tech rockets designed to blow apart a heavy bomber with a single hit.

Also of great concern were the German anti-aircraft defenses. While early flak guns relied on the skill of their operators, before the end of hostilities, the guns were of greater caliber and guided by radar. They were more accurate than their predecessors and far more deadly. Hiding in heavy cloud cover was no longer possible.

The 8th Air Force would lose more than a dozen bombers on the March 18 mission, a tiny fraction of the total deployment, but in comparison to the horrific death tolls of bombing missions two years earlier, these were "acceptable" losses. The *Lady Jane II* counted among those losses. She was first struck by flak, missing the ball turret gunner by inches, but severely wounding a waist gunner. She was also hit by jets of *Jagdgeschwader* 7 (JG 7), who chased her out of Berlin after she dropped her payload.

JG 7 was the result of the very first jet fighter group in the Luftwaffe, *Kommando Nowotny*, formed in 1944 around its very young and charismatic commander. Walter Nowotny was twenty-three years old when he was forced into the ground by an American P-51 pilot in November 1944. His

Kommando was reformed into JG 7. This group's ninth squadron, *Staffel* 9./JG 7, was equipped with the new R4M rockets. Like the jets, these rockets were the height of German technology and were incredibly deadly. It was a day of historic firsts as the 8th Air Force roared above Berlin and rained ruin upon the shrinking Third Reich.

As the crewmen of the *Lady Jane II* bailed out safely, several of the boys were captured by furious Germans on the ground and brutally murdered. Justice would elude two of the executioners, but one killer would find himself before an American war crimes tribunal.

This is the true story of nine men, some just teenaged boys barely out of high school, who volunteered for some of the most dangerous duty of World War II. There were no foxholes to jump into; there were no trees to crouch behind while under fire. These unbelievably brave men would ascend, day after day, week after week, in a thin aluminum tube as easy targets for enemy guns. They needed to fly straight and steady, into the very teeth of hell. While the bombardier peered into his bombsight, the crew knew that accuracy was paramount. They had to go slow and steady over the target—waiting to be blown out of the sky at any moment. Waiting to die. Their chances of making their combat tour were poor indeed. But they did it anyway, mission after terrible mission. Many of those that survived witnessed their crewmates, their family, their brothers blown to shreds by flak bursts, blasted out of aircraft without parachutes, bloodied, bruised, hideously wounded, maimed, and killed. Yet they continued to climb into their bombers and complete their combat tours. They carried the terrible emotional and physical scars for the rest of their days; haunted with survivor's guilt; driven to alcoholism for some; post-traumatic stress in one form or another for most. Few escaped unscathed.

While the *Lady Jane II* was not remarkable in the whole of the 8th Air Force, she was but one tiny cog in the greatest of all war machines to ever exist; her devoted crew did their duty and sacrificed all to help end the nightmare that gripped the world. They brought great honor to themselves and their country, even though they made little attempt to bring attention to their efforts. If asked, they would say they were just doing their duty; nothing more, nothing less. They truly were the greatest of all generations.

Chapter 1

THE MIGHTY 8TH GOES TO WAR

Strategic air assault is wasted if it is dissipated piecemeal in sporadic attacks between which the enemy has an opportunity to readjust defenses or recuperate.

—Gen. Henry H. "Hap" Arnold

On February 20, 1942, only two and a half months after the Japanese attack on Pearl Harbor and the entrance of the United States into the Second World War, the commanding general of the United States Army Air Forces (USAAF), Lt. Gen. Henry H. ("Hap") Arnold, deployed an exploratory mission to England to work out the logistics for an air campaign to be stationed in western Europe, and to provide a location for the nexus of that mission. The vehicle for this endeavor was the United States Army 8th Air Force (AF), which had been born the previous month via an order signed by Hap Arnold; he would designate Maj. Gen. Carl A. ("Tooey") Spaatz (pronounced "spots"), a respected World War I pilot and tactician, as commander of the USAAF in Europe. Spaatz, in turn, would designate Ira Eaker as the head of Eighth Bomber Command (VIII BC).[1] Eaker included six of his staff officers in his February entourage, all of whom were tasked with facilitating the development of the US bombing campaign against Nazi-occupied Europe. The goal was to work with the British Royal Air Force (RAF) to provide a united front against Germany, using bomber and fighter operations to be deployed in daytime.

The previous December, several weeks after the US declaration of war on Japan, President Franklin D. Roosevelt had met in Washington, DC, with British prime minister Winston Churchill in the ARCADIA Conference. The conference settled on the doctrine of "Germany first"; the Allies would prioritize defeating Germany while arresting the Japanese advance in the Pacific. The decision to send American bombers to England was agreed upon during the conference. The initial understanding was that American bombers would work under the auspices of the RAF, but this would later change, as Hap Arnold wanted US operations to conduct the war independently of the RAF, while working in conjunction with them.

Since Germany's invasion of Poland on September 1, 1939, the War Plans Division of the US War Department, renamed the Operations

Division in March 1942, had been formulating five strategies, code-named Rainbow, for implementation upon US entry into the war. Rainbow No. 5 was concerned with an offensive in the European theater and a defensive operation in the Pacific. In the No. 5 directive, the strategy was explained: "The building up of large land and air forces for major offensive operations against Germany will be the primary immediate effort of the United States Army. Its initial tasks are limited to such operations as will not materially delay this effort."[2] This plan was finally fleshed out by the spring of 1941 and further revised in November to provide for reinforcements in China and the Pacific and to bolster the initial numbers for forces in Britain. It would quickly become superfluous as the needs in the European offensive outstripped its provisions.

Operation Bolero was the code name for the US military build-up in Europe. It mandated troops for all services to be deployed to the European Theater of Operations (ETO) for the planned invasion of the mainland in April 1943 (Operation Roundup), although this invasion didn't actually take place for another year. The Bolero numbers are interesting in that they set a figure for the manpower estimated for the early stages of the "Germany first" strategy. Hap Arnold recommended in the spring of 1942 that 240,000 air force personnel, 525,000 ground forces, and 235,000 supply corps personnel, a total of 1,000,000 men, would be needed for Bolero to accomplish the invasion in Roundup. For the USAAF, these numbers translated into twenty-one heavy-bomber groups, eight medium, and nine light-bomber groups; also included were seventeen fighter, eight transport, and six reconnaissance groups.[3] All of these units would need to be in theater, trained, and operational by April 1, 1943. This was an ambitious plan to say the least given that the USAAF had no aircraft in the UK in June 1942.

At the onset the 8th AF was posted at the headquarters of the RAF Bomber Command at High Wycombe in Buckinghamshire, and on February 22, the VIII BC came into being. The 8th AF would site its offices in Bushy Park at Teddington, which the Americans would code-name "WIDEWING." Later, in mid-April, the British Air Ministry would assign Eaker and his staff the Wycombe Abbey Girls School, some 30 miles west of London, code-named "PINETREE," as the headquarters for the VIII BC. The VIII Fighter Command (FC) would be headquartered at Bushey Hall, near London. Both the VIII BC and VIII FC were located adjacent to their RAF counterparts. Over the next three years, the "Mighty Eighth" would develop into a massive war machine, the likes of which had never been seen before, nor observed since. Through subsequent organizational, operational, and technological improvements, it would become increasingly lethal to the Nazi war of expansion.

Initially, Ira Eaker and his staff worked carefully with the RAF. The British had been at war with the Germans for more than two years and had a wealth of experience to share. They knew what worked and what did not. Eaker would base much of the 8th AF organization structure on the British model and take inspiration from the Sir Arthur ("Bomber") Harris, head of the RAF's Bomber Command. Eaker was actually returning to England on that February day in 1942. He and his old buddy Tooey Spaatz had previously spent time studying RAF operations during the Battle of Britain and were familiar with their concept of nighttime bombing. However, the US Air Corps was proposing to divert from this model and operate by day. The British were very skeptical of the idea and let Eaker and his staff know of their opinions. Both the RAF and the German Luftwaffe had discovered, the hard way, the limitations of daylight bombing. While accuracy might be improved, casualty ratings were higher for attacking forces in daylight bombing. As a result of prohibitive losses during daytime sorties, both antagonists performed most of their operations at night; however, wartime improvements in radar technology made even this option extremely hazardous. Eventually, to help limit risk to their bomber crews, the Germans would increase their unpiloted missions over England through the use of unmanned missiles fired from mainland European launch sites with their Vengeance rocket program.

The British and the Germans would sacrifice daytime accuracy for nighttime area bombing to reduce losses. However, area bombing is not strategic if the objective is to spread terror and not destroy military targets. The American model was to hit military targets to reduce Germany's ability to wage war; area bombing did not pursue this goal and was to be avoided.

• • •

The concept of strategic bombing was not new. It grew during the bloodletting of the First World War, when aerial warfare was in its infancy. Italian Colonel Giulio Douhet was court-martialed during the conflict for condemning his government's management of the war. While bored and unoccupied in a fortress prison cell, he was rather busy thinking about aerial warfare. It was within these stone walls that he polished his revolutionary concept of strategic bombing. Command of the air was imperative to ending the stalemate and carnage of the trenches. The Allies, he postulated, should focus air power on destroying the "vital centers" of the Central Powers. This would include not only obliterating physical targets but destroying the people's desire to resist, even if it meant killing civilians, traditionally considered to be non-combatants. In 1921, Douhet would publish his philosophies in *Il Domino dell Aria*.[4]

During the First World War, the United States did not have aircraft types that could perform in a strategic bombardment capacity; any bombing missions were conducted with borrowed European models such as the Italian Caproni bomber, the British Airco, or the French Voison, among others. The first American bomber, the Martin MB-1, would not come into production until nearly the end of hostilities, and only a handful would be built.[5]

In the interwar years, a voice would call out, sometimes boisterously, to implement his vision of strategic bombing theory. William (Billy) Mitchell was an aviator during the Great War who was promoted to Aviation Officer of the American Expeditionary Force (AEF) by Maj. Gen. John J. Pershing in 1917. For several months before Pershing's arrival in Europe in June 1917, Billy Mitchell had studied aerial warfare as a guest of British aerial tactician Maj. Gen. Hugh Trenchard, commander of the Royal Flying Corps (RFC) in France. Trenchard, a strong proponent of strategic bombing theory, believed that the stalemate on the Western Front could be broken with air power. Mitchell gained deep insight in his meetings with him. The limiting factor for the RFC was the same issue hindering the American's: lack of aircraft capable of carrying out meaningful raids deep into enemy territory. Mitchell also spent time with French aviators in Paris and Italy; two of his contacts were Giulio Douhet and Italian aircraft developer Gianni Caproni. The latter was one of Douhet's staunchest cheerleaders and traveled to Paris in 1917 to advocate on Douhet's behalf while his friend languished in prison. Strategic bombing was not, at this point, gaining any fans with the Western allies.

Mitchell pressured Washington in numerous missives to increase support and funding for an AEF air force program using available French aircraft designs until US factories could produce reliable American models. Many of his requests were ignored, primarily because he was not considered an expert in this fledgling field. The US War Department planners were far more interested in using aircraft not for defensive or offensive deployments, but for reconnaissance and artillery spotting.[6]

In late spring 1917, Pershing proposed creating the Air Service of the AEF, separating the Air Corps from its previous attachment to the Signal Corps; however, the action was not finalized until the following year by President Woodrow Wilson. This was the first in many steps to create a wholly independent US Air Force, something that would not occur for another thirty years under President Harry S. Truman. This topic would consume much of Billy Mitchell's professional career and later personal efforts as he pushed for an independent Air Force. But during the Great War, Mitchell was concerned with strategic air power.

In June 1917, around the same time that Pershing arrived in France, a commission of aviators and engineers, led by Maj. Raynal Bolling, landed in France to investigate aeronautical theory and practice undertaken by the Allied powers. The Bolling Mission was pressed by the British Air Board not to focus on the creation of an equal deployment of reconnaissance, pursuit (fighter), and bombing missions, but instead to focus on bombers. Bolling's commission was convinced by the idea after seeing Caproni bombers in action in Italy. Upon his return to the United States, Bolling urged the Aircraft Production Board to prioritize bombers. But the infrastructure to accomplish this simply didn't exist, and the United States would need to purchase the European models. Hence, the United States would end the Great War with no effective bombing mission.

In the postwar 1920s, Billy Mitchell did not temper his tone on aerial power; if anything, he grew louder. He prophetically believed that air supremacy needed to take on a role equal to that of the Army and Navy. If the Great War had not ended when it did, he believed the United States would have adopted a greater aeronautics program. Mitchell continued to serve the nation following the Armistice, first as the director of military aeronautics, then as the third assistant executive and chief of the Training and Operations Group. These positions allowed him to maintain his stance and to push his theories on defensive and offensive aerial operations.

In July 1921, Mitchell published *Our Air Force: The Keystone of National Defense*. In this work he outlined what he felt was strategic bombing at its most basic tenet: "It may be at times the best strategy to damage and destroy property, and to kill and disable an enemy's forces and resources at points far removed from the field of battle of either armies or navies. The forces that are attacked may be composed largely of women and children and other members of the nation's industrial and economic armies not capable of bearing arms, but extremely important as manufacturers of ammunition, and many other necessities that are equally important as carrying rifles in the trenches."[7] In other words, everything and everyone was a fair target. He insisted that all countries participating in aggression should expect that "the entire nation is or may be considered a combatant force." He further stated that it was unconscionable "for a nation not to prepare for the destruction of enemy combatants and property of all classes." Everything was a target within the enemy's borders. Those targets should not be affected by the "swaying of the battle lines." The air force that conducted the war in this fashion should be fully independent of the army. This philosophy required a much-larger standing army than existed following the drastic military drawdown at the end of the Great War.

Even after the First World War, there was skepticism that bombing from aircraft could be achieved with any accuracy. Mitchell needed a demonstration to forward his message, and a defunct battleship was a ready sacrifice. On July 21, 1921, he presented a powerful validation of his ideas when his pilots destroyed the captured German battleship *Ostfriesland* while using Martin bombers. Following the demonstration, the board evaluating the tests suggested that aircraft carriers be added to the Navy's arsenal. This success prompted Mitchell to issue a treatise titled "Notes on the Multi-Motored Bombardment Group" in 1923.[8] This manual was not published and was specifically geared toward pilots; it was a "how to" manual on aerial offense. He advocated the use of pursuit (fighter) aircraft to support bombing missions. This lesson would be learned the hard way, and with tragic consequences, in the world war to come. Mitchell reiterated his message that bombing the opposition included destroying targets that Douhet had referred to as "vital centers." Mitchell also proposed the use of defensive flying formations within bomb groups so that "converging fire" would provide mutual defense to each aircraft in the formation. Years later this philosophy would be further developed to protect American bomber formations over German-occupied Europe.

As early as the mid-1920s, Mitchell saw conflict brewing in both the Pacific—with the Japanese—and in Europe; he pushed hard for new legislation and was frustrated by the refusal of the War Department to take him seriously. So he circumvented them and presented his case directly to President Calvin Coolidge. As a result, Mitchell was court-martialed for insubordination and forced to resign his commission as brigadier general. He died in 1936, before his visions would be realized in the Second World War. Billy Mitchell was prophetic and certainly brilliant, but he was a man far ahead of his time and lacked the footing he needed to implement his ideas. His theory on heavily bombing civilian areas was dismissed early in the air campaign in World War II, but this tactic was taken up during the final months of the war, with tragic consequences, in the destruction of Hamburg, Dresden, and other civilian centers. Had he lived, and perhaps not aggrieved his superiors so severely, he may have been instrumental in the build-up and preparation of the US Army Air Forces for World War II.

• • •

By the time of the entrance of the United States into the Second World War in 1941, the Americans had technology that allowed them the means they needed to perform accurate strategic bombing; however, the Norden bombsight could be operated only in daylight, requiring a skilled bombardier. The British had requested access to this early analog computer when the war began, but the USAAF would not give up its secret weapon.

The Norden bombsight was developed by Swiss American engineer Carl L. Norden in the 1920s and 1930s. He immigrated to the United States shortly after the turn of the century and had settled in New York. One of the projects he worked on was the first gyrostabilizer for use on ships. Additionally, he developed systems for launching deck-to-sea torpedoes from ships. He also began working on specialized equipment for the US Navy, earning a number of patents. Norden, a devout Christian, had wrestled with the morality of indiscriminate bombing and wanted to find a more humane method for delivering ordnance.[9] He used his knowledge of gyroscopes and began work on his most famous invention. The bombsight would enable the United States to deliver bombs directly on target and theoretically limit the suffering of those on the ground. It used a twenty-power telescope, which by itself wasn't terribly potent, but it was adequate for locating a factory in a crowded urban area. The bombsight used a primitive analog computer to calculate for wind drift, airspeed, and groundspeed of the bomber. The bombardier twisted knobs that were wired into the automatic flight control equipment (AFCE), allowing him to guide the bomber to the target while lining up crosshairs in the viewfinder. The device may have helped settle Carl Norden's conscience, but it really wasn't as accurate as he would have liked to believe; theoretical "pickle barrel" bombing was just that, a theory.

Photographs taken of bombers during the Second World War commonly show the bombsight obscured by a flier's jacket or a stitched cover. Despite all the secrecy, the Germans did gain access to its design before the war in 1938 via a German-born employee of the Norden Company, Herman W. Lang, who stole the designs and turned them over to his intelligence handlers.[10] However, the Germans would never make use of them; the Norden was far more complicated than their bombsight, the Lotfernrohr ("Lofte") 7. While the Lofte contained the gyroscopic platform similar to the Norden, it did not have an electronic interface with the aircraft's autopilot system. The British Mark XIV bombsight also lacked this important connection, and neither bombsight was as accurate as the Norden. But despite its accuracy shortcomings, the Norden was still very advanced for its time and would continue service in both the Korean and Vietnam Wars.[11]

The Norden gave the United States the tool it needed to carry out its revolutionary and "mad" plan of daylight bombing. Until operations could begin, however, much needed to be accomplished in logistics for the 8th AF to become the hugely successful organization it would be in the three years to come. But in February 1942 there were no aircraft or personnel to staff this effort and, much to Hap Arnold's frustration, the build-up would take time. The first bombing sortie would not be until July 4 and would be performed with light bombers borrowed from the RAF. Prior to that time, the Air Corps effort in the Atlantic was confined to anti-submarine patrols off the coasts of the United States, Caribbean, and Central America.

American manufacturing had been on a war footing relatively early in the conflict under the Lend-Lease program. Strategic planning in 1940 by the American administration was implemented in the event that Germany conquered Britain along with the whole of western Europe, leaving the United States to fight the Axis powers by herself; hence, aid was granted to her allies to stem the hemorrhaging as Germany overran the western allied nations. Officially titled "An Act to Promote the Defense of the United States, and for Other Purposes," it was signed into law by President Roosevelt on March 11, 1941. This act gave aid to US allies before her entry into the war, essentially negating any "neutrality" that FDR sought to project to the Axis forces. Already, American manufacturing was churning out Jeeps and bombers, but many of these items were being sent to Britain and China in support of their defense. The epic manufacturing effort characterized by America's industrial might that would eventually win the war wasn't quite up to steam yet, but the first steps had been taken. In the meantime, Hitler's scrapping of his 1939 non-aggression pact with Stalin, and subsequent invasion of the Soviet Union in June 1941, added Russia to the list of Lend-Lease clients. While FDR was thus far keeping the United States out of the European conflagration, coupled with Japan's increasing aggression, he knew it was just a matter of time before American involvement would mean more than shipping trucks and rifles overseas. As a result, on September 16, 1940, Roosevelt signed the Selective Service and Training Act requiring all American males between the ages of twenty-one and thirty-five to register with their local draft boards. It was the first peace time draft in US history. There was little objection to the legislation from the public, and the law itself was probably unnecessary given the overwhelming response to the attack on Pearl Harbor on December 7, 1941. Young men flocked to their community recruitment offices to sign up in the thousands.

In early 1940, prior to America's entrance into the war, the US Army Air Corps was a poor specimen indeed, with only 51,165 men and 2,588 aircraft.[12] In January through March 1941, the Americans and British met in Washington, DC, to discuss wartime strategy, should the United States be pulled into the conflict. Called the American, British, and Canadian Conference (ABC), it had called for an increase from fifteen to thirty-two squadrons to be deployed to England in 1941. When Eaker arrived at High Wycombe in February 1942, there were some 14,420 aircraft in the whole of the USAAF; by the end of the European conflict, there would be 63,715 aircraft in total for both the Atlantic and Pacific theaters of operation.[13] The existing British air bases were inadequate for the needs of the USAAF and the enormous influx of personnel and equipment that was on its way by the spring and summer of 1942. The British Air Ministry, therefore, authorized the construction of dozens of new airfields in East Anglia, an agricultural area with wide-open spaces suitable for runway construction. The 8th AF would occupy these bases and the RAF would concentrate their squadrons to the west. The United States would also send numerous engineer companies of construction GIs to build even more airstrips. The airfields were of a standard "A" shape, with three intersecting runways at 60 degrees from each other and a perimeter track where the aircraft would taxi to hardstands for parking. A US bomb group consisted of four squadrons and would normally occupy a single airfield. Two other associated groups would be stationed on nearby air bases and the three would make up a "combat wing." These three groups would be deployed together during an operation and assemble at the same location above a radio transmitter. Five combat wings would make up a "bombardment wing," later to be renamed a "bombardment division," shortened to bomb division (BD). By the end of the war, there would be three bomb divisions, the 1st, 2nd, and 3rd BDs. The 1st BD was made up entirely of B-17s, the 2nd was issued B-24s, and the 3rd was a mixture of both aircraft types. Many of the medium bomber models, the B-25, B-26, and A-20, ended up in Italy and North Africa as part of the 9th, 12th, and 15th Air Force organizations. The British also made use of the twin-engine Douglas A-20 Havoc light bomber, which they nicknamed the "Boston." It was a frequent component of the Lend-Lease program, and many models would be flown to England. It would be RAF Bostons that would be borrowed for the 8th AF's first mission in July 1942.[14]

The first installment of the 8th AF, some 1,800 personnel, sailed from Boston Harbor on April 27, 1942. The headquarters companies of the 8th Air Force, the VIII Fighter, Bomber, and Base Commands, the 15th Bombardment Squadron (Light), and the 2nd Air Depot Group all boarded a ship for Liverpool. The 97th Bombardment Group (BG) was placed on alert and instructed to deploy to England by June 1. The 97th, 301st, and 303rd BGs had been activated in February 1942, and the 92nd BG in March; all were equipped with the B-17E model. Two B-24 Liberator groups were formed as well; the 44th and the 93rd BGs were activated in February and March, respectively. It would be summer before these groups arrived in East Anglia.

The aircraft were normally flown to England in a northern route via Newfoundland, Greenland, and Scotland; however, there were other routes as well connecting the US to the Middle East and Europe. If harsh weather in the North Atlantic prevented delivery, then two other routes could be considered. A south Atlantic course left from southern Florida with refueling stops in Puerto Rico, Antigua, Trinidad, and British Guiana; there were multiple landings in Brazil before the long trans-Atlantic flight to the Ascension Islands and West Africa. A central route was additionally used to ferry aircraft from Florida through the Caribbean and then on to North Africa.[15] These routes were set up prior to America's entry into the war to deliver aircraft to Lend-Lease clients.

Sometimes an air crew would shuttle their own ship across, or, more often than not, they would deliver an aircraft assigned to another bomb group. Ground personnel normally traveled via ocean liners converted for troop transport. Many of these former ocean liners, such as the *Queen Mary* and *Queen Elizabeth*, were pressed into service as troop carriers because they moved faster than enemy submarines and could cross the Atlantic without an escort of destroyers. Often air crews would travel across the Atlantic aboard ships, sans aircraft, as would the crew of the *Lady Jane II* in February 1945. If an aircrew did not fly a plane across to Europe, shuttle pilots of the Air Transport Command (ATC) would deliver the aircraft.

Before flying to England, most bomber crews met at training bases in the United States. As the war progressed and the blood-letting reduced manpower, replacements would fill in aircrew vacancies as men were lost. But for the most part, crews trained together after completing their primary schools.

The officer candidates were sent to various facilities for pilot/co-pilot, navigator, or bombardier. Passing the requirements of these schools led to a commission in the USAAF. The enlisted men of an air crew would attend gunnery school, radio operation, or mechanical instruction, sometimes all three. At the onset of the war, there were ten men aboard a B-17: pilot, co-pilot, navigator, bombardier, a radio man, an in-flight mechanic (engineer), and four gunners (two in the waist area and one each in the ball turret and tail positions). The radio operator and engineer were also trained in gunnery school and operated weapons near their duty stations onboard the aircraft; however, the radio operator's gun position was eliminated in the B-17G in 1944, due to its poor range and the gunner's tendency to damage his own aircraft by inadvertently shredding the vertical stabilizer. Later in the war, the bombardier was replaced in many aircraft with a "togglier," a gunner who sat in the bombardier's position and toggled the bomb drop switch when a leading aircraft with a trained bombardier dropped his payload. The togglier would also man the "chin turret" twin .50-caliber machine guns when they were introduced with the B-17G model in 1943. The USAAF would make extensive use of toggliers as the war advanced and Pathfinding Forces (PFFs) were employed.

The PFF aircraft was a standard bomber with an onboard radar dome installed. One of the greatest problems faced by both the RAF and the 8th AF was the English weather; countless missions were scrubbed because heavy cloud cover prevented the employment of their respective bombsights. The British had developed the "Height to Slope" (H2S) air to ground radar system in 1941 following its attacks, and mostly misses, on German cities. This system used a 10-centimeter frequency pulsed from the aircraft-based unit, which consisted of a revolving transmitter, usually under the aircraft's nose. This antenna would send high frequency pulses toward the ground where they would be reflected back toward the unit's receiver, a scope resembling an early cathode ray tube television set, but with a monochromatic display. The scope would render the returning signals as rough images of the ground surface. It was initially developed for use on Halifax, Sterling, and Lancaster British bombers. In March 1943, Ira Eaker was impressed enough with the H2S (code-named "Stinky") that he requested a number of units be installed on B-17s.[16] The first B-17 to receive a unit was an F model. The Massachusetts Institute of Technology would further develop this ground-mapping device and name it the "H2X," with heavy testing of the units in the latter quarter of 1943. The H2X used a 3-centimeter microwave signal as opposed to the British 10-centimeter; it was generally considered more accurate than its predecessor. The H2X was code-named "Mickey," after Lt. Col. Fred Rabo of the 482nd BG stated that the radome looked like a "Mickey Mouse" setup. The moniker stuck, and an aircraft bearing one was referred to as a "Mickey ship." The Mickey ship bombardier would drop colored flares to notify aircraft in his formation of a drop; each togglier in that particular formation would then drop his payload after the lead PFF ship fired off a signal flare and released his load.

The British had also developed radar guidance technology to assist in assembly of formations and directing them to their targets. "Bunchers" were used to assist in assembling fighter escort or bomber groups. The "Splasher" was a series of three, later four, ground-based transmitters that broadcast with the same call-sign but on different frequencies. The radar groundcrews changed the frequencies daily to prevent the Germans from jamming the signals. The navigator onboard the Allied aircraft could locate his position despite England's infamous "pea soup" fog. Splashers were also used in assembly and would assist groups forming into their combat wings.

The "Oboe" system was radar-based, allowing the ship's navigator to position his aircraft accurately within 250 miles of the transmitter. The signals were distinct sounds received with a steady tone indicating to the receiver unit that the aircraft was on course; the tone would interrupt and change if the receiver moved too far to the left or right. The Grid or "Gee" system was employed by the 8th AF as a navigational tool used by some of the B-24s of the 2nd Bomb Division, initially planned for a squadron of the 44th BG, but then the 93rd. It consisted of a radar transmitter onboard the aircraft, where it would converse with several transponders on the ground. A visual indication was received back in the aircraft via a scope. The number of seconds it took for the plane's receiving unit to collect signals from two transmitters on the ground gave the aircraft's position. It was developed so that missions could be deployed on particularly cloudy or foggy days. The effective range of the Gee system was approximately 200 miles, so it was useless once the formations were over the European continent.

The most important technology at the disposal of the VIII BC was the heavy bomber itself. The Boeing B-17 Flying Fortress and the Consolidated Aircraft B-24 Liberator were two main participants throughout the American bombing effort in the ETO. The first Boeing bomber was built in 1935 (the 299 model). The term "Flying Fortress" was coined by a reporter who was astonished by the bomber's armament and the name stuck. Subsequent upgrades were termed the B-17A, B, C, D, E, and F models, with each improvement advancing the limits of technology for its day. The war would end with the G model.

Three main plants produced the Flying Fortress. The Boeing factory in Seattle manufactured aircraft that were identified with a "BO" code, short for "Boeing," following a bomber's model type. The Douglas Long Beach, California, plant produced B-17s under contract for Boeing; its planes were identified by a "DL" code. Finally, the Burbank, California, Lockheed Vega factory produced B-17s designated with the code "VE." Hence an aircraft's model designation might be B-17G-BO for an aircraft manufactured in Seattle.

The first B-17 to see combat was a B-17C model sent to the RAF in 1941.[17] The aircraft, nicknamed the "Fortress I," was not successful as a daylight bomber, so the RAF discontinued its use for that purpose. It was mechanically unreliable and a number of aircraft were lost to crashes. The B-17D model, with more armament and airframe upgrades, was a minor improvement over the C model. The early B-17s, the 299 model, B-17A, B, C, and D models all had the old style "shark fin" tails, unsuitable to stabilize the aircraft at high altitude; as a result, the B-17E was introduced with the larger vertical stabilizer so familiar in wartime models. The E model also had an extension in the fuselage.

Forty-two E models would reach England in the middle of 1942; these were primarily assigned to the 97th BG.[18] The E model was replaced in the summer of 1942 by the F, and most bomb groups reaching England would be issued this upgraded aircraft. The E model was essentially obsolete by the time the VIII BC deployed to Britain. A tiny handful has survived into the twenty-first century, but most were scrapped for recyclables after the war. A single B-17D exists today in the "Swoose" (registration no. 40-3097), manufactured in 1941 at the Seattle Boeing plant. It was rescued from the scrapping facility at Kingman, Arizona, by her pilot, Col. Frank Kurtz, in March 1946. She is currently being restored for display at the National Museum of the US Air Force in Dayton, Ohio.

The B-17F and G were 74 feet, 8.9 inches long; 103 feet, 9.4 inches wide; and 19 feet, 1 inch in height.[19] They were powered by four Wright Model R-1820-97 radial air-cooled, nine-cylinder, supercharged engines producing 1,200 horsepower each. The Wright engine consumed 100 octane gasoline. The G model was an improvement over the F, as it could carry a higher bomb load, 13,600 lbs., theoretically, versus 9,600 lbs. However, operational bomb loads were usually around 4,000 lbs., to provide for the added weight of increased fuel capacity. The G model received decreased fuel economy due to the increase in weight from upgraded armament: twelve .50-caliber. machine guns with two in a "chin" turret; the installation of clear plastic covers for the waist gun windows also added weight. Later, the aircraft would roll off the assembly lines sans paint due to the weight it added to the frame, and plain aluminum ships took to the air. Improvised G model aircraft first began reaching England in the fall of 1943 in the form of F models with chin turrets welded onto the nose.[20] Douglas, Boeing, and Lockheed-built B-17Gs were delivered the following spring. The F model would be considered obsolete by this point, so production was ceased. By war's end, some 6,500 G models, combined from all three manufacturing plants, were delivered to the 8th AF.[21]

It must be remembered that American bomber aircraft were barely twenty years old when Boeing sent the first Flying Fortress into the air. By the conclusion of hostilities, bombers were at the pinnacle of technology with computers, advanced electronics, and autopilot flight controls onboard. In addition, jet engines were in development, but primarily for use in pursuit aircraft, rather than bombers. Technological advancement was on a fast track necessitated by war. While introduced in the early 1940s, the first US jet fighter, the Bell P-59, would not complete its development and deployment by the end of hostilities, but the British and the German jet fighters would; more about that later.

In addition to the B-17, the USAAF accepted deliveries of the Consolidated Aircraft Corporation's B-24. In 1938, Consolidated was asked to produce B-17s for the US Army Air Corps. Instead, it submitted its own design for a heavy bomber, and the contract was accepted. The B-24 saw extensive service in the war with the 2nd and 3rd Bomb Divisions. The B-24D was first received in the ETO in late summer 1942. It was a hardy aircraft and, like the B-17, could take a lot of pounding and still bring her crew home. But the B-24's best operational ceiling was less than that of her Fortress sibling and tended to be squirrely above 23,000 feet. Normal operating altitude was usually 18,000 to 22,000 feet, whereas the B-17 was stable at 28,000 feet. For the purpose of this narrative, the B-17 is in focus. The *Lady Jane II* was a B-17G built at Boeing's Seattle plant in 1944.[22]

A radio-controlled drone developed during the latter stages of the war was another interesting variation on the B-17. The use of drones in the Second World War was, in part, a response to the German's "Vengeance" missile program. At the time, the Allies did not have the technology to advance their ballistic missile capabilities, so manufactured variants in the form of drones were used. American development of missiles would come at the end of the war, when the threat of Soviet intercontinental ballistic missiles was more acute.

The Germans had borrowed some of their theories on rocketry from the late American physicist Robert H. Goddard, but he died during the war without having benefited from the German advances in missile development. German scientists had become leaders in this technological breakthrough, particularly the brilliant engineer Wernher von Braun. After the war, he was brought to the US under Operation Paperclip to work on the American missile and rocketry programs. Von Braun would later gain American citizenship and become a distinguished engineer with NASA and develop rockets to send the United States into space.

Drones in the twenty-first century are often tiny affairs with whirling propellers and minute cameras installed; sometimes they are full-sized aircraft such as the Predator drone, operated by a pilot with a joystick controller hundreds of miles away. A drone in the Second World War might consist of a huge bomber packed with explosives and controlled by a pilot following close-by in another aircraft. Since these drones couldn't be launched by themselves, a human pilot would board the ship, lift it off the runway, and once on a correct trajectory, bail out while still over friendly territory. A second pilot, operating a radio controller on a pursuit aircraft, would then take over and steer the guided missile to its target. Since these drones needed no crew, ammunition, machine guns, an oxygen system, or other heavy equipment, they could carry far more explosives than a manned bomber, up to 20,000 lbs. versus 13,600 lbs. that the B-17G could (theoretically) carry. Aircraft chosen for drone duty were usually battle-weary B-17F and G models too worn out to continue missions, and were thus expendable.

After the war, most of the surviving bombers were sold to third-party nations, scrapped out at the Kingman recycling facility, or converted to peacetime roles such as Coast Guard patrol craft or firefighting bombers. A precious few exist today in museums.

CHAPTER 2
OPENING FIRE

To conquer the command in the air means victory; to be beaten in the air means defeat.

—Giulio Douhet

The opening shots of the "Mighty Eighth" were accomplished by a squadron of Douglas DB-7 twin-engine light bombers, also known as the A-20 Havoc. The heavy bombardment groups were still in transit when Hap Arnold, out of frustration and perhaps a little pressure from the American press, demanded action. The date was set for America's birthday, July 4, 1942. The aircraft, nicknamed "Bostons" by the British, were borrowed from the RAF, as the American crews were, at that time, without their own planes. The Bostons were repainted in American colors and sent into action with the 15th Bombardment Squadron. The 15th BS had been pulled out of the 27th Bomb Group (Light) and sent to England for conversion to a night fighter squadron in the spring, but this plan was eventually abandoned.[1] The squadron would serve in the British Isles until November when it was transferred to the 12th Air Force in North Africa.

The July 4 mission hit Luftwaffe airfields in the occupied Netherlands and was more of a publicity stunt rather than a meaningful strategic accomplishment, but the mission would temporarily help calm the American public's impatience while the 8th AF gained strength. Additionally, the strike was not terribly successful: two of the Bostons were felled by flak and one was severely damaged; few of the light bombers actually hit their targets. The "real" fight would begin on August 17, when the 97th BG lifted off from its East Anglian bases at Polebrook and Grafton Underwood to bomb marshalling yards in the Rouen/Sotteville area of occupied northern France. Two squadrons, the 340th and 341st, provided decoys for the German fighters to chase while the main bulk of the formation mangled the tracks at the rail yards. In the formation was the 97th BG commander Col. Frank A. Armstrong, flying on-board the B-17E *Butcher Shop*, piloted by Maj. Paul Tibbets; VIII BC leader Brig. Gen. Ira Eaker was a passenger aboard *Yankee Doodle*. The group was escorted by four squadrons of RAF Spitfires. One USAAF gunner, Sgt. Kent R. West, was credited with shooting down a Luftwaffe defender and was thus given the honor of becoming the first VIII BC gunner to score a kill in the ETO.[2]

The August 17 mission was a success in that it confused the Germans, who thought it was an RAF formation, thus were not expecting a daylight bombing effort, and assumed the formation was just passing through. Additionally, many of the bombs fell where they were aimed, not something that concerned the RAF with its nighttime bombing runs. None of the aircraft were lost on the August 17 flight and all returned to base. If not for these achievements, the mission might have gone down as another publicity stunt. The slow build-up to the European operations was the driving factor for this effort. A complete bomb group, including air crews and ground support, was not even available in the ETO until July 27, when the 97th BG arrived in Britain.

The poor training the air crews had received in the States prior to deployment contributed to the 8th Air Force's molasses inauguration. Gunners and radio men were simply under-trained for their jobs, so extensive remedial preparation was required before the crews could be turned loose to wreak havoc on the enemy. However, the VIII BC was able to send another bombing mission out on August 19, in a diversionary tactic to occupy the Luftwaffe while Canadian and British troops landed at Dieppe, France. The 97th BG dropped 34 tons of explosives on occupied Abbeville/Drucat area airfields. One of the American escort pilots managed to shoot down a German fighter, becoming the first 8th AF pursuit pilot to do so.[3]

Success in engaging enemy defenders was categorized by how many enemy fighters were destroyed, how many were probably destroyed, and how many were damaged after an encounter. A returning airman, whether a gunner on a bomber or an escort pilot, might report his successes as 2-3-2. However, several gunners on different bombers might claim the same downed aircraft as their kill, artificially raising these figures. Also, enemy fighters assumed to have been shot down might have merely been wounded and were able to peel away from the attack, retreat, and land safely at their bases. In January 1943, the confusion created by enthusiastic gunners prompted the VIII BC to institute new guidelines for reporting downed fighters. For an enemy plane to be considered "killed," it must have been observed to explode in air, disintegrate in air, descend completely in flames, strike the ground, or the pilot had been seen to bail out. The category of "probably destroyed" would include aircraft that were obviously seriously damaged but were not observed to strike the ground, or the pilot seen to bail out. An enemy aircraft observed to be struck without apparent mortal wounding, and no sign of a parachuting pilot, would be counted as "damaged." While the new standards for reporting lowered the sometimes-outrageous bomber crew tallies, the real figures would not be known until the end of the European conflict, when Luftwaffe records were acquired by the Allies.

The RAF had preferred nighttime bombing even before the outbreak of the Second World War, due to their theories in area bombardment. After the success of the 97th BG's August missions, RAF planners began to see the advantages of daytime strategic bombing theory, but not enough, apparently, to change their tactics. The British also had an experience not shared with the USAAF—the Blitz. The Blitz, short for the German *Blitzkrieg*, was the nighttime bombing of British cities during the Battle of Britain, from June 1940 to June 1941.

The German air attacks on Britain were originally begun in preparation for "Operation Sea Lion," the Wehrmacht invasion of the British Isles. In 1940, Hitler proposed the offensive after his successes in overrunning the Netherlands, Belgium, Luxembourg (i.e., the "Low Countries"), and France. Britain remained a malignant tumor in his conquest of Europe. The best way to excise the malignancy was to invade and conquer; or better still, force the British to come to the negotiating table and allow the Third Reich a free hand in the remainder of Europe. But this could not be done while the RAF drew breath. So, Hitler instructed his Luftwaffe commander *Reichsmarschall* Hermann Göring to destroy the British air forces and compel a negotiated settlement with their government. Thus began the Battle of Britain, fought entirely in the air over English country estates, villages, farmlands, and cities. Operation Sea Lion would eventually be scrapped as the logistics for moving hundreds of thousands of German troops and supplies over the Channel could not be implemented. Additionally, the invasion would fail unless the Luftwaffe controlled the airspace; Germany was unable to accomplish this feat, as the RAF beat back every attempt. But the bloodletting over Britain would continue with bombings and aerial carnage between the RAF and Luftwaffe.

Originally, the German tactic was toward daylight strategic bombing in hitting critical targets such as the port at Liverpool and industrial centers. But as learned with the RAF, the Luftwaffe was incurring too many losses to continue with daylight raids and moved to night operations, resulting in area bombing, also known as "terror bombing" because of its indiscriminate nature. The Battle of Britain ceased in June 1941, as Hitler wanted to focus on "Operation Barbarossa," the invasion of the Soviet Union. Any plans for the land invasion of Great Britain would never again be seriously considered by the German high command. Since British air defenses were fairly strong, the Luftwaffe's losses forced a change from daytime to nighttime bombing of British targets. British anger had seethed over Germany's indiscriminate bombings of London; area bombing on Britain, they rationalized, would justify area bombing on Germany. The British had no desire to cease arbitrary destruction of German cities while they themselves were similarly being assaulted from the air.

The 301st BG had arrived in England in August 1942 but did not remain long. It, along with the 97th BG, was sent to North Africa in early September to support Operation Torch, under the leadership of Brig. Gen. James H. Doolittle. Both of these groups would be assigned to the 12th AF before being transferred to Italy with the 15th AF, for operations in southern Germany and eastern Europe. In the meantime, more bomb groups and support units arrived in England. In September the 303rd, 305th, and the 306th Bomb Groups were assigned to the 8th AF.

Early in the war there was no combat tour of duty requirement for air crews other than that specified for all active duty service members, who were expected to serve throughout the duration of the conflict. But one issue apparently not considered by the USAAF planners was combat fatigue. Severe stress was a prevalent concern as crews went up multiple times per week in thin-skinned aluminum shells with little armor and no defense from flak bursts. The pilots had steel plating under their seats, but the gunners, radio man, navigator, and bombardier had precious little protection at the onset of bombing operations. Unlike an infantryman in a foxhole, there was nowhere to hide from artillery bursts. Airmen would suffer from the shits and shakes with no end in sight to the horror. Many would crack under the pressure of endless missions with no goal. To ease this problem, a tour of duty requirement was established. The 8th AF chief surgeon, Col. Malcolm C. Grow, recognized the issue with fatigue and recommended a specified mission limit for combat crews. Ira Eaker agreed, and in early 1943, a limit of twenty-five combat missions was instituted. Dr. Grow would gain further fame around this time for developing body armor that included flak suits and steel helmets.[4] A study performed in late 1942 demonstrated that some 70 percent of wounds to combat crews were caused by shrapnel and bullets hitting the aircraft. Dr. Grow had approached the Wilkinson Sword Company of London requesting aid to produce the flak suits. The suits were hugely popular with the aircrews and were further developed during the war to reduce weight and increase comfort. This effort, along with the definition of a combat tour of duty, helped increase morale with the airmen. Finally, there was a light at the end of a terrifying tunnel.

However, considerable stress was endured by combat crews. Airmen suffering from mission anxiety were often sent to rest camps, referred to as "Flak Farms." These camps were often large English country estates lent by their owners or the British government to the USAAF for rest and relaxation. If a crewman appeared to be suffering from combat fatigue, his group surgeon would recommend a short vacation from the flying schedule and would send him to a retreat. These mansions were often equipped with Red Cross ladies to serve the boys coffee and donuts; badminton and/or tennis courts, croquet, soccer, or football fields might also be included. More than a few baseball diamonds were no doubt scraped from the English grass by American players. Horseback riding trails, bicycling, hiking, and/or other outdoor activities were also included. The shell-shocked troops could play board games, eat superb meals, and mingle with fellow airmen, swapping stories and experiences as a way to relieve the tension and find kindred spirits. One was not alone in his anxiety if others shared in it. There was also the oft welcome ability to just keep to oneself and enjoy peace and quiet. Several days or weeks later, the crewman would return to his unit. Such retreats were critical, in many instances, to keep airmen in the fight and not breaking down. If a combat airman did experience a breakdown, especially after he had honorably served his unit, he was not ostracized. The claim of lacking "moral fiber," or being a coward, would not be applied to men who had faced a number of tough missions. If, however, a crew member "cracked up" after one or two missions, he was removed from flying status and sent to a ground unit immediately, usually with a demotion. Men with no stomach for combat could not be allowed into units where their influence could damage the morale of other fliers.

In 1945, two USAAF doctors produced a volume of case studies regarding the terrible impact of combat fatigue in air crewmen. *Men under Stress*, by Lt. Col. Roy R. Grinker and Maj. John P. Spiegel, gives details on the sufferings of these men and the diverse ways they expressed their fears. Some men who failed in performing their duties had arrived at their units already emotionally unsuitable for combat stress, but most others developed problems after entering combat. The authors referred to this as "external harassment." A man's ego, they state, can tolerate only so much "pounding" before weakness seeps in; everyone has a limit to the amount of stress he can withstand.[5] Every human being experiences daily challenges—stress that comes in measured doses throughout one's life.

Those persons who have experienced great trauma at one or two points in their lives normally experience these events as isolated incidents. In some ways they make us stronger, mature us, and make us who we are; more alert, more cautious perhaps, and responsive to the world around us. What happens when those "measured doses" are not measured, but come in torrents, streams, one upon the other, day after day, month after month? Some people are strong enough intellectually to cope inwardly to continue to do their jobs, to grow with the demands of the job and be strong for their crewmates. Others, not so much. Sometimes the stress comes so severely that even the strongest can no longer place one foot before the other and keep moving forward; they simply collapse. The Flak Farms were then the destination of these men.

Relentless diarrhea and vomiting before a mission were several of the most common expressions of combat fatigue.[6] But a case of the screaming runs was no excuse to relieve a man from the duty roster. As long as he could still perform his job, he flew. If he had a fever, then he might be excused. But an upset stomach was most likely simple stress, and the crewman had to suck it up and keep going. Besides, many of the men stayed with the same crew and wanted to finish their tour of duty with their buddies and not be delayed. Combat stress was one obstacle they tried not to think about.

• • •

At the onset of the American air war in Europe, fighter escorts were initially provided by the RAF, using their Spitfires in close air support for USAAF bombers while the VIII Fighter Command built up strength.[7] Many of the targets were in France, the Netherlands, and Holland, so the limited ranged fighters were able to cover the bombers for most of the effort. However, as the bombing missions traversed farther into occupied Europe and Germany, the range of the fighter escorts was reached. They would have to return to their bases, leaving the bombers to the mercy, or lack thereof, of the Luftwaffe. If bomber losses exceeded 10 percent, this was unsustainable and unacceptable.

Early in the war, USAAF planners regarded the Flying Fortress as capable of defending itself with its batteries of .50-caliber machine guns. But this theory was soon put to rest as the Luftwaffe figured out how to bypass the Fortress's defenses. The B-17E and F models were weak in forward defenses, and it did not take long for the Germans to find a way to assault the formations with less risk to their fighters. Initially, two "cheek" guns were installed on the Forts, where the bombardier and/or the navigator would operate them. The guns were only .30-caliber and had limited range in both distance and direction, given their restricted mount locations. A desperate crew would modify their Fortress to accept single or twin .50-caliber machine guns by cutting holes in the plastic nose of their bomber and stuffing the barrels through. The more potent firepower would not become standard on the B-17 until late in 1943, when the G model was rolled out with a remote-controlled chin turret equipped with twin .50s. Until then, the gunners would have to make due to defend their planes.

An experiment to shield the formations before long-range fighter escorts were available was the inclusion of bombers with upgraded armor and armament. Developed late in 1942, the so-called "YB-40" was a Flying Fortress F model bristling with sixteen .50-caliber machine guns instead of the usual twelve, including a chin turret that would become standard on the G model. There were also upgrades in steel plating to protect the crew. Eighth Bomber Command had assumed that formations could be seeded with these flying machine gun platforms to defend the bombers. Unlike existing fighter escorts, they would have the range necessary to accompany the bombing formations deep into German-occupied territory, then return with them. It was a brilliant concept. But a simple calculation that could have saved much money and energy was not included in the calculus of this program: more guns and armor meant more weight. The hefty YB-40 was unable to keep up with the bombers after they dropped their payloads on the target. Consequently, the YB-40s would lag behind and become easy targets for the Luftwaffe. The experiment failed and the program was discontinued. The need for long-range fighter escorts was acute and pressing.

Once the VIII Fighter Command began building up strength, it sent Lockheed P-38F Lightning models on escort missions with the bombers. But like other fighter aircraft (also known as "Pursuit" aircraft, hence the "P" in front of the model number), it had limited range. The P-38 was a superb fighter; with its with its two powerful 1,325 hp engines and twin tailed design, it was maneuverable and fast and could hold its own against the primary Luftwaffe fighters the Messerschmitt Bf 109 and Focke-Wulf Fw 190. The Germans also had excellent twin-engine fighter/bombers, the Bf 110 and Me 210, among others. The Republic Aircraft Corporation's P-47, made famous by Hubert Zemke's 56th FG, was also a tremendous asset in the ETO. Called the "Jug" by its pilots, the P-47 Thunderbolt was very large for a fighter and could be squirrely to control. Those that did master this beast loved it and were apprehensive when their units were re-equipped with P-51s later in the war.[8]

The Jug was a gas hog with its single Pratt and Whitney R-2800 supercharged engine, so its range was also limited. Like the P-38, it could carry a drop tank for longer missions. The problem with drop tanks was that they could interfere with the fighter's performance in combat and needed to be ejected if the Luftwaffe showed up for a shootout. The Germans figured this out and would often feint an attack to prompt the escorts to eject their spare tanks, then peel off; after that, the Luftwaffe fighters would wait for the escorts to turn back when low fuel necessitated a return to base. The bombers would then be without their protection and easier to pick off. The need for a long-range escort fighter would lead to the development of the North American Aviation Corporation's P-51 Mustang.

The British had initially requested a high-performance fighter in 1940. But the stock engine for the P-51 was an under-performing Allison engine that was almost useless above 15,000 feet. The British installed a more powerful Rolls-Royce Merlin engine, and the fighter would gain an almost mythic reputation as a result. But the engine was not ready until late 1943, long after the VIII Bomber Command commenced operations. Until the 8th AF had long-range escorts, the attrition rate would be ghastly. In short, the developers of the Flying Fortress and the Liberator were horribly wrong when they insisted, early in the war, that these aircraft could defend themselves. They could not.

• • •

During the waning weeks of August 1942, the 8th AF would send bombers to shipyards in France and the Netherlands. The pace was still slow as new groups arrived in September and came up to speed on training and operations procedures. Additionally, the planning for Operation Torch in North Africa triggered a build-up for the Twelfth Air Force in Algeria, diverting needed resources from the 8th AF.

However, in October several missions were dispatched to occupied France. While many efforts were scrubbed due to weather concerns, on October 9, 1942, multiple bomb groups took off to strike the Compagnie des Fives steel plant and the Ateliers d'Hellemmes locomotive works, both at Lille. It was the first 8th AF mission to send more than one hundred bombers with the inclusion of the 92nd, 97th, 301st, 302nd, 306th Bomb Groups and Liberators of the 93rd. Accompanying the bombers were P-38 escorts.[9]

The 305th BG was commanded by Lt. Col. Curtis LeMay, a brilliant strategist and tactician who would gain the respect of 8th AF brass with his ideas on protecting bombers in "combat box" formations. LeMay was a cigar-chewing hard ass that changed the way the USAAF conducted its missions. He was both admired and detested by the men that served under him, collectively referring to him as "Iron Ass," "Iron Eagle," "The Big Cigar," "Bombs Away LeMay," and other perhaps less forgiving monikers. He rode the 305th BG hard, upgrading their training, and ultimately their confidence, to increase their survival chances and mission success. His leadership style dictated that he head up many dangerous missions into which he was sending his boys, including the August 17, 1943, mission to Regensburg.

LeMay's philosophy on bombing grew out of interviews with combat bomber pilots. Bombing accuracy was poor when pilots engaged in evasive maneuvers to avoid flak damage. He theorized that accuracy would increase if the pilots flew straight and level courses while on the bomb run from the Initial Point (IP) to the point of bomb release. Of course, this idea was not widely appreciated by the bomber crews, who saw it as suicide. But accuracy over the target would shorten the war, and wails of protest would be replaced by feelings of pride and confidence as missions were completed and accuracy was improved. Air reconnaissance flyers would verify success following the bombing effort and submit their photos to USAAF intelligence staff and mission planners. "Iron Ass" would man the helm of the 305th until May 1943; in September 1943, he would lead three bomb groups as the commanding officer of the newly created 3rd Air Division. In 1944, his success as strategic planner gained him yet another promotion to lead the bombing campaign against Japan. His planning and influence resulted in the fire bombings of Japanese cities.

The October 9 mission would cost the 8th AF four heavy bombers; since it was the inaugural mission of the 93rd and 306th, with so many rookie crews, the success of the strike was not as good as it could have been.

A second notable October effort was a bombing mission to the submarine pens at Lorient in northern France. The Germans had seized the peninsula in 1940, and under direction from *Großadmiral* Karl Dönitz built an enormous concrete-reinforced bunker to house up to thirty submarines. The Allies would make many attempts to smash the pens, with the first American effort on October 21, 1942. Fifteen B-17s from the 97th BG released their ordnance from 17,500 feet. Greeting them were thirty-six German defenders. The effort was not successful even though many of the bombs, some thirty 2,000-lb. high explosives, hit close to the location where the bombs were planned to strike, the mean point of impact (MPI). The submarine pens themselves were not terribly damaged due to the 16-foot-thick concrete. Three bombers tumbled from the sky on their return to East Anglia as the furious Luftwaffe caught up with them. The Allies would return and repeatedly smash the surrounding town and port facilities to isolate the submarine base and disrupt its resupply, but the base would not fall until Germany's surrender in May 1945.

In an age before "bunker buster" bombs were effective, lower altitude might provide more blast for the buck; this thought encouraged Gen. Spaatz to propose a drop from a much-lower altitude. The submarine pens at Saint-Nazaire, France, would provide the location to experiment with lower drops and, hopefully, more damage to heavily reinforced concrete.[10] Since the pens were beyond the range of fighter escorts, the mission would be without protection. While Spaatz was well aware of the increase in potential losses, he opted for the risk.

On November 9, the VIII BC dispatched the mission to Saint-Nazaire on the west coast of France. The bombers left England and skipped over the Channel at 500 feet to avoid enemy coastal radar; they skirted around the Brest Peninsula before rising to their assigned elevations. The RAF flew a diversionary mission to successfully draw the Luftwaffe off, but the anti-aircraft batteries at Saint-Nazaire were prepared and mangled the formations. Some twelve B-24s from the 44th and 93rd BGs dispensed their payload from between 17,500 to 18,300 feet elevation and escaped serious damage, but thirty-one low-flying B-17s from the 91st and 306th BGs were heavily opposed and many damaged by 20 mm and 37 mm flak batteries. The 91st operated from 10,000 feet and the 306th from 7,500; the latter would lose three of its aircraft and crews. Severe damage to twenty-two surviving aircraft ended the poor experiment, which would later be represented in the 1949 Hollywood feature *Twelve O'Clock High.* While the VIII BC would strike Saint-Nazaire many more times, low-altitude bomb runs would no longer be considered, for any operation. Analysis experts would determine that operating at low altitudes did not improve accuracy for the simple reason that increased flak strikes and explosions threw off the bombardier's concentration and aim. At this stage of the war, flak guns did not yet have high-altitude radar-directed accuracy; that would change. But for now, the crews were a little more protected at 20,000 feet. On a positive note, at least for the Allies, repeated strikes against the submarine bases kept port facilities out of commission and reduced the operational success of the pens themselves.

During a November 23, 1942, mission to again hit the Saint-Nazaire sub pens, the Luftwaffe began greeting the 8th AF with a new tactic, the frontal assault.[11] It had not taken long for the Germans to find holes in the defenses of the American bomber formations. Georg-Peter Eder and Egon Mayer, of Jagdgeschwader 2 (JG 2), were pioneers in destroying four-engine bombers with the frontal attack. The preferred method had been to come from behind and slightly above the bomber to avoid the ball turret gunner and focus on the tail position.[12] If the tail gunner could be taken out, the attacking fighters reduced their risk. With the B-17F model's poor forward-facing protection, a frontal approach made more sense, but it also required nerves of steel by the German fighter pilots. JG 2, with its Fw 190 fighters, would streak in, at a combined closing speed of well over 500 miles per hour, and fire on the bomber's nose, in an attempt to kill the flight crew. These new attacks were fairly successful; bomber losses rose from about 4 percent in November 1942 to nearly 9 percent by January 1943, an unacceptable figure.[13] The introduction of chin turrets on the bombers made this approach more hazardous for the Luftwaffe attackers, but these were not widely available early in the war. The aircraft crews improvised in many cases with the installation of handheld .50-caliber machine guns shoved through a hastily drilled hole in the plastic nose of the plane; groundcrews would then weld together simple frames for the gun mount. While this gave a little more protection, it certainly wasn't enough. By mid-January 1943, the forward-facing machine guns became more common, and the bombers were better able to protect themselves. The Germans were forced to improve their ground-based anti-aircraft defenses to protect their cities and war industries as the new frontal assault became more perilous for the Luftwaffe.

At the onset of hostilities in 1939, the Luftwaffe, which administered the air defense batteries, had approximately 6,700 20 mm and 37 mm flak guns and 2,600 88 mm and 105 mm.[14] The Luftwaffe had access to radar, but radar-directed flak guns were not used regularly during the opening phase of hostilities. In January 1943, the German defenses surrounding Saint-Nazaire were improved with more accurate fire. The Germans developed *großbatteries* with dozens of anti-aircraft guns. Before the use of radar-directed fire, the large batteries would fire in unison, sending up boxes of potentially lethal flak. While these boxes were fairly inaccurate, they were certainly unnerving to aircraft crews navigating toward their targets; they were also treacherous to tight formations. Saint-Nazaire's flak guns were increased and radar added to guide searchlights and the fire; American airmen would label the place "Flak City." With so many of the German men in combat on the eastern and western fronts, many of the *großbatteries* were manned by women and children, with Hitler Youth making up a large contingent of flak gun operators. As the war progressed, the Luftwaffe was largely defeated and became scarce over German cities and industrial centers; the anti-aircraft defenses became more important, and accurate radar-controlled searchlights and flak guns became more prevalent.

In the meantime, the buildup continued. By November 30, 1942, the Eighth Bomber Command numbered around 10,000 officers and enlisted personnel. During the first six months of 1943, aircrew and staff numbers swelled to 40,000 as the surge progressed.[15] More aircraft and crews also meant increased losses. Additionally, the Luftwaffe was becoming wise to the USAAF operational habits. In the early stages of the daylight bombing campaign, the Germans were caught off-guard, and mission success for VIII

BC was fairly good. By early 1943, the Germans were more aware of American brashness to confront them in broad daylight and faced the threat accordingly, and losses for the Eighth increased.

In late 1942, the 303rd BG would make its debut in the ETO; the 97th and 301st would leave at about the same time, heading to the 12th AF and Operation Torch in North Africa. The 303rd called themselves "Hell's Angels" after one of their B-17s with the same moniker. Many history buffs can state the claim to fame for the *Memphis Belle* (41-24485) and her crew, the B-17F of the 91st BG that would be the first 8th AF bomber to complete twenty-five missions and return to the United States. But they were not the first to complete their combat tour; the crew of the *Hell's Angels* (41-24577) B-17F held that honor on May 13, 1943.[16] The *Memphis Belle* crew completed their combat tour six days later; that bomber was made famous by filmmaker William Wyler when he accompanied the men on their last few missions. This recognition obscured the accomplishment of the 303rd BG for being the first to complete their tour, but it brought important attention to the daily perils the 8th AF crews faced.

• • •

Curtis LeMay wasn't the only commander interested in defensive bomber formations. Brig. Gen. Lawrence Kuter put LeMay's philosophies to use when he took over the 1st Bombardment Wing in early December 1942, which, at that time, consisted of the 91st, 92nd, 303rd, 305th, and 306th BGs. Kuter's plan included increasing the LeMay combat box into as many planes as possible, with each box formation consisting of an entire bomb group of three squadrons, or eighteen to twenty-one planes. The basic unit of these boxes was a three-plane chevron, used throughout the war.

However, early in the 8th AF's deployment, squadrons were well spaced apart, sometimes by miles of airspace, providing no interlocking fields of fire between group elements. LeMay helped rectify this within the 305th BG, but implementation was initially slow across the whole of the USAAF. Brig. Gen. Kuter was appalled by losses during a December 30, 1942, mission to the Lorient U-boat pens. Aircraft from the 91st, 306th, and one from the 305th, all left their respective formations for one reason or another and were shot down by German fighters. It was crystal clear that leaving the protection of the formation was a potentially lethal decision. Aircraft crews were directed to stay in formation regardless of the circumstance. One aircraft leaving the group to cover for a straggler was forbidden. Stragglers, at least before long-range fighter escorts were available, were to be left to their fate. It was a hard choice but necessary for group survival and mission success.

The box structure itself consisted of staggered configurations within the larger formation. Lead planes would cause turbulence for those in their wake. Contrails would also provide visibility problems for those farther back, so groups were staggered with high, center, and low groups in each combat box. Additionally, staggered formations would allow for most of the turrets to be free to engage enemy defenders. If all the aircraft were at the same elevation, top and bottom turrets would be useless should the German fighters come in at the same elevation; staggered elevations meant some of the bombers could use more of their turrets. There was approximately 1,000 feet of elevation difference between the high group and the leading element and another 1,000 feet between the lead and the low group. Squadrons would make up four three-plane chevrons; the lead squadron would be in the center location with another squadron in the high position, and a third in the low. This arrangement would make up a complete thirty-six-plane bomb group. The most dreaded location was the low group, normally in the rear of the formation. The airmen called this the "tail-end Charlie" position, and many aircraft in this location were tempting targets for Luftwaffe fighters; the crews dreaded being there. Often the only protection a dead last bomber had against rear-approaching German defenders was the tail gunner.

The combat box techniques would change over the course of the war as threats evolved. Early in the bombing campaign, the major threat was from the Luftwaffe. Missions that went no farther than northern France, Belgium, or the Low Countries could include Spitfire escorts, and bomber formations didn't need the close fire support that would be so critical on longer missions. At this stage of the war, there were few escorts that could penetrate deep into enemy territory and the defensive box was the only option to limit losses. So on January 3, 1943, the Eighth returned to Saint-Nazaire using a new tactic of bombing "on the leader," rather than individually. This was one of Curtis LeMay's defensive tactics for improving bomber survivability and was part of the combat box strategy. An experienced bombardier would be employed in the leading aircraft. When he released his bombs, the entire box would release theirs, usually upon signal flares or smoke grenades released by the lead bomber. The planned MPI and the actual bomb dispersal were the guiding numbers for determining release accuracy. If most of the bombs hit within 1,000 to 2,000 feet of the MPI, this was a good release pattern; if not, then more training would be needed. If the lead bomber was shot down, an alternate aircraft, usually within the same leading three-plane element, would take its place; therefore, lead aircraft would need to include experienced personnel. The tactic limited the danger of collisions, as would happen if each plane jockeyed for position over the target. The method also added more protection from defending fighters as each combat box maintained integrity over the target. Ira Eaker would adopt the procedure for 8th AF missions. This would, in part, lead to the replacement of a skilled bombardier on each plane with a gunner trained to toggle the bomb release switch and not man a computerized bombsight.

Following the improving success the combat box afforded to group firepower, in February 1943, the Luftwaffe attempted to disrupt bomber formations by using timed ordnance dropped from aircraft above the formations. This again was inefficient but pointed to the healthy respect the German pilots had for 8th AF gunners. But the head-on tactic developed by Eder and Mayer would continue, even after the installation of forward-facing machine guns on the bombers.

CHAPTER 3
BLOOD AND TREASURE

A man's courage is his capital and he is always spending.
—Charles McMoran Wilson

Despite the culmination of strategic planning and increasing success in targeting, 1943 would be a hellish year for the Army Air Forces. It cannot be said that Hap Arnold, Tooey Spaatz, and Ira Eaker were not aware of the risks involved; they knew there would be losses. But they also harbored the misguided idea that their tools of aerial warfare, the heavy bombers, could defend themselves. It took the blood-letting of this year to demonstrate that they had been naïve in their original assessments; they were certainly unprepared for the monumental task before them. The technology they required, the long-range escort fighter, was not yet available, and it would take the horrific attrition of 1943 to hammer this point home. The P-47 Thunderbolt was readily available in three fighter groups by the spring of that year, but this gas hog had limited range.[1] Regardless, planning and mission deployment would continue until hideous losses forced a temporary cessation of operations in the fall.

Mission planning by 8th AF brass was in coordination with the RAF Bomber Command and was comprised of staff forming the "Committee on Coordination of Current Air Operations." The Committee met weekly from August through December 1942; after that, they met as needed until the Casablanca Conference with President Roosevelt, British prime minister Winston Churchill, and the Combined Chiefs of Staff in January 1943. The main objective of each mission followed the prescriptive doctrine of destroying the enemy's ability to wage war. The Committee met many times to determine which targets would meet this objective.

In the spring of 1943, this planning would be refined into the Combined Bomber Offensive (CBO). The dual efforts of the USAAF strategic bombing by day and the RAF area bombing at night kept relentless pressure on military targets such as U-boat pens and supporting docks, ports, and workshops; munition plants; aircraft and ancillary manufacturing plants supporting the aircraft industry; and lines of communication such as roads and rail lines in Germany and occupied countries. Since the RAF bombed at night, they could not do much more than attempt to affect morale rather than destroy specific targets. The hope was that the pounding would weaken the Luftwaffe enough that an invasion of mainland Europe would be possible in late 1943 or early 1944. The embodiment of the CBO, the "Pointblank" Directive, would be initiated in June 1943. It would include some seventy-six different targets within six different industries: aircraft factories, submarine pens, oil production, ball bearing factories, railroad marshalling yards and related communication systems, and other war-related industries. But the main focus was to eliminate the Luftwaffe so that the land invasion of Europe could proceed.

Operation Pointblank, the zenith of months of discussion and planning, was meant to support the invasion of the continent, but Supreme Allied Commander Gen. Dwight D. Eisenhower's ground forces were simply not ready within the desired timeframe. Also, the destruction of war manufacturing would take some amount of time to be felt in the enemy's economy; indeed, this consideration was taken into account when mission planners decided upon targets. The sooner the loss was felt by the German war industry, the greater the priority given to the VIII BC. Additionally, larger amounts of time and human resources needed to repair a damaged facility were also important. More resources diverted to rebuild destroyed infrastructure resulted in fewer hands making planes and bombs. Sadly, the Germans would make great use of forced labor to repair the bombed facilities. Millions of enslaved people were transported from conquered territories and made to replace track and rebuild ancillary structures damaged or obliterated by Allied ordnance. Manpower for such efforts was not normally as strong a consideration for the Germans as were raw materials. A damaged marshalling yard could be back in operation within a few days following a visit by the 8th AF.

The submarine pens, such as Saint-Nazaire and Lorient, were an early consideration of the 8th AF as the war in the Atlantic was costing the Allies dearly in shipping losses. But the CBO brought much more industry into focus. While the plans called for lofty goals in Pointblank, the USAAF's strength was still low by the spring of 1943, as missions were hampered by the limited availability of operational aircraft and crew numbers. This time period saw only six bomb groups in any state of readiness at a given moment.

One new piece of technology successfully finding its way into the fight was the AFCE. Automatic pilot systems had been in use since their development in the 1930s. The AFCE allowed the aircraft's bombardier to take control of the plane while on the bomb run; cables tied into the Norden bombsight allowed the manipulation of flight controls while the bombardier twisted the knobs. On a March 18, 1943, mission to bomb submarine pens at Vegesack, Germany, the AFCE saw its first successful use in combat.[2]

However, with the implementation of "bombing on the leader," such equipment would become useful primarily to the leading bombardier. The March 18 mission was also notable in that the 305th BG would display "pickle barrel" accuracy and drop some 76 percent of its ordnance within 1,000 feet of the MPI. For the time, this was extremely accurate. While seeming to be less accurate at first glance, bombing on the leader turned out to be an excellent experiment and increased overall accuracy for the groups.

The March 18 mission was also testament to the incredible fortitude needed by the fliers to carry out their duties. The nation's highest military honor was issued to an 8th AF airman as the result of this sortie. Twenty-one-year-old Jack W. Mathis was the lead bombardier in the 303rd BG as it deployed to the sub pens. The first lieutenant was one of two Texas-born Mathis brothers who signed up to be bombardiers in the USAAF; his brother Mark had been flying in B-26s in North Africa and came to Molesworth to visit his younger brother, who apparently attempted to talk Mark into transferring to the 303rd. Jack was tasked with one more mission before he and Mark were promised a weekend pass to get caught up with each other. Mark wanted to fly the mission to Vegesack but was denied due to red tape; he would have to wait for Jack to return. He would never see his little brother again.

Being the lead bombardier meant a lot of responsibility. The entire squadron would be looking to Jack to sight correctly on the bomb run; they would toggle their bombs as he released his. He could not make any errors. As the run started over the sub pens, Jack was bent intensely over his Norden bombsight, twisting the dials and making adjustments, when a large flak burst exploded just next to his position in the nose of his B-17, *The Duchess*. Jack and the navigator, Jesse Elliott, were blown to the rear of the nose compartment. Plexiglas and metal tore through the area. Elliott did not realize his crewmate was wounded, as Jack crawled back to his bombsight and bent once again over the viewfinder. He released his payload and uttered a single word, "Bombs...." The crew had been expecting the normal declaration of "Bombs away," but Jack collapsed before he could finish. When his crewmates pulled him from his station, he was dead; there was a large hole in his torso and his right arm was nearly severed above the elbow. The rest of the squadron had successfully released their payloads.

Upon return to Molesworth, *The Duchess* touched down with a red flare deployed to indicate wounded on board. Mark was waiting as she landed, no doubt immediately disturbed by the severe damage to the front of the ship. Knowing his brother was stationed in the destroyed nose, he must have been terror-stricken as she coasted to a stop. He was utterly devastated upon seeing his brother dead, but he knew what he had to do as he requested that transfer to the 303rd BG that Jack had wanted. Mark Mathis replaced his late brother at the very same position on board *The Duchess* and became her bombardier. Jack would be granted a posthumous Medal of Honor for the accurate placement of his ordnance while mortally wounded. His sacrifice would not be the only one endured by USAAF fliers; much more blood and treasure would be expended to bring Hitler to heel.

On May 29, 1943, nearly 280 aircraft were dispatched to Saint-Nazaire, La Pallice, and Rennes; of these bombers, only 238 actually attacked the targets with a number of aircraft forced to abort.[3] By war's end, one mission could see more than 2,000 aircraft dispatched, but for now, the North Africa campaign, Operation TORCH, would continue to divert precious resources of men and equipment, as it had done in the previous year. The May 29 mission was notable in that it was the first time the 8th AF made use of the YB-40 escorts (see chapter 2). Seven of these converted B-17s were dispatched to provide security for the mission.[4]

By this time, the Germans were beginning to withdraw aircraft from the eastern front to defend against the steadily increasing threat from the 8th AF. Until this time only two defensive Luftwaffe units were available to greet the 8th AF, *Jagdgeschwader* (JG) 2 and JG 26. Soviet Premier Joseph Stalin had wanted a second front in the west to take pressure off his troops, but the actual implementation of the second front was still over a year in the future with the Normandy landings. A minor fulfilment of Stalin's desire did come with Torch as the Allies landed in North Africa and then Sicily (Operation Husky) in November 1942 and July 1943, respectively. However, the redirection of the Luftwaffe from the Russian Front did ease some of the stress on the Red Army. Due to the bombing campaign in Germany and the occupied countries, the Germans were thus forced from an offensive posture in Russia to a defensive stance in its own territories to protect its war industries. The 8th AF was letting its presence be felt.

• • •

While the build-up continued, additional heavy bomb groups were added in the first half of 1943: the 94th, 95th, 96th, 351st, and 379th Bomb Groups became operational in May.[5] The 100th, 381st, and 384th would fly their first missions in June. The second half of the year would see the addition of the 385th and 388th in July; the 390th and 482nd in August;

the 389th and 392nd in September. The 401st flew its first sortie in November; the 445th, 446th, 447th, and 448th Bomb Groups were flying missions in December.[6] More groups would be added in the following year. And because crews required training upon arrival, assignments did not necessarily mean immediate inclusion into the mission roster. It might take a month or more for a bomb group to begin missions following their arrival in theater. New groups would also need to be assigned to one of several bombardment wings.

Earlier in the war, prior to the buildup, the VIII BC had new groups assigned to one of two bombardment wings (BW), the 1st and 2nd. Most of the pioneer groups, deployed with B-17s (the 97th, 301st, and 92nd) were assigned to the 1st BW. The 2nd Bombardment Wing would incorporate units equipped with the B-24 Liberator. In September 1943, a restructuring of the 8th AF would designate the bombardment "wings" into "divisions." Three bomb divisions would result when the 4th Bombardment Wing was renamed the 3rd Bombardment Division. Part of this action was due to the numbers of units being added and the increasingly unwieldy nature of the enormous expansion that was being undertaken in the summer of 1943. The bomb divisions were further divided into "combat bombardment wings" (CBW), with each division made up with four to five combat wings, each wing consisting of two to three bomb groups. By the spring of 1944, there would be some fourteen CBWs, which represented the final configuration for the VIII BC divisional organization. The complete structure was as follows:

CBW	1st Division[a]	CBW	2nd Division[b]	CBW	3rd Division[c]
1st	91st BG	2nd	445th BG	4th	94th BG
	381st		453rd		385th
	398th		44th		447th
40th	92nd	14th	392nd	13th	95th
	305th		492nd		100th
	306th		93rd		390th
41st	303rd	20th	446th	45th	96th
	379th		448th		388th
	384th		489th		452nd
94th	351st	95th	491st	92nd	486th
	401st		458th		487th
	457th	96th	466th	93rd	34th
			467th		490th
					493rd

a. Designated with a triangle on the tail fin and equipped with B-17s

b. Designated with a circle and equipped with B-24s

c. Designated with a square and contained a mix of B-17s and B-24s

By July 1943, each division was given a specific geometric shape so that bomb groups could be recognized as belonging to one of the three divisions. The 1st Division was designated by a triangle, the 2nd Division was identified with a circle, and the 3rd Division with a square. Letters within the shapes identified to which group the aircraft was assigned. For example, the 91st BG aircraft displayed a triangle "A" on its vertical stabilizer. The tail markings were not universal in the 8th AF, and many aircraft would not display these geometric shapes but would be identified by paint combinations on the vertical stabilizer, as was common in the 2nd Division with their B-24 Liberators.

In the meantime, the blood-letting continued. On a May Day mission to Saint-Nazaire, the 91st and 306th BGs would suffer more losses as they unloaded on the submarine pens again. One Fortress assigned to the 423rd Squadron was piloted by 1Lt. Lewis Johnson. On board was a short attitude-ridden staff sergeant by the name of Maynard "Snuffy" Smith. Smith, on his first mission with the 423rd, was the assigned ball turret gunner. Due to his diminutive stature, he was suited to the cramped space of the turret. Upon the group's return to base following the ordnance release, the Johnson crew was subjected to intense flak from the Brest Peninsula over France. The aircraft was solidly struck mid-ship and began burning furiously when a fuel tank ruptured. Three crewmembers bailed out over the Channel and were never seen again. Smith stayed onboard and began a ninety-minute battle against Armageddon. He tended to wounded gunners who were not able to bail out, while manning fire extinguishers and tossing flaming debris through a huge hole burning away the side of the aircraft. When enemy fighters assaulted the doomed B-17 to finish her off, Smith manned the waist guns to fend them off. When the extinguishers were emptied, he urinated on the conflagration. Somehow, he managed to beat back the fire to a standstill, ward off the Luftwaffe, and save the lives of his six remaining crewmates. The severely damaged aircraft crash landed on the first available English aerodrome. The scrappy little attitude monger would be awarded the Congressional Medal of Honor by Secretary of War Henry L. Stimson some weeks later.[7]

Prior to the May Saint-Nazaire mission, many of the original crews who had been flying since 1942 were exhibiting signs of combat fatigue, but there was nothing to be done about it at this time due to the immense build-up underway for the USAAF. The early crews of the 8th AF suffered tremendously, as there was no designated combat tour at that time. The men had no idea how long they would have to endure the terrible trials of combat flying. It would be many months before the 8th AF brass would implement a mission goal for airmen to complete to finish their combat tours. Until then, the Flak Farms would be the only outlet for shell-shocked troops.

On July 24, 1943, the Allied air forces initiated "Blitz Week." Weather for the previous few months had prevented all but a few missions where possible; now, with clear weather, General Eaker decided it was time for a big engagement. The operations of this maximum effort began with American strikes in Norway to eliminate metal industries and U-boat facilities in Heroya and Trondheim. This mission marked the successful use of splasher beacons for formation assembly. The uncooperative English weather often resulted in scrubbed missions when heavy overcast prevented bomber pilots from seeing their squadron mates as they rose from airfields. The splasher was a British invention and allowed crews to form up when they couldn't see each other (see chapter 1).

But it was the planning of the RAF Bomber Command that would include what today would most likely be considered a war crime. RAF Bomber Command chief Bomber Harris had made plans to strike a German city with intense ferocity, presumably to bring the German High Command to its senses. On the night of July 24–25, Bomber Harris dispatched his forces to Hamburg in what was titled Operation Gommorah. In addition to high explosives, the bombers would also release incendiaries over civilian targets. The goal was to create such a firestorm that the city center would be obliterated. It was the first use of this tactic, but would not be the last as Japanese cities would also feel equal wrath from the 20th AF later in the war.

For Bomber Harris, it was an exclamation point to be hammered home. For the 8th AF, Hamburg was a legitimate military target, as it contained war industries including engine plants and U-boat construction yards. So the Eighth followed the RAF and bombed Hamburg the next morning. Great plumes of smoke rose from the city as the American bombers passed overhead, obscuring the visibility of the bombardiers. Still, the Fortresses were able to unload their payloads and add to Hamburg's misery.

Two nights later, the RAF returned and unleashed more hell. Flames engulfed previously unburned structures, and humans, with hurricane force ferocity. People dove for the presumed safety of basements and bomb shelters only to be suffocated by the fire's ravenous appetite for oxygen. Hundreds upon hundreds of lifeless corpses would be found sitting quietly in bomb shelters without a scratch on them. People caught in the open were incinerated with no hope of later identification; some were reduced to amorphous scatterings of ash and charred debris. Gommorah would conclude in early August. The final death toll was estimated at 30,000 to 40,000 for the four raids, July 24–25, July 27–28, July 29–30, and August 2–3.[8] But the complete total will never be known, as Hamburg had been swelled beyond its normal population with internally displaced German citizens, refugees, and forced laborers from occupied countries The death toll may have been well over 100,000. We will never know the extent of the tragedy.

During the Blitz Week push, VIII BC dispatched 303 bombers to assault targets in Hamburg and Hanover on July 26; some twenty-four aircraft would be lost.[9] One of the attacking planes to survive, miraculously indeed, was *Ruthie II* of the 92nd BG, piloted by 1Lt. Robert L. Campbell and co-piloted by 1Lt. John C. ("Red") Morgan. This was the second "*Ruthie*" to be named for the pilot's wife, the first having been scrapped following too much battle damage. While in route to the target in Hanover, the formation was greeted by a furious flight of Fw 190s that careened nose first into the 92nd, spouting sheets of 20 mm cannon fire. Campbell was hit in the head but did not die instantly; the top turret gunner, Staff Sergeant Tyre Weaver, was also struck, severing his left arm below the shoulder. He collapsed unconscious onto the deck and was quickly attended to by the navigator, 2Lt. Keith J. Koske. Since the wound was so close to the shoulder, Koske was unable to staunch the heavy bleeding with a tourniquet. He knew if his friend was to have any chance for survival, he would need immediate medical assistance not available onboard a crippled bomber. He adjusted Weaver's parachute and, with some difficulty, shoved his buddy out the bomber's hatch. The intense cold on his drift to the ground no doubt helped slow the heavy bleeding. Miraculously, Weaver was found by the Germans in time and taken to a hospital, where he recovered.

The same happy ending could not be said of *Ruthie*'s pilot. With the back of his skull blown away, Campbell's death throes included a vise grip upon the flight controls. Morgan tried to dislodge the hold in order to keep the aircraft in the formation. For two solid hours the co-pilot fought a physically and emotionally exhausting battle to remain with his squadron and complete the mission. Morgan had considered removing Campbell's oxygen mask and allowing him to die, thus ending the terrible struggle, but he was unable to condemn his friend to death and instead fought to keep him alive and maintain position in the formation.

Morgan was unable to contact the rest of the crew over the interphone, as it had been fatally damaged, so assumed they were all dead or had bailed out. Equally, the crew was unable to speak to the flight deck and had no idea of the epic struggle underway in the cockpit. Many of the gunners had in fact passed out due to anoxia when the oxygen system in the rear of the plane was shot to pieces. The aircraft was at that time at approximately 24,000 feet of elevation. Koske and the bombardier, 2Lt. Asa J. Irwin, were fine in the nose compartment and still unaware of Morgan's distress until after the bomb drop on Hanover. While close to the channel, on the way home, Koske finally clambered up to the flight deck and discovered the nightmare Morgan was enduring. He assisted the co-pilot in pulling Campbell out of the pilot's seat so that Morgan could move over; the windshield had been all but destroyed and was too damaged for Morgan to see through. It was then that Koske learned that Morgan had been fighting with Campbell for two hours and *still* managed to complete the bomb run and stay in formation. The gunners were revived in a frozen state but were still alive. Morgan made an emergency landing at the first RAF base he could locate after the battered *Ruthie* crossed the Channel. Campbell had clung to life for only a few hours more before finally expiring. For his incredible feat of physical and emotional fortitude, Red Morgan was awarded the Medal of Honor. Humble to the core, Morgan argued that the award should have gone to Koske for both saving Weaver's life and helping to get the bomber under control. In March 1944, while serving as co-pilot with the 482nd BG (Pathfinder), Morgan was shot down in his H2X-equipped B-17. He would spend the remainder of the war as a guest of the Luftwaffe at Stalag Luft I in Barth, Germany, the only Medal of Honor recipient of the war to hold that distinction.[10]

The Blitz Week effort continued on July 27, when eighteen B-26 Marauders of the 323rd BG lifted off from their East Anglian base at Earls Colne to smash the runways at Tricqueville in Normandy. No losses were reported. Deep penetration into Germany occurred the next day, when seventy-seven bombers attacked the aircraft factories at Kassel and Oschersleben. The airborne defenders managed to shoot down a number of American bombers using air to air rockets. Twenty-two bombers were lost on this deployment, an intolerable and unsustainable 28 percent loss rate.[11] On July 29, the 8th AF attacked the U-boat pens at Kiel and aircraft factories at Warnemünde. No losses were reported. The same could not be said for the last mission of Blitz Week. On July 30, Gen. Eaker dispatched two more efforts to Kassel to continue with the disruption of its aircraft industry. The bombers were escorted this time by P-47s equipped with drop tanks, surprising the Luftwaffe with such deep incursion into German airspace. Despite the escort, of the 134 bombers attacking, twelve were shot down.[12]

July 30 would mark the end of Blitz Week for the 8th AF; the heavy-bomber crews were exhausted and needed rest. The first half of August 1943 would see a number of missions to shipyards at Le Trait, France (August 4); industrial targets in the Ruhr Valley of Germany (August 12); airfields in France and the Netherlands (August 15); and airfields in France (August 16).

But it would be a mission to central Germany that would be the first of several to a location few Army Air Force crewmembers had ever heard of and would elicit forebodings of certain death in many. Before the missions to the ball-bearing plants at Schweinfurt were over, the losses sustained by the bomber crews would force the 8th AF brass to rethink their methods. The men aboard the bombers simply could not endure the slaughter at such a horrific scale.

Missions to destroy railroad marshalling yards, submarine pens, aircraft factories, and ancillary support facilities were intuitive to planning for the Combined Bomber Offensive. But there were other factories integral to the smooth operation of Hitler's war machine. The humble ball bearing was critical to allow armies to roll. Germany had a large facility in the center of the country in the small town of Schweinfurt, far from the range of escorting fighters. Gen. Eaker opposed the mission. He did not feel the Eighth had the manpower to attempt such an endeavor and wanted to wait until more bomb groups were operational. Indeed, his caution would cause great friction with Gen. Arnold in the coming months and lead to what Eaker considered a demotion. Regardless of his reservations, the mission would go forward.

The weather had cleared for the Blitz Week push, but by the end of July, the crews were too exhausted to include a long mission deep into Germany; the second week of August 1943 was selected. The flight, Mission 84, would lift off on the first anniversary of the inaugural deployment of the 8th AF. Added to the target planning was the Messerschmitt factory at Regensburg in the south of the country. Such long distances were now possible with the addition of "Tokyo Tanks," additional fuel capacity installed in the bomber's wings which granted the aircraft longer flight times. These tanks were made up of nine fuel cells in each wing for a total of eighteen cells; each was rubberized and designed to be self-sealing. The cells were connected to each other and to the main fuel tanks via lines draining by gravity from the wings to the main tanks. The increase was an additional 1,080 gallons and allowed the two flights ample fuel to reach their objectives.

This would be a maximum effort for the 8th AF; 376 bombers were planned with 230 dispatched to Schweinfurt and 146 tasked for Regensburg. However, a number of aircraft were forced to abort, or otherwise did not reach the target, and the final tally was 183 attacking Schweinfurt and 127 assaulting Regensburg.[13] Fighter escorts would accompany the formations, at least initially. P-47 Thunderbolts and Supermarine Spitfires would provide cover for the very beginning and end of the mission for bombers returning to England. The 1st and 4th Bombardment Wings (at this time informally referred to as the

1st and 3rd Air Divisions, respectively) would be tasked with this largest deployment yet of the war, with Brig. Gen. Robert B. Williams commanding the former and Col. Curtis LeMay the latter. Williams would be tasked with hitting Schweinfurt, and LeMay Regensburg. Given the long distance from its bases in East Anglia, LeMay's strike force would not return immediately to England but would fly on to North Africa over the Alps to bases belonging to the 12th AF for refueling and eventual return to England. The mission was deployed as a "double-strike" to try to split the German fighter defenses. In theory, LeMay's group would pull fighters away from Williams and allow the Schweinfurt raid a margin of success it might not have achieved otherwise. Unfortunately, that's not what happened.

Timing was *everything* in this massive effort. The 1st Division would need to leave within ten minutes of the 3rd Division's entrance into enemy airspace. The 3rd would then occupy the Luftwaffe while the 1st flew on to the ball-bearing factories. But Mother Nature intervened and kept Williams's aircraft grounded with fog and cloud cover. The 1st Division would not ascend until more than three hours after their prescribed departure. By then, the 3rd had moved deep into Germany and the Luftwaffe's air defenses were in full force to greet the 1st Division. The P-47s and Spitfires were able to deploy with the 3rd Division bombers, and many returned after escorting the early phase of the Regensburg mission to fuel up and rearm. The escorts then ascended again and attached themselves to Williams's formation, flying as long as their drop and main fuel tanks would allow before returning to base. Additionally, diversionary sorties were dispatched to French airfields to confuse the Luftwaffe.

But the German air force was not as confused as the bomber groups would have liked. The formations, especially on the Schweinfurt leg, were assaulted with wave after wave of defenders, in all some 300 enemy fighters. Many of the German pilots had plenty of time and attacked the bombers, ran low on fuel, returned to their bases to refuel and rearm, then ascended aloft to hit the Williams's formation again. By the time all was said and done, the 1st Division would lose thirty-six aircraft of the 183 deployed, some 20 percent of its attacking force. The bombing patterns were not very accurate, but several of the main plants were heavily damaged.

The Regensburg raid was slightly more fortunate, though not by much. It lost 24 of the 127 planes that bombed the Messerschmitt plants, close to 19 percent. One of the units suffering the most was the 100th Bomb Group. They were in the unfortunate low position, called by the crews "Purple Heart Corner," and took the brunt of the Luftwaffe's attention; close to half its number never made it home with nine planes downed, more than any other group. Additional bad luck in coming months would earn them the unfortunate moniker the "Bloody Hundredth."

LeMay's group scored excellent hits on the Messerschmitt plants, damaging nearly all of the most important buildings. They then turned south to fly on to North Africa to refuel. After reaching the base there, Col. LeMay complained about this first "shuttle mission" and the difficulty in keeping the bombers flying without their ground crews. As a result, many aircraft too damaged to be returned to service without extensive repairs had to be left behind in North Africa, their crews climbing aboard airworthy bombers for the long flight back to England.

While bombing patterns were considered good, especially on the Regensburg leg, Mission 84 was not considered a rousing success due to the high loss rate. Ten percent losses for any deployment were unsustainable; the combined attrition rate on August 17, 1943, was a total of sixty aircraft lost with 600 men, some 19 percent of the attacking forces; many more bombers had to be scrapped upon landing due to fatal battle damage, becoming "hangar queens" for parts distribution. The final cost of aircraft for Mission 84 was approximately 40 percent. Fighter escorts were the key to mission survivability, but the technology just wasn't available … not yet.

• • •

The 8th AF took a brief respite from long range deployments to lick its wounds and allow the traumatized crews to collect themselves. Smaller missions were dispatched to assault German airfields and industries in the occupied Netherlands. On August 19, ninety-three heavies were tasked with smashing airfields in Gilze-Rijen and Vlissingen. A day later, the Donier bomber factory at Vlissingen was attacked by A-20 Bostons and B-26 Marauder medium bombers. The mediums would continue to keep up the pressure on the twenty-second and hit airfields in France at Beaumont le Roger.

Some eighty-four of the heavy bombers parked in North Africa following the Regensburg mission were returned to East Anglia on the twenty-fourth with a brief fly-over of Bordeaux to release high-explosive greetings to the German occupiers of a local airfield. Ware industries in Villacoublay and airfields in Conches and Évreux, all in France, were also hit on the twenty-fourth. With the exception of the North Africa flight back to Britain, all of these latter August 1943 sorties for VIII BC were within range of fighter escorts with minimal losses. Even the 3rd Division's shuttle back to East Anglia was relatively inexpensive, with three bombers lost en route; one bomber was downed on the Conches and Évreux segment.[14]

The VIII BC planners received word on a Vengeance weapon launching site, located in France at Watten, in late August, and sent a large deterrence of 180 heavies to address the issue and discourage the assembly of further facilities. The launch site was still under construction and had not yet been commissioned. The V-weapon sites would become a primary target for the 8th AF. This was the first of many missions to obliterate them as soon as they were discovered.

In late August, a milestone in the VIII BC's ability to operate in poor weather was reached as the first Pathfinder bomb group became operational. The Alconbury-based 482nd BG was equipped with H2S/H2X air-to-surface radar as well as the Oboe system developed by the British. Three squadrons of B-17F bombers were tasked with pioneering the skill of blind bombing in what was primarily a testing and training period. Their first mission was on September 27, 1943, when they led 244 heavies to the Port of Emden in northern Germany. This testing period would lead to full mission deployment of the H2X on B-17G models in February 1944. Another milestone was achieved on this mission as P-47s equipped with drop tanks escorted the bombers the entire length of the effort. However, the sortie was not without loss; seven aircraft did not return to England.

Not only were the British and Americans developing enhanced technology to fight the war; the Germans had introduced more devastating defensive measures with the deployment of air to air rockets. Aircraft-launched rockets had been in use since the First World War. The main German defensive aircraft-based weapon during 1943 had been the 20 mm cannon. With the initiation of head-on attacks by Egon Meyer's unit, the skill needed to accurately aim air cannon fire at 500–600 mph closing speeds was daunting. Additionally, the range for the cannons was similar to that of the bomber's .50-cal. guns. With enough fuel, rockets could be deployed behind the bomber from a safe distance, thus avoiding its defenses. These weapons were devastating; they could take down a heavy bomber with a single strike. Early Second World War versions of air defense weapons included the Luftwaffe's Werfer-Granate 21. It was in use by 1943 and consisted of a single tube-mounted projectile under each wing of a Fw 190. Fortunately for bomber crews, these rockets were extremely inaccurate, but should they strike a B-17, the result was complete loss of life aboard the aircraft. The much-vaunted German air-to-air missile, the *Rakete, 4Kilogramm, Minenkopf*

(R4M), was still in development and was not yet deployed for normal operations. It would prove one of the most devastating defensive tools in the Luftwaffe's arsenal for confronting the bombers.

Meanwhile, the strikes would continue. Given the strategic importance of the ball-bearing industry, the VIII BC mission planners continued the war against the factories. Hitler had by now realized the peril of having above-ground facilities.[15] He would eventually get the message and begin dispersing factories, especially the aircraft plants, to hidden underground locations masked by deep woods. But until that time, German industries would take a terrible beating. The VIII BC decided that Schweinfurt was due for a second visit in October 1943. The bearing factories would be hit on the fourteenth in what would be stamped "Mission 115."

Mid-morning on October 14, 1943, hundreds of bombers from the 1st, 2nd, and 3rd Air Divisions lifted off from their bases in East Anglia; mechanical problems and other snafus would ground or send many back to their airfields, with 229 finally airborne over Germany. Elements from the 2nd Division became lost in the Channel fog and ended up performing an impromptu diversionary mission off Germany's northern coast. Many of the Schweinfurt-bound aircraft would never reach the target, despite the deployment of P-47 and Spitfire fighter escorts; the bombers' "little friends" could not remain with their charges for long and the heavies were soon on their own. The VIII BC brass knew that many Luftwaffe fighter bases were well within range of the bombers' flightpath, but this could not be avoided. As soon as the escorts turned toward home, the Luftwaffe fell upon the Americans with a terrible ferocity. The VIII BC planners were fairly ignorant of just how well prepared the German defenders would be in opposing the mission. Wave upon wave of single and dual-engine fighters hit the bomber stream, knocking down their targets with machine guns, 20 mm cannon fire, and rockets, with the latter being deployed primarily by twin-engine fighters.

As with the August mission to Schweinfurt, the German defending pilots had ample time to assault the bomber stream, return to their bases to refuel and rearm, ascend again, and pummel the bombers a second time. With no fighter protection, the 8th AF finally reached its target with a nasty bloody nose; some seven aircraft, seventy men, from the 40th Combat Wing tumbled to earth before reaching the initial point. Despite the trauma, the hits on the ball-bearing plants were generally well-placed, resulting in extensive damage. The bombers then limped toward home only to be hounded, slapped, smacked, and blown apart on the long and terrifying flight back to

East Anglia. The 1st Division would lose a total of twenty-nine bombers before the day was finished; thirty-one more aircraft from the 3rd Division would also be shot down. The losses equaled those of the August raid. Twenty-six percent of all the attacking bombers were destroyed. Seventeen aircraft that did, miraculously, return to their bases had to be scrapped, becoming "hangar queens" for spare parts; 121 more needed repairs before being deployed again. Some 600 men became POWs or were killed as a result of the second Schweinfurt raid. The day would go down in 8th AF history as "Black Thursday."

Such horrendous losses could not be sustained. The cost for Mission 115 was so great in lives, equipment, and crew morale that the VIII BC ordered a temporary halt in operations. Combat crews, especially those who suffered through both Schweinfurt missions, needed rest, with many, undoubtedly, reporting to flak farms. Even top USAAF brass had to admit that the deep penetrations into Germany could not be undertaken without the protection of "little friends." The Army needed a long-range escort, and after the attrition rate of the past few months, it needed more bombers and more crews. It needed both badly.

Chapter 4

BOMBER BOYS

Nothing is as strong as the heart of a volunteer.
—James Doolittle

As with so many of the "Greatest Generation," Rodney Alverson Williams rarely spoke with his children about his war experiences. Like so many traumatized veterans, he kept his nightmares to himself. He was born on October 14, 1911, the son of Harry Frank Williams and Elizabeth Alverson Williams; they were married on October 3, 1906. Rodney and his older sister Louise grew up in a middle-class Spokane, Washington, neighborhood until Harry, a salesman by trade, moved the family in the mid-1930s to follow better job prospects during the Depression. Family lore has it that Harry paused at a highway intersection where he flipped a coin to decide whether the car would be turned east to head to the Atlantic coast, or south to stay on the west coast. The coin toss determined a southern route; the Williams family ended their journey in Long Beach, California.

Rod worked as a restaurant bus boy before landing a job as a machinist at J. A. Campbell Company in Long Beach, in 1938. He quickly rose to master machinist, and for four years prior to his enlistment in the US Army Air Forces, he stamped sheet metal for boiler parts. The company made process control instrumentation such as water level control mechanisms and other essential boiler accessories, as well as equipment for the petroleum industry. Rod never said so, but his late 1942 entry into the service could have been delayed due to work Campbell may have been doing for the war effort, but Rod never commented on this to his family. On October 19, 1942, he joined the Army Air Forces, and at thirty-one years of age, he was much older than the young kids he met in basic training.

Recruits were given a litany of tests to determine their fitness for service in the Army Air Forces, with psychological toughness at the top of the list; they were also tested for motor skills, mental acuity, and physical condition. The Office of the Chief of Air Corps (OCAC) Medical Division developed a psychological study in June 1941. The goal was to systemize the process of selecting men, particularly pilots, mentally capable of combat air service. A testing program was the fruit of this study and was implemented in September 1941. Pilot training candidates were sent to the psychological screening center at the Maxwell Field Air Base in Alabama; later, screening programs were installed at San Antonio, Texas, and Santa Ana, California. A thirty-hour in-processing regime was faced by each man selected to attend the program. The procedure included a six-hour psychological screening process, broken down into three two-hour sessions. The idea was to muster out underperforming aircrew candidates by subjecting them to high-stress conditions and monitoring their reactions.[1] The testing at Maxwell proved to be so useful that a longer study was conducted, using the results of the preliminary screening.

The tests consisted primarily of written exams and "psychomotor" skills determinations (i.e., the coordination between thought and the necessary physical response to a specific stimulus). The candidate's reflexes and response times were measured; balance and equilibrium were tested; and the ability to think clearly and respond with purpose in times of extreme stress were all measured to see how the candidate reacted.

A tough set of standards grew from all this testing; a man seeking to be posted on a bomber had to successfully complete each exam. Men not meeting those strict standards were quickly dismissed or sent to an Air Corps ground crew or even an Army infantry unit. Those scoring high on their tests could be considered for pilot, navigator, or bombardier schools. The original educational requirements for men to qualify for these advanced schools, two years of college or the passage of a difficult written exam, were eased to allow for a greater pool of recruits. By 1941, the two-year college requirement was abandoned in favor of the possession of a high school diploma and passage of written and physical exams. Therefore, a fully trained bomber pilot could be a teenager or a young man barely out of his teens, a common situation during the Second World War, especially in the latter stages of the conflict. Desperate for pilots, the Army Air Force would recruit kids fresh out of high school. Like young men everywhere and throughout the long expanse of human experience, these boys no doubt were anxious to shake the dust of their tiny hometowns from their feet and leave home for an adventure. They were completely ignorant of the trials and terrors that lay ahead.

Basic training for Air Corps recruits was not very different than regular Army training. The prospective airmen would learn military discipline, physical training, close order drill, first aid, use of firearms, and other basic skills required for a soldier of the US Army. The difference was in the advanced training each future airman received. Basic instruction lasted four weeks before newly minted GIs were sent to advanced individual training schools.

Rodney spent a month in Army basic training at Buckley Field Air Base in Colorado before moving on to Lowry Field, Colorado, for three months of Airplane and Mechanic School, where he learned basic procedures with the function of the aircraft. Following that stint, he was transferred to Las Vegas for five months of Aerial Gunnery School, where he was promoted to buck sergeant and stayed on for a year to train more airmen to operate .30-cal. and .50-cal. machine guns, as well as 20 mm and 37 mm aerial cannons. Shortly thereafter he was promoted to staff sergeant.

In November 1944, Rod met with his permanent crewmates for the first time at Biggs Field Air Base at Fort Bliss, Texas. Biggs served as a training base for heavy-bomber crews. Men transferred here trained together and shipped out as a cohesive team; they became familiar with their crewmates as well as their aircraft. It was here that Rodney met his pilot, twenty-year-old 2Lt. David E. Vermeer, the son of Dutch immigrants, Peter and Rena Vermeer, who teased a living from rich Iowa farmland. The co-pilot, 2Lt. John J. Thompson, nineteen years old, was a high-spirited, good-natured kid from Dexter, Michigan. The navigator, 2Lt. Eugene ("Gene") E. Holley, also nineteen, hailed from Windsor, Ohio. Second Lt. John Sites, twenty years old, called Tennessee home and manned the Norden bombsight.

SSgt. Williams was assigned to the crew as a waist gunner. The other gunners in the aircraft's self-preservation team included Chicagoan radioman/gunner twenty-year-old Sgt. Milan Basara, the son of Yugoslavian immigrants; Wisconsin native Sgt. Harold ("Hal") Churchill, age twenty-one, served as the flight engineer (the onboard mechanic) and top turret gunner; Chicago resident Sgt. Fred A. Gerhardt, age eighteen, regularly mashed his 6-foot-plus frame into the cramped ball turret; he and Rodney later switched places as Rod was a slight 5 foot, 8 inches and more suited to folding himself into the tiny ball turret. Rounding out the bomber boys was twenty-eight-year-old Wisconsin resident Sgt. Harold L. Babcock, who manned the uncomfortable banana seat at the tail gunner's position.

Gene Holley's path to Biggs Field as a young officer was via the USAAF Miami Beach Training Center, where he underwent basic training in July and August 1943. Gene disliked the facility and the location in general and was happy to be sent to Allegheny College at Meadville, Pennsylvania, only 40 miles from his Ohio hometown. At Meadville he took college classes and flying lessons where he learned to fly the Piper Cub. He was then sent to Texas, to the San Antonio Aviation Cadet Center.[2] It was here that he further enhanced his flying skills while awaiting a slot in navigator's school. He was also most likely subjected to the psychological screening as discussed above, as San Antonio had such a program at that time. Navigation school was at Ellington Field near Houston. Gene graduated and left Houston on October 2, 1944, with shiny new navigator wings pinned to his uniform. He met with his wartime crew at Biggs Field in November.

The boys trained together and formed a close bond, with several deciding on nicknames for their new buddies: Rodney became "Willy," Fred Gerhardt was called "Hardtack," John, J. Thompson was "JJ," and Milan Basara was "Bas." The crew flew practice missions while at Biggs Field, getting to know each other's habits and idiosyncrasies. Second Lt. Sites, as bombardier and flight armorer, was required to learn each gunner's position and the functions of all of the .50-cal. machine guns onboard. He trained on the loading of the bombs and the procedures required to arm and set the fuse; he learned of the physics required to release them from the racks successfully. Dave Vermeer was an excellent pilot and very familiar with the B-17G.[3] Gene felt the crew was in good hands with Dave at the helm. Gene also felt that JJ served a crucial role as the crew's comic relief and kept the boys smiling, whereas Dave was all business during training. Gene honed his navigational and flying skills while the gunners practiced their aim.

The new crew all trained hard on a B-17G that was not the ship in which they would be sent to the war. The aircraft at Biggs Field were assigned as trainers. The boys stayed at Biggs until January 1945, when they were transferred to Lincoln, Nebraska, ostensibly to pick up the ship they would be flying to Britain, but such was not the case. They were trained as a replacement crew and would be flying aircraft already on location in Britain. On February 2, 1945, they found themselves boarding an ocean liner, the *Île de France*, after a short stay at Camp Kilmer, New Jersey, a staging area for troops before deployment to the ETO. Despite the liner's enormous size, some 791 feet, the boys were stuffed into cabins with beds stacked three high and little elbow room. Most of the long hours spent onboard ship would have included chess and poker tournaments, dice-rolling crap games, long discussions with new-found friends on food, girlfriends, wives, pre-war jobs, parental duties with small kids at home, and everything in between. They would have had manhood-measuring contests with arm-wrestling, body-wrestling, impromptu boxing matches, and so on. The trek across the Atlantic would have been exceedingly long and boring for hundreds of young men itching for "adventure." By the end of it, tempers were short and gratitude upon finally landing at port was long.

Despite the long days of boredom, the *Île de France* was fast, far more so than any enemy submarine and most US Navy escorts, so she traveled alone across the Atlantic, under constant blackout conditions so that enemy craft could not spot her. John Sites served as a "blackout" officer during the voyage, keeping curious GIs and sailors off the top deck at night. The crew landed in Glasgow, Scotland, on February 11, incident free. The relief at making it across safely must have been tremendous for the boys. Everyone knew how dangerous the German U-boat wolfpacks were to Allied shipping.

The newly arrived airmen would have immediately noticed the dampness and cold air of the British Isles in February. Scotland and England are nestled in the North Atlantic, where cold and damp are a constant discomfort during the winter months. The ubiquitous fog, rain, and chill would rest uncomfortably for many of the boys throughout their tours. Airmen from Seattle might feel at home, but most others would feel they were in a never-ending drizzle; clouds would cover the sky most of the time. As they grasped their duffle bags and strolled down the ship's gangway to waiting trucks, they might have wondered if the clouds were always there, or if this was just a particularly moist day. Indeed, this very weather was so ubiquitous, particularly in the time of year that Dave's crew exited the *Île de France*, that crews throughout England had learned to fly their missions by taking off in nearly blind conditions with heavy fog, seeing the sun only when forming up above the clouds. It was a skill that would serve them all well. But there were also many tragedies as pilots lost their way on the path to formation. This thought may have crossed Dave's mind as he clambered aboard the transport vehicle with his crew. JJ was probably cracking jokes at the time, and while he frequently had a smile on his face, Dave was often quiet and pensive. He probably had a myriad of questions roaming through his head as he looked out of the rear of the truck.

Upon reporting to the US Army Air Force Assignment Depot at Stone, England, on February 13, the boys learned of their posting. They would be sent to Station 128 at Deenethorpe, in Northamptonshire, 65 miles northeast of London, the home of the 401st Bombardment Group. The 401st was considered one of the most accurate bomb groups of the 8th Air Force and was one of the most decorated. Gene Holley remarked in his memoirs that the posting was a fortunate one with such a distinguished unit.

The 401st had four bombardment squadrons: the 612th, 613th, 614th, and 615th; Dave's crew was assigned to the 613th. The 401st flew the B-17G and was part of the 1st Bombardment Division. Upon their arrival, Dave and the boys would have immediately noticed the tail markings on the bombers, a broad yellow stripe with black borders and a black triangle near the tip of the tail displaying a large "S." At this point in the war, B-17s sent from the States were no longer painted in ubiquitous olive drab but were shiny, factory-fresh aluminum. Paint weighed down aircraft and affected their speed, critical to survival in enemy airspace. Additionally, there was little evidence that camouflage paint actually protected the bombers.

The squadron markings for the 401st were based on the British habit of displaying an alphabetic code in the center of the fuselage of the ship. The 613th squadron was identified in large black paint by "IN" forward of the waist windows. The other squadrons were 612th with "SC," 614th with "IW," and the 615th with "IY." Behind the waist windows was the ship's individual alphabetic code, its place in the squadron was marked by a large black letter, "A," "B," "C," etc. The letters were painted both at the waist area and under the aircraft's serial number on the vertical stabilizer.

The boys would spend some time in orientation and training before being placed on the mission roster. They would not be assigned a specific aircraft until their missions were scheduled, and even then, they would be allocated different bombers. As a replacement crew, they were bounced around a bit; they would spend their missions having to get acquainted with four different aircraft. This was often problematic for crews, as they could not become fully in tune with one bomber, learning her strengths and weaknesses, knowing her timing, responses, and quirks. As flight engineer, Hal Churchill would have to carefully check out each unfamiliar aircraft to make sure he was fully aware of any mechanical issues, regardless of complexity, before every mission. He would speak to the ground crew mechanics and perform meticulous systems checks, as well as physically check the aircraft with the crew chief in tow. The crew chief, as the head groundcrew mechanic, would know each ship in the squadron individually. Hal would need to understand any issues that might come up during the flight and how to respond to them. He would also need to ensure he had the pertinent knowledge required to deal with any problem that might arise during a flight. Hal's job was critical and his skills and knowledge were essential to the success of each mission and the well-being of the crew. Every other mission Dave's crew was assigned a different B-17G, initially a nameless bomber (43-38791), then *Morning Star* (42-31730), *Southern Comfort* (44-8767), and finally the *Lady Jane II* (43-38607). The boys would have to adjust; having a regular bomber would be a luxury Dave's crew would not know.

• • •

The 401st Bombardment Group was formed in April 1943 as part of the buildup of the Mighty Eighth. On April 1, 1943, while several of Dave Vermeer's future crew were still in training, General Order Number 46 was issued, and the 401st was born, initially headquartered at the Ephrata Army Air Base in Washington State. Seven weeks later, the unit moved to another Washington air base at Geiger before transiting to Great Falls, Montana, for yet more training. Many of the air crews and ground personnel traveled to Britain via the *Queen Mary* while their B-17G aircraft were ferried to the ETO through Iceland in October 1943 by male and female pilots of the ATC. The delivery pilots would often fly another aircraft back to the States or, more often than not, hop aboard a ship to return home, grab another aircraft, fly it to England, and repeat the process, again and again. The men and women of the ATC are truly unsung heroes, as they kept the flow of planes to airbases as the losses of combat aircraft mounted; they are often forgotten in too many histories of the Second World War.

The 401st BG arrived at Deenethorpe by November 3, 1943. On November 26, the new bombardment group flew its first mission to hit the center of Bremen, Germany. According to the after-action report, the 401st managed to get lost during assembly and mixed with an "unknown" combat wing, eventually determined to be the 388th BG.[4] Some twenty 401st bombers were dispatched, but one was forced to return to Deenethorpe due to a mechanical issue. The remaining nineteen bombed Bremen on a PFF signal and returned to base with fairly light flak damage. It was an encouraging beginning; no aircraft were lost, but a mid-air collision over the target with a 388th B-17 cost the life of a gunner in the ship *Fancy Nancy* when the ball turret was torn away. The unlucky occupant was a waist gunner who had shimmied into the turret to clear a fault with the .50-cal. guns with which the assigned ball turret gunner was having difficulty. Both aircraft eventually returned to base, but *Nancy* was scrapped.[5] Lt. Scribner Daily, her pilot, would fly three more B-17s named *Fancy Nancy.* He would lose the second one as well when she ran out of fuel; the crew was forced to bail out near Kimbolton, Cambridgeshire, following a December 31, 1943, mission to Cognac, France. The remaining two *Fancy Nancy* bombers that would grace the 612th Squadron were numbers III and IV, with number III being shot down during a mission to Brunswick on January 30, 1944. Fortunately, the *Fancy Nancy IV* was reassigned out of the 401st and spared Lt. Daily's apparent curse with the name.[6]

On December 5, 1943, the small village of Deenethorpe was reminded just how perilous it was to have a heavy bombardment group for a neighbor. Assigned to the 613th BS, the oddly-named B-17G *Zenobia El Elephanta* was taking off for a mission to Paris when her pilot, 1Lt. Walter B. Keith, was unable to gain altitude and quickly lost control of the fully-loaded bomber. An investigation later concluded that icing on the wing and prop wash triggered a loss of power; the imbalance to the engines caused the left wing to dip, striking the runway as the ship lifted off. The *Zenobia* listed to port and headed straight for Deenethorpe, where she crashed into an unoccupied cottage and proceeded to burn. Airfield personnel sprinted to the site while local villagers hastily pulled the crew to safety. The crewmembers then ran around the village frantically imploring residents to evacuate before the bomb load cooked off and exploded. They were successful; no one was hurt. But the village was leveled; not a building escaped damage. Few could have predicted that such severe bomb damage would be caused by friendlies and not by avenging German raiders.[7]

The 401st developed a reputation for accurate bombing; it received two Presidential Unit Citations in quick succession in January and February 1944, only a few months after arriving in theater. As a result of their quick learning and adaptability, they were often the lead element in many missions, as was the case on a January 11, 1944, mission to Oschersleben, Germany, a fighter production factory complex 90 miles west of Berlin. The 401st led the 94th CBW. While all three divisions were dispatched, 8th AF weather watchers urged a recall due to heavy rain clouds; the 2nd and 3rd Divisions heeded the call and returned home. But the 1st Division was closer to their goal and remained in the fight. Disregarding the recall, they rumbled on toward the aircraft factories.

At this point in the war, more P-51 Mustangs were available in the ETO, but certainly not enough. These long-range fighters were welcome companions for the American heavies. However, only a single group of Mustangs from the 354th FG was available to escort the remaining elements of the 1st Division to the target. P-47s accompanied the bombers as far as their fuel tanks would allow; then the Mustangs would provide security to the Focke-Wulf plants and back. But coverage was not constant, so as soon as the P-47s peeled off to head home, Bf 109s, Fw 190s, Bf 110s, Me 210s, and Ju 88s assaulted the bombers. The enemy would do what it must to protect their war industries, and the 8th AF knew the Germans would put up a stiff resistance. The 94th CBW followed the 41st CBW into the heavily contested airspace, not knowing just how stiff that resistance would be.

Thick cloud cover added to the problems of the day and most of the 354th was separated from the bomber stream; many of the fighters were separated from each other as the Luftwaffe closed in on the 1st Division.

While flak was light over the target, the Germans pounded the bombers for two hours, knocking down four B-17s from the 401st and six from the 351st BG. When it looked like the bombers would be fatally punished for their deep incursion into German airspace, a single P-51 roared from behind the enemy formation, immediately sending several Luftwaffe defenders spinning to earth. Thirty-year-old Maj. James Howell Howard had found the bomber stream in the thick clouds and for some thirty minutes protected the heavies as a one-man air force, engaging some thirty to forty enemy fighters and shooting down at least four of them. Upon his return to his base, he simply shrugged off the feat as being part of his duty. Five months later, he was awarded the Medal of Honor. Additionally, for its excellent accuracy and performance on this mission, the 401st was awarded its first Presidential Unit Citation.

• • •

By this point in the war, the various Air Forces in Europe had fallen under the auspices of a much-larger organization. The missions of the bombing and fighter groups were intrinsically tied to the invasion of the European Continent (Operation Overlord). All of the Allied bombing missions were tasked to support this goal with Pointblank well in mind. Around the summer of 1943, Hap Arnold began to think that the entire US mission in the ETO would be best served under a single command structure, in cooperation with the objectives of Overlord, which was scheduled for the spring of 1944. Arnold was getting impatient; he realized that Pointblank was stalling. By late 1943, he noted that the Luftwaffe was still too potent a force to ensure even a modicum of success for the cross-channel invasion.

During the Tehran Conference between the Allies in November and the Cairo Conference in December, Arnold brought up his concerns. Given his anxiety about the slow pace of Pointblank and the need for greater coordination for the bombing missions, he had decided to combine the entire USAAF European mission into a single command for easier synchronization of missions between the 8th and 9th AFs (Britain), the 12th AF (North Africa), and the 15th AF (Italy). "Bomber" Harris of RAF Bomber Command, who had previously been apprehensive on being subservient to Arnold's proposed organization, made his case for RAF independence.

With the support of President Roosevelt, on January 1, 1944, the United States Strategic Air Forces (USSTAF) in Europe was born, at least on paper.

The VIII Bomber Command was dissolved and rolled into the 8th AF when Jimmy Doolittle took over; he moved the 8th AF headquarters from Bushy Park to High Wycombe Abby. USSTAF headquarters would reside at Bushy Park. The change was needed as Gen. Eisenhower was made Supreme Allied Commander. It also required his blessing, or that of his representative Maj. Gen. Walter B. Smith. It was granted in early January. Hap Arnold selected Tooey Spaatz to head the new organization as its commanding general. Additional complex administrative alterations took place that exceed the scope of this narrative.

• • •

Operation Argument, famously known as "Big Week," kicked off on February 20, 1944. The weather over western Europe had been fickle at best, impossible at worst for the USAAF to carry out missions in January and most of February. In a time before accurate weather stations and computer-driven modeling, meteorologists were heavily depended upon to "get it right" so that the missions to Germany could be carried out with minimal weather-induced recalls. While many, if not most, of the bomber pilots were skilled enough to take off on instruments, bombing still required decent weather; landing the bombers after missions was also problematic in the foggy English winter.

Bombing via H2X and Mickey aircraft was certainly an option, but *accurate* bombing still required visible targets; high winds, rain, and sleet could make even PFF-guided missions immensely difficult. Gen. Spaatz was fully cognizant of the importance of Pointblank to Overlord, which could not be successful until the Luftwaffe was no longer a concern. Good weather and multiple maximum-effort missions were necessary. Finally, on February 19, the USSTAF meteorologists delivered the good news. While the English fog might not cooperate, the cloud cover over Germany appeared to be thinning out. Argument would migrate from paper planning to the air.

Twelve targets were selected, primarily to hit aircraft assembly plants in the Leipzig-Brunswick, Posen, and Tutow areas in Germany. The 401st was tasked with hitting aircraft factories at Leipzig. More than 1,000 heavies total were dispatched to cripple Hermann Göring's aircraft production, the greatest deployment of the war to date. Some sixteen combat wings of B-17s and B-24s and seventeen groups of USAAF fighter escorts from both the Eighth and Nineth Air Forces were assigned.[8] Additionally, the RAF deployed sixteen of its fighter squadrons. The 401st, once again leading the 94th CBW, made up two combat boxes of eighteen aircraft each. Col. Harold W. Bowman, commander of the 401st, led the formation to the target. There was one loss for the group on the opening Big Week mission; 2Lt. Edward T. Gardner, of the 615th BS, piloting *Doolittle*'s *Doughboys*, following repeated assaults by German fighters, stayed at his controls to keep his fatally damaged bomber level while his crew bailed out. In doing this, he lost his chance to escape the ship and perished with her as she blew apart.

The 401st had once again performed magnificently on February 20, earning their second Presidential Unit Citation, a marvelous achievement for such a young green combat group. Their motto, "The Best Damned Outfit in the USAAF," was well deserved.

As part of the Pointblank Directive, the philosophy of Operation Argument was to use the bombers as bait and let the fighter escorts knock down the German defenders as they rose up from their bases. It was the result of brainstorming after Jimmy Doolittle was placed in command of the 8th AF. Hap Arnold had expressed exasperation with Ira Eaker in 1943 with his reluctance to deploy the bombers. With the backing of Gen. Spaatz, Eaker was sent packing to command the US Army Air Forces in the Mediterranean in January 1944; this act triggered no little amount of bitterness on Eaker's part. Even though the transfer was technically a promotion, Eaker never saw it as one, and he was furious. The many delays and recalls of missions were not necessarily his fault or that of the of the 8th Air Forces' leadership, but the result of the terrible English weather.

With an aggressive commander now at the helm of the Mighty Eighth and a break in the sour European weather, a major offensive could now kick off and, hopefully, diminish the Luftwaffe in the run-up to the Normandy invasions scheduled for the spring. Under Ira Eaker, the escort fighters were restrained to stay near to the bomber stream. Under Jimmy Doolittle, they were now free to chase and destroy the enemy fighters, whether in the air or on the ground. It was open season with no bag limit. The change in tactic was a surprise to *General der Jagdflieger* Adolf Galland and his Luftwaffe fighter squadrons. And since the planned targets were primarily in the central and south portions of the Third Reich, the Italy-based 15th Air Force was also tasked with mission assignments; the Third Reich was being assaulted from north to south. But the Fifteenth was also heavily involved in the defense of the Anzio campaign, which had kicked off a month earlier. This forced the Fifteenth to split its forces in support of both tasks as it began flying missions into Germany on February 22.

Big Week was the first time 150-gallon drop tanks were employed on the P-47 escorts.[9] The tanks were limited in size, as the space beneath the Thunderbolts would not allow for larger containers. Invented by the British, these disposable tanks were constructed primarily of cardboard-like heavy paper pulp and paper-mâché. Initially, the tanks were designed to be released upon entry into hostile airspace, but later fuel shortages mandated that the tanks be retained for as long as possible before ejection. The use of paper products to build these tanks was a response to both the need to reduce weight, as this would conserve fuel, and was also due to wartime metal rationing. The loss of valuable aluminum on disposable vessels made little sense, whereas cardboard was cheap and plentiful.

Big Week continued for the 401st on February 21, with the 8th AF deploying 764 heavies to Germany to flatten targets of opportunity at Achmer, Bramsche, Hannover, Lingen, Hopsten, Rhein, Quackenbruck, Vorden, Ahlhorn, and Hesepe. The primary objectives were Brunswick's aircraft plants and an airfield at Diepholz, but overcast protected these targets for the time being. The 401st was tasked with cratering the airfield at Lippstadt, Germany. The 613th Squadron comprised the lead box formation with Maj. Edwin W. Brown in the fore.[10] However, upon reaching the IP, Major Brown determined that visual bombing could not be accomplished, due to cloud cover, and ordered the group onto a target of opportunity at Emlichheim near the Netherlands' border.

On the third day of Big Week, the 1st BD, including the 401st BG, returned to Oschersleben, Germany. The 613th BS again led the pack. The bombing was accurate but 2Lt. Loy M. Shanks's B-17 was shot down by flak and defending fighters. Most of the crew were interred in a POW camp save top turret gunner/engineer William H. Jarrett, who did not survive the incident.

It was on day five of Big Week, February 24, that the 8th AF returned to Schweinfurt. The previous October saw the most damaging raid on the ball-bearing works of the war. Army Air Force planners estimated, through reconnaissance photography and intelligence, that some 75 percent of the plants had been rebuilt and were back in production. This was unsettling, and despite the horrific cost of the October mission, a return was unavoidable. The 8th AF dispatched 231 heavies to disrupt production once again. The 401st supplied eighteen bombers and three spares for the low combat box. All four squadrons deployed, with four heavies returning due to mechanical issues, leaving seventeen bombers to complete the mission. Of the 231 total aircraft, eleven were lost, a far less painful penalty than the previous

Schweinfurt sortie when sixty aircraft were destroyed; all of the 401st bombers returned to base. The RAF followed up on this success that evening, and the next, releasing their bombs by using the light of the fires as aiming points. Reconnaissance flyovers confirmed that the target had been thoroughly crushed and out of commission.

At 9:15 a.m. on February 25, the 401st lifted off from Deenethorpe for the last of the Big Week missions. The 613th BS supplied six aircraft for the lead box element. The goal was to smash the Messerschmitt plant at Augsburg, deep into Germany, nearly to the Alps. The target was well hit and mangled in the effort. In all, the 8th AF had deployed a total of 680 heavies to bomb Regensburg, Augsburg, and Furth, all aircraft plants; the ball-bearing facilities at Stuttgart were also heavily mauled. The 401st did not lose any aircraft but three were forced to land at other airfields, presumably due to battle damage.[11]

With the courage of the bomber crews of all participating groups, and the leadership of the 401st BG, Big Week was a big success. An estimate of the Luftwaffe's strength following this important effort in the Combined Bomber Offensive described a much-reduced force.[12] The hellish pressure by the USAAF and RAF on both the aircraft industries and on operational aircraft had weakened the Germans to the extent that there was a poor response to the D-Day landings three and a half months later, achieving one of the main goals of the CBO and, by extension, Pointblank. The Luftwaffe could mount a determined response, but it would be feeble in numbers. The oil campaign, relentlessly prosecuted by the USAAF at Ploiești, Romania, and other sites, was steadily shutting off the tap for sea, land, and air forces of the Reich. Before long, even trained pilots would be in alarmingly short supply. By the spring of 1944, things were looking up even while the carnage continued in foxholes, on destroyers and carriers, and in thin metal tubes cruising at 25,000 feet.

• • •

The CBO officially ended on April 14, as the US Strategic Air Forces were placed under the command of the Gen. Eisenhower in the run-up to D-Day.[13] The Supreme Allied Commander would best determine the overall deployment of the 8th AF from this point forward. Generals Spaatz and Doolittle had done a splendid job softening up Göring's forces and armament's minister Albert Speer's plants. But more difficult work was pending, and the 401st had many more trials ahead.

On March 6, 1944, they joined the 8th AF for its first visit to Berlin. They were yet again in the vanguard for the 94th Combat Wing, with Erkner, near Berlin, as their primary target. Unfortunately, bad weather forced them to focus on the secondary target at Templin northeast of Berlin. Some 60–150 enemy aircraft greeted the formation and managed to shoot down a 401st bomber piloted by 2Lt. Claude M. Kolb of the 615th Squadron. The crew survived and were made guests of the Luftwaffe until the end of the war.

The 401st would continue to distinguish itself while Dave Vermeer's crew worked to complete their individual training. On March 24, 1944, the 401st led the 94th CBW over Schweinfurt again. This time, a Pathfinder B-17 dropped first into heavy cloud cover. It was wise that Albert Speer had begun scattering crucial war industries to remote, and in many cases underground, manufacturing facilities. Regardless, the Mighty Eighth kept up pressure on known, and largely destroyed, above-ground targets.

By the time Dave's crew had received their orientation and training and were placed on the duty roster, the 401st had completed 218 missions in the ETO. On March 1, 1945, Dave's crew finally lifted off from Deenethorpe in an unnamed B-17G, serial number 43-38791, to bomb the marshalling yards at Heilbronn, Germany. The boys were together for their first mission, with the exception of JJ. He was temporarily swapped with another aircrew so that the green-around-the-gills replacements could ride with an experienced flyer, 2Lt. Thomas J. Skiffington, who had some four missions already under his belt and had been on the roster since the Big Week kickoff. JJ rode with the crew of 2Lt. Jacob N. Shepherd Jr. in *Bottle Baby*, serial number 43-38458. To make sure the untested flyers were well secure in their mission goals, they were placed on the port wing of the flight leader, Lt. John W. McGoldrick, in the Mickey ship. Technically, John Sites didn't need to be there since his job was to release his bombs on the PFF signal. But all of Dave's team needed experience, and this was a good way to successfully complete their first mission.

Gene Holley stated that the run-up to the mission went well with only light flak encountered. Unfortunately, shortly before the IP was reached, Hal Churchill called out over the interphone that there was a fire onboard. Currently unoccupied as a navigator, Gene sprang into action. He grabbed a walk-around oxygen bottle and a fire extinguisher, quickly locating the problem. The issue was an electrical spark triggered by an overheated pump motor that drove the hydraulic system. Losing hydraulics could be a fatal affair for the bomber; normally the system is shut down during a bomb run and restarted after the bomb load was delivered. But this time, the lines were drained, the pump was not turned off, and the motor got red-hot, triggering the fire. Hal and Gene each sprayed the fire into oblivion, and the ship was able to continue on its mission. Unfortunately, Gene had overextended his walk-around oxygen bottle and collapsed from anoxia. John Sites dropped the bombs and rescued Gene, plugging him back into the ship's oxygen system. The bomber had lost its hydraulics and was not able to land at Deenethorpe. The huge aircraft needed a long runway, as there were no flaps and no brakes; friction was required to stop the squirrelly beast. Dave's skills shined brightly as he landed the big bird at the Woodbridge airfield north of London, free of complication. The bomber required repairs and was removed from the mission roster for a period of time; the boys were transported back to Deenethorpe the next morning. All of the assigned aircraft except for Dave's had returned safely from this mission.

The scary incident, and the professional response to the emergency, earned Dave's crew a three-day pass on March 2. Dave, JJ, Gene, and John all took off for London to see the sights, despite a strict blackout in the big city. No one recorded what Willy, Hal, Bas, Hardtack, and Harold did on their three days off. Presumably, they too had a chance to do some sight-seeing in London or the English countryside. As with so many of the East Anglia airbases in World War II, Deenethorpe was located in idyllic farm country, surrounded by green fields of hay with grazing horses, cows, sheep, and goats. Some of these local critters made a nuisance of themselves as they wandered the base, creating hazards for bombers on runways. Rod reported that goats were a real evil for post inhabitants as they entered barracks and ate pillows, sheets, equipment, and any other munchable treats they could procure, earning the wrath of howling GIs as the offenders were chased out of living quarters.

After the three-day leave, Dave's boys assembled on March 7 for their second mission. Since the nameless bomber was probably still grounded (it does not appear in any mission roster for a period of time), they were assigned to man 42-31730, *Morning Star*. This was to be a run to Dortmund in the Ruhr Valley to hit marshalling yards and a roundhouse maintenance facility. But due to malfunctions in two separate Gee radar units, the secondary target at Siegen, also in the Ruhr, was selected. Siegen also had extensive railroad servicing facilities and was chosen for this reason. John released his bombs on the flare from a Mickey ship. Solid cloud cover prevented any sight targeting and the formation headed for home with no losses; indeed, no flak or enemy aircraft were encountered. It was a milk run and an easy addition to the thirty-five missions required for an airman's combat tour.

The third mission for Dave's crew occurred the next day on March 8. Mission 224 for the 401st BG was to Essen, Germany, to bomb an oil refinery. Again, the boys were assigned to the *Morning Star* as their chariot for the day, but again, nature prevailed, and solid cloud cover protected the target. The refinery needed to be hit by visual means; this was not possible, so the quaternary target of the Essen marshalling yards was settled upon. Once again John's skills with the Norden were not required, as bombing was done via a PFF ship set of flares. The cloud cover was so thick, the after-action reports stated that the town of Wuppertal, rather than Essen, may have been bombed. *Morning Star* flew in the back of the 613th with the high squadron, free of incidents. It was another easy milk run with three feathers now in the crew's cap.[14]

Mission 225 went off on March 10; it would not be a milk run this time for Dave's crew, but another nerve-wracking flight. They were issued an unfamiliar bomber, *Southern Comfort* (44-8767), while *Morning Star* was assigned to 1Lt. James H. May and his boys. Again, Hal Churchill would have had to do a thorough go-over with the ground crew chief to get used to yet another strange lady. Yet, even this precaution did not identify a potential in-flight problem. Dave held the *Southern Comfort* in the back of the 613th, the lead squadron for the day. The bomber was loaded with 3,100 pounds of ordnance. John Sites performed his duty at the appointed time, pulling the cotter pins from the bombs to arm them. The release switch was toggled at 25,000 feet and John waited for Milan Basara to call "Bombs away." Instead, Bas reported a problem. As the radio operator, his position was closest to the bomb bay, and it was his job to call out successful armament deployment. However, this time only one side of the bomb racks released properly, the other was a tangled mess. Some 1,300 pounds of high explosives were jammed up in a rack designed to hold 500 pounds.[15]

The bombs were armed. Inrushing air from the open bomb bay doors could cause the tail spinners on the high explosives to begin the countdown to rupture, destroying the *Southern Comfort* and killing Dave's crew. John stared in horror as one of the vanes was beginning to spin. He had to act fast, not only to avert potential catastrophe, but also because his walk-around oxygen bottle was good for only three minutes. As he investigated the mess, he noticed that all of the bombs, except the bottom one, had released from the shackle, clogging the system. At this point, the bomber stream was turned toward home, with *Southern Comfort* in tow. John reported the situation to Dave and JJ over the interphone, frantically searching for resolution. Any air turbulence could jolt the bombload and blast the aircraft and her frightened crew to glory. Dave eased *Southern Comfort* away from the formation to mitigate potential damage to the rest of the 613th, while John waited until she was over the English Channel. Although he did not record it in his memoirs, he had most likely found a way to stop the vanes from spinning in the inrush of air and had returned to his station. John then most likely plugged back into the ship's oxygen system until they reached the Channel. Once over the Channel he shimmied into his parachute harness, and with Hal holding onto the straps, he eased down below the catwalk and managed to wriggle the obstruction loose, releasing the load into the cold water. The pucker factor had been mitigated, and the boys landed safely at Deenethorpe.

The crew would obtain a two-day reprieve before taking off again, this time in another unfamiliar bomber. The assignment for their fifth mission was aboard the *Lady Jane II*, serial number 43-38607. She was named after another, rather unfortunate, B-17G named *Lady Jane*, also of the 613th Bombardment Squadron. On November 6, 1944, the *Lady Jane I* had lifted off from Deenethorpe with pilot 1Lt. Raymond H. Hillestad and co-pilot 2Lt. John H. Emch at the helm. In November 1995, navigator Frederick L. Campbell provided an account of the fate of the *Lady Jane*. While on the bomb run over Hamburg, she was hit by flak, losing the number 2 engine. Hillestad feathered the engine (i.e., stopped the blade from spinning freely and causing drag) and struggled to stay with the safety of the formation, but the wounded bird simply couldn't keep pace and dropped back. As she flew over the North Sea, she began losing altitude. The pilot lowered her to 10,000 feet so that the crew was able to take off their oxygen masks. Unfortunately, lower altitude meant the bomber was easier to hit with ground fire, and the number 3 engine was shot out and disabled. She was going down. Hillestand and Emch crash-landed her in a Dutch field near Medemblik, allowing all nine crewmen to exit safely. Unfortunately, they were all rounded up quickly, as a German radar station was nearby, and they were taken off to be guests of the Luftwaffe for the remainder of the war.[16] The *Lady Jane* was destroyed by the Germans where she lay as she was far too damaged to salvage. Had she not been so severely damaged, she would most likely have been repaired and used by the Luftwaffe to design assaults on the heavily armed bombers, as had been done with previous American heavies that were surrendered intact.

On March 12, the *Lady Jane II* (*LJ2*) carried Dave's crew on Mission Number 227 to hit the naval facilities at Swinemunde, on the Baltic coast. She lifted off with five 1,000-pound bombs and 2,780 gallons of fuel shortly before 8:00 a.m. Assembly went well, and the formation was on its way with no complications. Due to heavy cloud cover, the formation had several PFF ships that were used to deploy target flares. While the overcast prevented visual confirmation of bombing success, crews were satisfied with the mission; all ships returned to Deenethorpe, incident free. Dave's crew could chalk up another milk run.

The *LJ2* was an experienced bird. She had been in the fight since October 7, 1944, when she flew her first mission to bomb one of Hitler's many synthetic oil plants at Pölitz, Germany. The crew manning *LJ2* was headed by 1Lt. Luther N. Douglas for this trip. That mission, number 154 for the 401st, was especially costly and five of its bombers were brought down, but the *LJ2* survived and brought her charges home safe and sound. She would be bounced around from crew to crew, but her "normal" team was headed by 1Lt. Herbert P. Cox. He and his crew would pilot her fulltime from New Year's Day 1945 to February 21; then they would be assigned to her sporadically from then on until Dave's boys took her for missions 227 and 231. She was off the roster for missions 228–230. Her last two missions would be headed by Dave's now experienced band of bomber boys.

But it was Mission 231 that would bring the *Lady Jane II* to her fate, testing Dave and his crew to their very limits. Disaster was coming, and these boys, like so many of their compatriots, whether in foxholes, on Navy vessels, or in flying aluminum tubes, would become men in an instant and learn what they held the most dear was not their own lives, but those of their brothers-in-arms.

CHAPTER 5

MISSION: BERLIN

Offense is the essence of air power.
—Gen. Henry H. "Hap" Arnold

After their fifth mission, Dave's crew was rewarded with a three-day pass to London, wherein they took in "all the usual sights." Dave, JJ, Gene, and John all stayed at the Van Dyke Red Cross Club just outside of London. John Sites complained that the "buzz bombs" spoiled some of the trip, as they landed too closely. But it reminded the bombardier that the ordnance released by his own craft must have equally produced fear and terror for those beneath his toggle switch.[1] The English Bomber Command, with their own horrific early losses, had resorted to area bombing long ago to try to mitigate their numbers of dead and wounded with night bombing. The Germans at the receiving end called this wide area disbursement "*terrorangriffe*," terror bombing.

On Sunday, March 18, the morning after their return to Deenethorpe, Dave's crew was selected for Mission 231. They were again assigned the *Lady Jane II*, their bomber from the previous flight. The boys were knocked out of their bunks at a blurry-eyed 2:30 a.m. for a 3:00 breakfast. Upon arriving at the briefing hut, John Sites was surprised to see that his name was not listed for the mission; the rest of the crew was listed, but not the bombardier. Bewildered, he found an officer who was able to explain that bombardiers were no longer required, as PFF ships were now the norm and highly-trained Norden operators were superfluous except on lead bombers. John was out of a job. He didn't record his movements for the day, but he may have returned to his hut, perplexed and deeply disappointed at this separation from his friends for what was to be a maximum effort for the Mighty Eighth, indeed, the largest of its history. Several days later, John found himself being retrained as a navigator and remained assigned to the 613th squadron; he flew his first sortie on March 24, with the crew of 1Lt. Audrey J. Bradley for one mission as a substitute navigator. His next assignment was with the 615th Bombardment Squadron crew of 2Lt. Fred Eglin. With this team, they all trained as a lead bomber crew, with John once again leaning over a Norden bombsight, this time for mission 248, to bomb enemy gun positions at Royan, France. John flew three more missions before the 8th AF stood down to allow Allied ground forces to complete their penetration into the dissolving Third Reich. John would not see his brothers aboard the *Lady Jane II* again.

• • •

The briefing for Mission 231 was one of suspense, shock, and fear. As the assembled crews looked on, the group commander stood up and removed the curtain over the large map board at the front of the briefing hut. Until this point, the men didn't know where their target was located. On the map, a fat piece of colored yarn stretched from Deenethorpe to Berlin; an audible gasp emanated from the crews. They would be flying to the "Big B," the hardest and most terror-stricken location of the war. JJ later stated that he learned it would be a rough mission when the co-pilots were handed the crews' in-flight lunches: an "old timer" had informed him that Hershey bars and cookies were reserved for "tough" missions. Normally, the airmen were given Clark Bars or Milky Ways; coveted Hershey bars were issued only for the "biggies" and were viewed as sort of a last supper. Following the main briefing, Gene Holley attended a special discussion for navigators, including any concerns with the weather, flight time information, and the location of the I.P. for the bomb run. Gene was also given a flak map showing the concentrations of anti-aircraft artillery to and from the target area.

After the briefing, Hal Churchill and Dave Vermeer met with the *Lady Jane*'s ground crew to discuss the ship's readiness for the rough task ahead. Since this was their second mission aboard this ship, they were fairly familiar with her and may have been hoping she would be permanently assigned to them, thus ending their perpetual state as vagabonds. While Hal and Dave spoke to the crew chief, Rod Williams (a.k.a. "Willy"), Fred Gerhardt ("Hardtack"), Milan Basara ("Bas"), and Harold Babcock all checked out their guns from the armory and installed them on the bomber. They examined the actions on the weapons, making sure to cock them and applying oil if they needed lubrication. Lastly, they each made sure they had the allotted amount of ammunition and stowed the cases in the correct locations at each firing station aboard the ship.

Also reporting to the flight line was a young kid from Connecticut, baby-faced nineteen-year-old Ernest James ("Jim") Butlin, who was reassigned from another crew to fill John's station and man the bomb toggle switch. As a trained "togglier," he was often bounced from one crew to another, from one squadron to another. The unfortunate kid didn't have a permanent home, a hard existence for a substitute crewman with a critical skillset.

Jim was born on Christmas Eve 1925, the younger of two brothers; his big brother Kenneth was seven years older. Both boys grew up in Fairfield, the children of Ernest, a bricklayer, and May Butlin, a homemaker. May passed away in 1935 and Ernie remarried. Martha Henrietta Kreutzfeldt Stone became the new Mrs. Butlin, providing Kenneth and Jim with a stepbrother, Bill, Martha's son from a previous marriage. Bill was two years older than Jim. The new family settled in Bridgeport, where Jim and Bill attended Warren G. Harding High School. Jim never attended college; he played few sports in high school but enjoyed the skillful aim, deployment, and resulting trajectory of a tennis ball, an ability which no doubt later assisted in the accurate placement of .50-cal. machine gun rounds and high explosives onto enemy targets. Shortly after D-Day on June 8, 1944, eighteen-year-old Jim entered the US Army Air Force as a private. On January 4, 1945, he was home on leave and was able to visit with the family. His stepmother Martha adored him; Jim reciprocated her affection and gave her a locket with his military picture nestled inside. She cherished it until the day she died.

Jim didn't know Dave's crew very well, but when he stepped into the nose of the *LJ2* on March 18, he took on his new assignment with the commitment and professionalism required of so deadly a purpose. For this mission Dave, JJ, Gene, Hardtack, Hal, Bas, Harold, and Willy were his family. These men were his brothers, if only for one mission.

As the crew prepared, they donned all their heavy equipment, the electric heated suit, "Mae West" inflatable vest, parachute harness, headgear, and throat mic. Since relieving oneself on these long flights involved peeing into a tube or out a hatch or window, the boys no doubt also voided as much used coffee as possible before shimmying into their heavy gear. At this point in the war, most crews had access to body armor, suits, and helmets. Willy, Harold, Jim, Bas, Hardtack, and Hal may have had to adorn themselves with this heavy paraphernalia in addition to the other items. The cumbersome nature of all this gear may have been oppressive, but it meant greater survivability and was well tolerated by the crews. Some of the men would stow the flak suits next to their stations as space allowed and would don them when close to enemy airspace.

Once they were all dressed, the aircraft had passed all of the pre-flight checks, and all the boys were at their take-off stations, they waited for the officer on the tarmac to fire off the "start engines" flare. Wheel chalks were pulled away from the big tires as Dave pushed open his sliding window and called out to any ground crewmen to stand clear of the propellers as he toggled each engine to life. JJ did the same for the right side of the big bomber. As Dave revved up the engines to push the big beast forward, he watched their squadron mates pull their B-17s off hardstands to line up on the perimeter track, waiting for their turn to position their ships on the main runway and take off. Gene quietly pondered the danger of this moment in a mission. A fully loaded bomber was a terrifying weapon both to the enemy and to any unfortunate crew, should the pilot not do his job correctly. But as always, Dave skillfully brought the heavily laden bomber up and lifted her, and her charges, safely into the air.

The *Lady Jane II* circled around the buncher beacon with good visibility as the 401st assembled. Once the formation was all present, and after several "doglegs" to pick up other groups, it headed north, then east. Dave and JJ had made sure to position the *LJ2* into her assigned slot in the massive formation as part of the 94th CBW, "C" group, in the rear of a three-bomber formation, just off the left wing of 1st Lt. Robert S. Jones and his crew in *Carrie B IV* (44-6588). The 613th BS lead the 401st with two PFF ships (a main and a spare) at the fore and one Mickey ship in each of the 612th, 614th, and 615th squadrons. The call sign for the four squadrons of the 401st was "Jabwock" for the 612th, "Macro" for the 613th, "Golfclub" for the 614th, and "Buzzard" for the 615th.[2] Using the last three numbers in the *LJ2*'s serial number, Dave may have reported his callsign as "Macro-607."

The flight to the Big B was fairly uneventful, although JJ reported some inaccurate flak off to the sides of the formation. One of the concerns was the presence of heavy contrails. These were a danger to the bomber crews, as they often could not see the aircraft directly in front of them. The warm engines mixing with very cold air at 28,000 feet produced water vapor and added to the complications of tight formation flying. The bombers were ordered to increase altitude to 28,500 feet to avoid the ground batteries that could now spot them so easily. The increase in altitude added to the misery onboard the aircraft as the temperature inside the bombers plummeted to 56 degrees below zero; Gene could not remove his heated gloves and write at the same time. Even though they were in formation, navigators had to know the exact location of the aircraft at all times, should they become separated from the formation.

The *LJ2* was one of thirty-six bombers deployed by the 401st BG that Sunday morning; only one B-17 was forced to return to Deenethorpe due to mechanical issues. This mission would be the largest maximum effort thus far in the Second World War. Over 1,250 bombers from all three divisions were dispatched with more than 600 fighter escorts; nearly two-thousand Allied aircraft would darken Germany's skies that morning. German farmers on their fields below may have looked up at the astonishing sight and marveled at the deep rumble of 5,600 engines when the long and vast formation passed overhead; it would most likely have been a terrifying sight, eliciting more than one "*Mein Gott*!" from the frightened civilians below. No European nation had ever fielded such a force before, nor since, the eighteenth of March 1945. The Mighty Eighth was just that, the mightiest combat unit in history. It would make history this day. The bomber stream was so enormous that the Germans were well aware of its location and, after reaching their airspace, its destination. They had been able to read formations by tapping into the radar used on the PFF aircraft since late 1944. The Berlin mission was no surprise. They would be ready to greet the 8th Air Force.

A few miles from the target, the cloud cover parted giving flak batteries much-better visual targeting, and the anti-aircraft defenses opened up in earnest. Since the Luftwaffe had been fairly well decimated (but decidedly *not* destroyed) by General Doolittle's campaign of search and destroy, flak was the primary defense of Germany at this point. The flak guns had gotten much more accurate and deadly with radar guidance. Even with this danger, Dave gave the controls over to JJ to allow him to guide the *LJ2* to the IP. JJ stated that Dave was a very fair and thoughtful pilot and shared much of the flying with his co-pilot. As JJ flew the aircraft, he felt Jim Butlin open the bomb bay doors. The drop was imminent. They just needed to get closer and wait for the PFF ship to send off a flare and signal the release.

Still approaching the target, the *LJ2* began to shudder as the rear gunner opened up on in-coming targets. Harold Babcock was positioned in the tail as he called out over the interphone, "Bandits, enemy fighters in the area!" At first, the crew didn't realize the terrible danger they were truly in; these weren't just Bf 109 or Fw 190 fighters, they were the cream of the Luftwaffe, Messerschmitt Me 262 jet fighters, the pinnacle of German engineering and technology. The American airmen called them "blow jobs," as not only would they blow past formations at impossible speeds, but they also blew hot air as propulsion. No P-51 Mustang, the cream of American engineering and technology, could catch them in a straight-up contest. Instead, US fighter pilots had to out-maneuver the jets to take them down. The "blow job" had a very poor turning arc and couldn't match the Mustang's, or the Jug's, agility. But a fully loaded B-17G had an airspeed of just 200 mph, while an Me 262 could roar past at more than 500 mph. All the bomber crews could do to defend their aircraft was to try to hit these revolutionary interceptors with machine gun fire; the only real way to accomplish that was by "leading" the jet and firing slightly ahead of it. Harold, Hal, Hardtack, Bas, and Willy were greatly tested as they tried to site their guns on fleeting specks hurtling at impossible speeds. Willy, who normally manned the waist guns, had switched with Hardtack on this mission, as he was much shorter than Fred and fit more easily into the cramped ball turret. (They had probably switched due to the long flight time and Hardtack most likely did not want to spend the long hours in the tiny turret.) Harold believed he had hit one of the jets as he saw a chunk of metal fly off the craft as a result of his fire. Fear spread about the *LJ2*, but each man kept his cool and did his job as JJ kept the ship steady and on course toward the IP.

The jets had crept up on the formation by hiding in the thick contrails. Gene looked out of the Plexiglas nose and saw several of the Me 262s beneath the *LJ2*. Meanwhile, the P-51 escorts had their work cut out as they whipped in and out of the bomber stream, struggling to catch the jets. Gene thought he saw a P-51 hit an Me 262, but for the most part, the greatly outnumbered German defenders were in command of the airspace above Berlin.

Intensifying flak exploded all around the *LJ2* and she rocked with each nearby concussion. Bright orange centers meant the explosions were too close. Then, suddenly, the ship lifted violently upward, rattling everyone on board; the noise was deafening. Bas, stationed in the radio room, called over the interphone that the ship had taken a direct hit and that Hardtack was down. Gene, assuming that one of the jets had fired on them, snatched up a walk-around oxygen bottle and his parachute, and moved quickly to inspect the damage and tend to the wounded man. JJ, still at the helm, suddenly lost control of the aircraft, Dave jumped in to help, the both of them struggling to keep the big bird level. She was violently shuddering out of their grasp when Dave hit the autopilot and the beast quieted down. The flak burst had apparently severed the cable that controlled the trim tabs. The secondary autopilot system was able to bypass this problem, calming down the *LJ2*; she came under control. Dave and JJ looked at each other and breathed in relief.

A little after 11:20 a.m., the bomber lifted again, this time from the ease of weight as Jim spotted the PFF signal and toggled the release switch. The payload headed for the target below, the Schlesischer Marshalling Yard very near the Tempelhof Airfield, one of the few rail yards left in Berlin that was still capable of handling traffic. While the 401st focused on the marshalling yard, other 8th AF squadrons unloaded over the airfield, severely cratering the runways and damaging the main terminal. Other targets that day were either in Berlin or areas near the city as two additional marshalling yards were bombed and two tank and armament plants were hit, along with several targets of opportunity.[3]

As soon as Gene saw the chasm in the floor of their ship, he realized the culprit was flak, not cannon fire from the jets. It had made an enormous hole near the aircraft's waist area, missing Willy by just a few inches and badly wounding Hardtack. Gene, as the aircraft's first-aid officer, needed to respond to the medical emergency as Fred lay on the floor near the radio compartment. Bas jumped out of the radio room to assist Gene. The explosion had occurred so close to the ball turret, it bent the twin Brownings and rendered them inoperable.

Dave called over the interphone, "What happened?"

He was answered by Willy, "We got hit behind the ball turret; there's a hole big enough to drive a jeep through. My guns are bent and I'm coming out!"[4] Rod Williams then hurriedly squeezed out of the turret and did what he could to help the others; in the rush of adrenaline, he didn't realize that he too had been wounded.

Hardtack was unconscious on the floor of the *LJ2* with a hole in his windpipe. Gene was surprised to see little blood but thought it was due to the lack of oxygen at nearly 29,000 feet; the intense cold was also contributing to the slow flow of blood as minus-50-degree air blasted through the huge crater in the aircraft's fuselage. The hole in Fred's throat meant that he was trying to breathe without benefit of the onboard oxygen system through his mask. Bas and Willy assisted while Gene bandaged the hole with tape that he had grabbed from the radio room. Hardtack quickly regained consciousness, then Gene saw additional holes in his legs. The man was a mess. Willy too was injured, but the wounds on the back of his legs were not severe enough to keep him from helping his friends.

Once Hardtack was stabilized, Gene returned to his navigation table and began plotting their course home. Willy continued to conceal his own injuries, which by that time must have been increasingly painful.

The *LJ2* appeared to be flying fine; she was not on fire and the engines were responding. The emergency appeared over, but the oxygen in the aircraft was steadily losing pressure as the system had been damaged by the flak explosion. JJ quickly took the battered bomber down to 13,500 feet before they all passed out from anoxia, while Dave called for fighter support. But in taking the *LJ2* down, they were forced to leave the safety of the formation. Until the escort arrived, they were on their own, alone and immensely vulnerable.

It was about at this point that an argument broke out in the cockpit. Dave and JJ were discussing their options. By March 1945, the Russians had penetrated deep into Germany, to the point that they had airbases to the east of Berlin. JJ wanted to fly to one of them. It would shorten their length of time in the air and get Hardtack the medical assistance he needed much sooner. But Fred Gerhardt was stable, and Dave was not keen on flying to Russian held territory. Dave was a deeply religious person and felt the Soviets persecuted Christians and others with whom they did not agree. Dave stated that they would *not* be landing at a Soviet airfield, under *any* circumstances. But Gene had already plotted a course to the Russian airfield and had given the coordinates to JJ. The latter then turned the bomber into that heading, causing a cockpit uproar when Dave realized what was transpiring. He put his foot down; they were returning to Deenethorpe. Period. Dave was a quiet man, never given to tantrums or swearing, but this upset him. He felt betrayed by JJ for attempting to thwart his original decision and let him know.

Gene plotted a new course for the wounded bird to follow, displaying his exceptional skill. While the heavies were in the bomber stream, flying in close formation, navigators needed to know their location at all times, but while at the IP, the navigator was jobless; it's why they were therefore designated as first aid officers in addition to navigation duties. So in the chaos of the flak damage, assessing the aircraft's condition, and helping stabilize Hardtack, Gene was away from his navigation table, unable to keep track of the ship's location. His ability to quickly locate the bomber's position and plot a course for home was a difficult task that he easily completed. Despite JJ's deep reservations about the *LJ2* surviving the trip home, he turned her into the wind and headed west per Gene's instructions over the interphone.

At around 12:20 p.m., the boys must have thought their prayers answered as five "Little Friends," P-51s, formed around the *LJ2* like a protective cocoon to escort her to the Channel. Despite the terrible day, they would be OK and sleeping in their bunks at Deenethorpe tonight; Hardtack would get the medical care he needed; everything would be fine. The escorts were all equipped with drop tanks, indicating they had had not been involved with the vicious fistfight over Berlin; if they had, they would have jettisoned the tanks upon entry into combat. Gene and JJ didn't note who these Little Friends were but expressed joy at their appearance. Occasional puffs of smoke around the tiny formation told everyone that that German ground crews were awake and responding to the American presence. But no flak reached the *LJ2* or her escort, and the flight continued as Gene navigated the little formation per his accurate flak map.

The six aircraft were headed home when about 100 miles west of Berlin, the P-51s detached their drop tanks and peeled off. As JJ was preparing to dispense the crew's lunch of Hershey bars and cookies, he wondered why their Little Friends were abandoning them. Dropping to his hands and knees, he began squirming through Hal's legs to dole out the treats when the top turret gunner put his hand down and motioned for JJ to go no farther. Something was wrong. Then Hal's machine guns erupted in a deafening roar, spent casings began raining down on JJ's head.

JJ hadn't even managed to back up when all hell broke loose. All the gunners started firing. The *Lady Jane* vibrated and rocked as every machine gun onboard opened up.

Unknown to the crew, *Jagdgeschwader* 7 (JG 7) had been following the *Lady Jane II* since Berlin. As soon as the P-51 escort left the wounded bomber, they fell upon her like lions on a half-dead wildebeest, proceeding to rend and rip her to shreds. Like the wildebeest, she stood no chance at all.

The crew of the *Lady Jane II* would not be asleep in their bunks that night. They would be in a fight for their lives.

CHAPTER 6
STORMBIRD

There stood two Me 262 jet fighters, the beginning and center point of our future and at the same time, our great hope.
—Adolf Galland

Before the term "blow job" became a common euphemism for an obscene act in the American lexicon, USAAF airmen used the phrase to describe an advanced type of aircraft. It was a piece of technology that was conceived in Britain in the 1930s, with an RAF engineer named Sir Frank Whittle. Whittle, born in 1907, was a brilliant engineer who cut his teeth in 1928 as a twenty-one-year-old RAF pilot. He had written a thesis while a cadet stating that current piston engines were not suitable for high-altitude operations that should be critical to modern flight. The less dense air high above means less friction, less obstruction, and greater distances on limited fuel capacity. The jet engine wasn't initially his first idea; turbo-driven radial engines piqued his interest, something that would indeed become commonplace in the future. He also considered rocket-powered engines. Rockets, of course, are believed to have been invented by Chinese engineers hundreds, if not thousands, of years ago. Rocket-powered engines had not yet been perfected by the early twentieth century, so Frank thought about them, a lot. But the more he considered them, the more his idea began morphing into something new, something different.

In 1928, while at the RAF college, Whittle submitted his senior thesis describing his vison of what was an early design of a jet engine. Initially, he was laughed at and openly ridiculed by the Air Ministry. Additionally, the British government and private industry also dismissed this hair-brained idea. His vision of an engine that used hot air for propulsion was scoffed at across the board; the boy was mad. Fortunately, this derision did not alter the course of history, and Frank pushed on. The first jet engine design included a centrifugal compressor and a large single chamber for the combustion of liquid fuel; it was submitted as Whittle's graduate thesis in 1930, which he quickly patented. In 1936, he created Power Jets Limited to protect and further develop his ground-breaking invention. But the first ground-based test of this early jet engine wouldn't occur until 1937. On that day, Whittle's jet engine roared to life. His theories finally began to attract attention and admiration. Maybe the man wasn't mad after all. The RAF became very interested and tasked Gloster Aircraft Company to design an airframe appropriate for the new technology.

In mid-May 1941, Whittle's design was used in the RAF's first jet-powered aircraft, the Gloster E.28/39. His design included not one but ten combustion chambers. Whittle had worked closely with Gloster's chief George Carter for several years prior, while they collaborated on an acceptable design for the airframe. The flight was successful, prompting the Gloster "Meteor" to be developed as an intercept against Hitler's Vengeance weapons, the V-1 and V-2 rockets. The US was also working on a jet-powered aircraft during this period with the Bell XP-59A Airacomet. Even though the Meteor was in the air before the end of hostilities, the RAF chose not to deploy it in combat against Hitler's jet aircraft. Had they done so, aerial combat between jets would have been a true contest between competing technologies long before the Korean War, where they became commonplace.

It would be a German engineer named Dr. Hans Pabst von Ohain who would expand on Whittle's 1930 design to produce the world's first combat-ready turbo jet engine.[1] Aircraft engineer Ernst Heinkel developed the rocket-propelled engine in 1939 with the He 176. He incorporated Ohain's engine design into the He 178 at the same time, much to the delight of Adolf Hitler and Hermann Göring, who were witnesses during the momentous maiden flights.

*Bayerische Motorenwer*ke (BMW) and *Junkers Motorenwerke* (JUMO) earned contracts to develop the jet engines, each producing their own variant on a similar design. But the brilliant engineers involved at all levels of this revolutionary engine design knew that the airframe of a typical propeller-driven plane would never stand up to the intensity of physical stresses at 500–600 mph. A new airframe would need to accompany the new engine. A number of different designs were tested, some based on the rocket technology prevalent in Germany's offensive weapons programs.

German engineer Wernher von Braun had been on the front line of development of rocket science at the research facility on the Baltic coast of Peenemünde. Research on missile aerodynamics led to the designs of early rocket-propelled aircraft such as the Me 163 ("*Komet*"), which resembled a squat, pregnant torpedo and was notoriously unpredictable and difficult to fly. In addition to being extremely hard to control, it burned through fuel so fast, it could only be airborne a few minutes to fire what amounted to a single burst of ammunition at an enemy aircraft before it was forced to return to base to refuel. In addition to flight limitations, it was a "widow maker," killing numerous pilots during test flights. It was not what Hitler wanted in a jet-powered fighter-bomber.

One initially promising design was based on the standard fighter with under-wing retractable landing gear and a tail wheel. As in von Braun's rocket designs, the wings were swept back approximately 35 degrees to reduce potentially lethal wing vibration at high speeds, and the Me 262, also called the *Schwalbe* (Swallow) and more commonly the *Sturmvogel* (Stormbird), was entered into trials. Aircraft engineer and manufacturer Wilhelm Messerschmitt had submitted the design in June 1939 for testing with a conventional, nose-mounted piston engine. The jet engine was still in development and not ready for air trials.

Another excellent design was the Arado (Ar) 234. This aircraft had twin turbo jet engines, tricycle undercarriage, and a Plexiglas nose to aid in improving pilot visibility. It would make a terrific "*blitzbomber*," something for which Hitler was hankering. During a conference with aviation and armaments ministers on May 29, 1944, the Führer mandated that the new jet designs be developed exclusively as bombers. But a number of factors such as cost of production, material scarcities, fuel cost and availability, and other concerns prevented the Ar 234 from achieving its full potential.[2] The Reich simply could not afford multiple jet aircraft and therefore decided to focus primarily on the Me 262. Still, some 200 Ar 234 jets would be deployed by the war's end.[3]

Hitler was far more optimistic about the Me 262 but did not see it as an interceptor/pursuit aircraft, a roll for which it was designed. Knowing that the cross-channel invasion was coming at some point, he felt that a fast bomber would be more useful for beating back waves of troops landing on French beaches than another interceptor aircraft. Against the advice of clearer minds, he insisted that the Stormbird be developed as a *blitzbomber*. In August 1944, Hitler had forbidden the Me 262 from even being called a *jagdbomber* (fighter-bomber); it was to be referred to and developed solely as a *blitzbomber*.[4]

Hitler's insistence and stubborn adamancy would lead to a delay in its development and further retard its entry into combat against the Mighty Eighth. Herr Messerschmitt did not help matters either, as he was eager for the government contract and faithfully told Hitler whatever he thought the Führer wanted to hear, promising that the design could sustain a bombing role. But it could not; it was simply not designed to be a bomber, but an interceptor, and attempts to redesign it led to delays. Historical hindsight has suggested that had Hitler not interfered with the development of the Stormbird, it may have been deployed sooner and been more effective against the 8th AF.

The lateness of the development of the high-tech engine was another huge problem. Had the turbo jet engine entered research and development even five years sooner, the war may have ended in an armistice, rather than full capitulation for Germany. The first full test flight of the jet-powered Me 262 wasn't until July 18, 1942. The man behind the controls was a gutsy Messerschmitt test pilot named Fritz Wendel. The first flights were to test the Me 262 airframe utilizing a prop engine. On this effort, there were two jet engines installed on the wings with a propeller motor in the nose as a backup, should failure occur with the new jet engines. Wendel's courageous flights led to necessary operational procedures and airframe upgrades to the revolutionary design.

The first planes had a tail wheel that unexpectedly retarded the aircraft's ability to lift during take-off. Wendel figured out that if he tapped the brakes, forward momentum would lift the tail off the ground and the ungainly beast could catch air and climb; otherwise, the plane would roar down the runway at 110 mph and never lift off, running out of concrete in the process. (Lift is provided by a propeller; if there is no radial engine, lift is much more problematic.) Wendel also learned that the thrust of the engines against the ground during take-off speeds led to more problems with lift, so the three-wheeled "tricycle" carriage, with the nose wheel, was quickly installed on the early jets. The more Fritz Wendel flew the plane, the greater his understanding of the physics involved with the aircraft's design. He would contribute to the upgrades after many of his flights.

While the airframe challenges were being addressed, there was a big problem facing the turbo jet engine itself, primarily a shortfall of technology. The engine worked by compressing air, heating it by burning fuel in a combustion chamber, then forcibly expelling super-heated air out the rear of the nacelle to produce thrust. The problem with the early designs was that the heat created by the burning fuel was not tolerated by the metallurgy of the time. The parts in the engine would grow extremely hot, then warp causing the entire motor to blow apart or, more commonly, seize up. The Jumo-004 engine, used primarily in the Me 262, had a limited lifespan, as the turbine blades would crack under the intense heat and vibration. The mild steel comprising the turbines needed to be tempered steel. Additionally, the turbines were coated with aluminum to resist oxidation. The soft metal parts simply melted in the jet's super-heated blast furnace. After approximately twelve operational hours, the engine was *kaput* and a replacement was required; late war metallurgical improvements would stretch this to twenty hours. Additionally, a skilled pilot could extend the life of the engine by measured use of the throttle and avoiding conditions that might cause the combustion chambers to become overheated.

The constant engine replacements, along with the relentless bombing campaign endured by the scattered factories and oil production facilities, meant that the Me 262 was immensely expensive to produce and operate. Expertly trained fighter jet pilots were scarce; these too, by war's end, were a rarity as the Luftwaffe was systematically obliterated by Gen. Doolittle's chase-and-destroy policies.

But the Stormbird did operate, at least in limited numbers. Luftwaffe units were formed that would fly the Me 262 exclusively. The first combat operational jet unit was formed in the fall of 1944 when the Führer finally caved to reality. Several of the arguments used to change his mind involved design specifications. The Stormbird had poor visibility for aiming bombs, as a bombsite would be extremely difficult to install on the aircraft.[5] The only method for turning the jet into something the Führer would be happy with would be to fit it as a dive bomber, similar to the role taken by the Ju 87 Stuka. But the Me 262 became unstable in dives at high speed; it would a be a deathtrap if fitted for diving attacks.[6]

Hitler had finally relented at the end of summer 1944 and agreed to release the Stormbird to the Luftwaffe's fighter arm after terrible losses in September from American bomber escorts.[7] The conventional German fighters did not appear up to the task of by-passing the escorts to pick off the bombers when the USAAF began beefing up escort numbers; there were simply too many of them now. Hitler realized his mistake and reversed his earlier declaration that the Stormbird be produced as a *blitzbomber. General der Jagdflieger* Adolf Galland was ecstatic.[8]

• • •

Prior to the deployment of a combat-ready Me 262 *Gruppe*, there had been a testing unit called *Erprobungskommando* ("Test Command") 262. In September 1944, Galland restructured this unit to make it combat ready, placing Walter Nowotny in command. Stationed on the Eastern Front, Nowotny was a fighter ace extraordinaire, having amassed some 255 aerial victories against Soviet forces by February 1944, flying conventional aircraft such as the Bf 109.[9] Propaganda Minister Josef Goebbels had convinced Hitler in February of the marketing value of the star ace. Consequently, *Hauptman* (Captain) Nowotny was pulled from the front and returned home. Months later, he would be promoted to major and find himself in charge of the former *Erprobungskommando* 262, now named *III.Gruppe* (Group 3) *Erganzungsjadgeschwader* ("Supplemental Fighter Wing") 2. It was quickly referred to as "*Kommando Nowotny.*"

Bases for the new jet fighters were at Lechfeld, Hesepe, and nearby Achmer, in Germany. Each of the three planned sixteen-plane *Staffeln* (squadrons) would be stationed separately. But even still, neighboring towns Achmer and Hesepe were close to the preferred route of the American bomber streams, so would be quicker to deal with them as they entered German airspace. Nowotny disliked this airfield placement idea and complained about it, to no avail. His argument was that "convenience" would also mean that these jets would suffer the brunt of the fighter escorts of the 8th AF. Lechfeld, farther away in the south of Germany, was a little more protected from the wrath of the American fighter escorts. Major Nowotny would be vindicated; the closeness of the airfields to the Mighty Eighth's navigation routes would prove disastrous.

The operational strength of Me 262 aircraft in the fall of 1944 was very poor. Of the 239 Me 262 jets manufactured between May 25 and November 4, 1944, only sixty were delivered to the new units.[10] The number of pilots trained to fly these revolutionary aircraft was even smaller. The preferred pilots to fly the new jets were those already familiar with twin-engine aircraft such as the Bf 110, Me 210, and Me 410. Nowotny's unit existed in print only until men could be found to man the machines. This would cause yet more delays in a program that had suffered unending delays in development, including the USAAF Regensburg raid on August 17, 1943, as Stormbird production had been temporarily halted when the Messerschmitt plant was hit.[11] However, it was in the fall of 1944 that Hitler was finally convinced to release more of the 262s to the fighter arm of the Luftwaffe.

By September 1944, Reich Minister of Armaments and War Production Albert Speer was successful in having the majority of the production shifted to Adolf Galland's section.[12] Part of the reasoning for this was the terrible damage taking place as part of the Allied bombing campaign. Major Walther Dahl, of *IV Sturmgruppe* (Storm/Assault Group 4), convinced the Führer that the bomber's escorts could be bypassed by the jets.[13] There was no more time. Germany was being bombed into rubble as the German

High Command argued about the best use of the Me 262. Hitler's acquiescence to releasing the jet as an interceptor was the catalyst that produced the fighter-jet units. At least one delay had been addressed.

Kommando Nowotny began to grow in personnel and equipment, but was still woefully understaffed for deployment. On October 7, 1944, Major Nowotny received word of a large bomber stream with a heavy fighter escort entering German airspace. His *Gruppe* was simply not ready to confront the Mighty Eighth at this point, but he dispatched what he could, successfully bringing down several B-24s. But while some of his jets were taking off from Achmer, fighters from the 351st Fighter Group spotted them. The American P-51s made short work of the vulnerable jets. The advanced aircraft were so easily defeated on take-off that additional security was requested and nearby airfields would send up conventional fighters to cover for them while they lifted off.

The first Allied aircraft to be shot down by a German jet was an RAF Mosquito on July 26, 1944, over the Alps.[14] The twin-engine Mosquito was the fastest aircraft flown by the Allies with the exception of the Gloster Meteor, the British jet, which had been in the air since 1943. The Meteor was never combat-deployed during the war but did perform many test flights. The first B-17 to be shot down by an Me-262 was on August 15, 1944.[15] United States intelligence had known of the development of the German jet fighter tests as early as the end of 1943, including the rocket-propelled aircraft such as the Me 163.[16]

The 8th AF would first encounter the "blow jobs" in massed combat in November 1944. The VIII FC would report the shooting down of eleven jets with another seven damaged.[17] This was the largest deployment of the new German aircraft thus far in the war. The pilots of VIII FC reported some 137 contacts with the 262s in November with twenty-nine actual dogfights; forty-one were destroyed on the ground at Achmer and Hesepe, and seventeen damaged.[18] If the American fighter pilots could hit the jets on the ground, it was a turkey shoot. But if the fight was in the air, it was a contest of skill and luck as the American fighters stood little chance in "catching" the jets. They had to out-think and out-maneuver their opponents. Additionally, the Allied air forces knew that jet fighter pilots were a rare commodity that required months of specialized training. So, upon losing their aircraft, the jet pilots were, tragically, targeted by both American and British airmen and killed as they helplessly dangled in their parachutes. It was a crime without honor in the German's eyes, and no doubt by the Allied pilots as well, but a necessary act to deny the Luftwaffe of specially trained airmen. Vengeance for such killings were taken out on de-planed American airmen by German pilots as well as civilians on the ground in tit-for-tat acts of violence.

One of the irreplaceable losses to the Luftwaffe in November 1944 was Major Nowotny himself. On November 8, *Kommando Nowotny* responded to a report of a large bomber stream crossing the Zuider Zee Bay in the northwestern coast of the Netherlands, the location of a major radar installation. Four Stormbirds lifted off from Achmer and two from Hesepe to meet the threat. The Me 262 pilots, along with numerous other conventional aircraft, rose from their bases with determination and courage. At Achmer, Nowotny's wingman, Günther Wegmann, was able to become airborne right away and sped off without his commander to intercept the bomber stream as quickly as possible. Nowotny had problems engaging the jet engines in his machine and was forced to move to another aircraft; this cost precious time, forcing him to take off alone without his wingman. Once he was able to catch up to the bombers, he managed to shoot one down, but was chased home by furious escorts. Adolf Galland was at Achmer for an inspection at the time when he and others could hear a terrible calamity unfold on a radio at the airfield. Nowotny's last radio transmission was reported as "I have just shot down my third… left engine is out… I am being attacked… I have been hit."[19] A bomber gunner had knocked out his number 1 engine. He tried to fly his wounded bird home when a P-51 from the 357th FG caught up with him and forced him into the ground. Witnesses stated that when the aircraft crashed, there was no fireball, or even a fire, just an audible "thud."[20] There was no time for him to bail out or respond in any way to the damage his aircraft suffered. Even if he had made it back to the airfield, he would not have been permitted to land peacefully. The VIII FC was well aware how vulnerable the jets were when taking off and landing. Instead he lost control of the jet. Death was instantaneous.

Adolf Galland and several others raced to the crash site in a vehicle and were devastated by the scene that greeted them. There were little recognizable features of either an aircraft or a human being other than a dismembered hand, a chunk of thigh muscle, and Nowotny's service medals, including his Iron Cross with Oak Leaves, Swords and Diamonds; there was simply bits and pieces of human flesh and jet pieces in a large crater.[21] Born in December 1920, Major Walter Nowotny was, remarkably, only twenty-three years old and had an astonishing 257 aerial victories at the time of his death.

The loss was terrible for the unit, which was forced to undergo restructuring. Thus far, the jet program was a disaster. *Kommando Nowotny* had lost twenty-six precious jets for only eighteen to twenty-two victories; eight of the losses were due to enemy action, the rest lost to training accidents.[22] The aircraft were simply not advanced enough for the intended task, nor were the pilots ready to fly them. General Galland sent the *Kommando* survivors to Lechfeld for intensive training. On November 19, 1944, Nowotny's command was redesignated *III. Gruppe/Jagdges-chwader 7* (JG 7), Group Three Fighter Squadron Seven; it was placed under the command of *Oberst* (Colonel) Johannes Steinhoff and transferred to Brandenburg-Briest. This unit had existed on paper since August of that year, but was not activated or staffed due to personnel and budget issues. The death of Nowotny allowed some positive steps for General Galland to finally use the designation and make sure the unit was equipped solely with Stormbirds.[23] More re-structuring rolled the unit into an entirely new and complete organization. Many of the changes made to JG 7 exceed the scope of this narrative, but by March 1945, JG 7 was finally ready for combat.

• • •

In addition to the re-vamped engines, lasting up to twenty operational hours by the end of 1944, and more trained pilots, some of the Me 262 jets carried a new type of weapon. Rockets had been in use for much of the war, but the height of technology was now found in the *Rakete 4Kg Minenkopf* (R4M) wing-mounted mortar-type weapon. Previously, air-to-air rockets were notoriously inaccurate and had to be fired from pointblank range to hit a bomber, placing the Luftwaffe fighters at great risk from the bomber's team of gunners. Something new was needed to reduce the risk to the German fighters. Development occurred throughout 1944 to design and test a deadlier weapon that could be fired from jets rather than conventional fighters, and from greater distances. The high closing speeds of jets could enable quicker deployment before the American gunners could respond from the targeted bombers.

In addition to improved combat tactics, the R4M was designed to fly straighter with eight blade fins that deployed upon firing. The weapon was approximately 814 mm (2 feet, 8 inches) and 3.5 kg (9 lbs.); the warhead was 55 mm with 520–530 g of HTA (hydrogen, TNT, and aluminum) explosive; it detonated with an impact fuse.[24] The rocket was designed to be fired from up to 800 yards, deployed from a wooden rack beneath each wing of the jet; it traveled some 1,700 feet per second. Each rack could carry up to twelve rockets. The R4M was a single-shot bomber destroyer. On March

18, 1945, JG 7 assigned an entire squadron to be armed with these killers; six Stormbirds from 9.*Staffel* rose up to deploy the R4M in combat for the first time, and by 11:20 a.m., they scored their first victories with the new weapons. Previous use of the weapons had been in practice flights from February to the middle of March, working out bugs and deployment issues. But by March 1, they were ready, and the results were catastrophic for the unlucky targets. Pilots of 9.*Staffel* reported devastation beyond their expectations as one hit would obliterate a B-17 into tumbling shards of aluminum, engines, human bodies, and mangled debris.[25] There were no survivors following such a hit.

If the *Lady Jane II* could avoid being caught by one of these killers in her weakened state, she just might make it home.

The crew of the *Lady Jane II*. *Standing left to right*: David Vermeer, John J. Thompson, Eugene Holley, and John Sites. *Front row*: Rodney Williams, Harold Churchill, Milan Basara, Fred Gerhardt, and Harold Babcock. This photograph was taken while the boys were training at Biggs Field Air Base at Fort Bliss, Texas, in late 1944. The B-17G in the background was a training aircraft. *Lorraine Williams*

Pilot David Elmer Vermeer. *David Elan Vermeer*

Co-pilot John J. Thompson. *Tom Johnson*

Tail gunner Harold L. Babcock. *USAAF*

Radio operator Milan Basara; "Bas" had apparently bailed out safely. *USAAF*

Navigator Eugene E. Holley at eighteen years of age upon entry into the USAAF. *Sue Holley-Suarez*

Waistgunner Rodney A. "Willy" Williams changed places with Fred Gerhardt on the March 18 mission. *Lorraine Williams*

Baby-faced togglier Ernest James Butlin. Jim had replaced John Sites on the fateful flight. *Martha Stone*

Teenaged newlyweds Elinor and Eugene Holley before his deployment to the UK. *Sue Holley-Suarez*

Rodney enjoying the sun and sand in Long Beach before his departure to the war. *Lorraine Williams*

Rodney and his cousin Russell Shaw before shipping out. Both men served in the USAAF. *Lorraine Williams*

Lt. Kenneth Speer's crew. *Standing left to right*: 1Lt. Kenneth D. Speer, 2Lt. James J. Kelly, TSgt. David Yohay, SSgt. William D. Gross, and SSgt. Jack C. Everett. *Sitting left to right*: 2Lt. Robert H. Simon, TSgt. Gordon C. Cupp, and Sgt. Jim Butlin. Jim would replace John Sites on the *Lady Jane* crew for her last mission. Missing in this photo is 2Lt. Wm. Scanlon, the bombardier. He is replaced here by Jim Butlin, a togglier. *USAAF*

The original *Lady Jane*, 42-107009, was shot down on November 6, 1944, following a mission to Hamburg. *USAAF*

The boys flew their fourth mission on 44-8767, *Southern Comfort*. As a replacement crew, they were rarely assigned the same bomber for each mission. This aircraft survived the war and met her fate at the recycling facility at Kingman, Arizona, in 1946. *USAAF*

The operations room at Deenethorpe. *USAAF*

Wartime censors scratched out the unit designation of these B-17G bombers belonging to the 613th Bombardment Squadron. *USAAF*

The Messerschmitt Me 262 was the world's first combat-deployed fighter jet. The first ever combat group to engage the enemy using this advanced technology was *Jagdgeschwader 7* in November 1944. It would change history and severely threaten the Mighty Eighth. *Public domain photo*

The Arado Ar 234 was the world's first jet bomber. Hitler had wanted a "blitz bomber" to halt the invasion of mainland Europe he knew was coming. Unfortunately, the German Reich could not afford multiple jet development programs, and the Ar 234 was sidelined in favor of the Me 262. *Public domain photo*

Major Theodor Weissenberger was among the group of jets that chased the *Lady Jane II* out of Berlin. While in the interrogation center, JJ Thompson met a man matching Weissenberger's description. The German officer said he had delivered the fatal fire that brought the bomber down. However, evidence suggests that it may have been Günther Wegmann who had shot down the *Lady Jane II*. Wegmann was seriously wounded in the encounter east of Uelzen and had lost his leg as a result. It is unlikely he was recovered enough to speak to JJ. The Luftwaffe officer who spoke to the captured American airman was apparently uninjured. While JJ couldn't remember the officer's name, it was most likely Weissenberger. *Public domain photo*

Historic composite images taken from Google Earth showing the assigned target of the 613th Bombardment Squadron on March 18, 1945. The Tempelhof Airfield can be seen in the southern portion and is pock-marked with bomb craters. The image of the railyard dates to 1943 while the airfield image is dated March 18, 1945, the day of the raid. It was most likely snapped by a post-raid American reconnaissance aircraft to determine the effectiveness of the mission. The railroad marshalling yard is now a quiet park-like area. Most of the track has been removed, with only the roundhouses remaining. *Google*

Aerial photograph of Deenethorpe Airfield, Station 128, taken shortly after the war. Note the hardstands scattered around the perimeter track. *USAAF*

The airfield today as seen in a modern image from Google Earth. The control tower is long gone but the main runway is still in use by a local flying club. *Google*

1945 image showing the exhumed bodies of the crew of *Wham! Bam! Thank You M'am*. Six of the nine crewmembers were murdered by villagers shortly after their capture. *US Army Signal Corps*

Wartime photo of Lt. Col. Siegfried Utermark. His chauffer at the time was a young man who identified this vehicle as the one used to carry the body of one of the murdered *Lady Jane II* crewmembers. Notice the "RAD" on the license plate designating it as belonging to the *Reichsarbeitsdienst*, the Reich Labor Service. *Court photo Case #12-1813*

The only known photographs of the *Lady Jane II* are pieces of her carcass as the tail section lay upside down near Wittingen, Germany, after the war (1946 or 1947). The child is playing on the vertical stabilizer. The aircraft's alphabetic designator, "H," is clearly seen on the left. The registration number, 38607, is partially visible beyond the child's feet. This photograph first appeared in *Between War and Peace*, by Johannes Plummeyer, in 2012. *Private family photograph, used by permission*

A post-war family outing on the tail section of the *Lady Jane II*. *Private family photograph, used by permission*

Andrey Andreyevich Vlasov. The *Lady Jane* crew believed their release from Russian custody was dependent upon the transfer of this man from American to Soviet control. This photo was probably taken during his Moscow trial. *Public domain photo*

US Air Force captain John J. Thompson in 1957. *Tom Johnson*

Maj. John J. Thompson in Vietnam. On May 16, 1965, JJ was having breakfast when a huge fire erupted on the flight line at the Bien Hoa Airbase. The resulting catastrophe killed twenty-seven Americans. *Tom Johnson*

Kingman, Arizona, 1946: Hundreds of B-17Gs, some brand new and never deployed into combat, await their fate. It took three years to reduce all these warbirds into aluminum ingots. *Army Air Force Museum*

The original grave markers from the Rosche Cemetery were kept in a small shed for many years. *Lorraine Williams*

David E. Vermeer's final resting place at the Ardennes American Cemetery. *Public domain photo*

Milan Basara's final resting place at the Ardennes American Cemetery. *Public domain photo*

Jim Butlin's final resting place at the Ardennes American Cemetery. *Public domain photo*

Rodney Williams's daughter Lorraine interviewed the *Lady Jane II*'s navigator Gene Holley at his Ohio home, in 2013. *Craig Holley*

CHAPTER 7
THE DEATH OF A LADY

The enemy fighters shot holes throughout the ship, injuring gunners and setting afire the gas tanks located at the number 2 engine.

—Gene Holley

Reichsmarschall and Luftwaffe chief Hermann Göring relieved *General der Jagdflieger* Adolf Galland of his command in January 1945. General Galland and Göring had been having an increasingly contentious relationship. The failings of the fighter arm of the Luftwaffe to counter the American daylight bombing campaign had greatly upset Hitler. He was furious with Göring for allowing Big Week to occur. The *Reichsmarschall* had promised the Führer earlier in the war that "not one bomb" would touch German soil. How wrong he was; finally, in light of the endless bombings and Galland's increasing criticism regarding the prosecution of the war, the "Fat One" had had enough and sacked the general, perhaps taking some of Hitler's rapprochement out on the Luftwaffe general. Göring yelled at Galland; Galland yelled back. The operations and course of action taken by Göring were counterproductive and essentially ineffective. The *General der Jagdflieger* let his boss know exactly what he thought, to the detriment of his career.

When Galland was sacked, *Oberst* (Colonel) Johannes Steinhoff was fired as well, losing his position as the head of *Geschwaderstab* (*Stab.*)/JG 7 (Headquarters Company). Steinhoff was a close associate of Galland's, and displeasure from Göring meant suffering for all. His replacement was Major Theodor ("Theo") Weissenberger.

Weissenberger had been *Kommandeur* of *Staffel* I./JG 7 before his abrupt reassignment. Steinhoff had been in charge of JG 7 since its reorganization following the death of Walter Nowotny. The sudden change in command was unexpected but, ultimately, not harmful to the operations and effectiveness of the unit. However, it may have delayed the deployment of the unit by some weeks while the reorganization proceeded.

By all appearances, Theo Weissenberger was a good leader and administrator. He placed Major Rudolf Sinner in charge of III./JG 7. Weissenberger worked hard and was able to bring JG 7 to full combat readiness, for the first time since its inception. By March 18, 1945, they were finally ready. When the huge bomber formation was spotted via radar in the morning, he alerted his pilots, briefed them, and sent them aloft, en masse, thirty-six jets in all. After deploying his troops, Weissenberger hopped into his private Stormbird "Green 3," fired her up, and led his men into battle. The R4M-equipped jets of 9./JG 7 were delayed on take-off but joined the melee by 11:15 a.m. in the skies above Berlin.

• • •

The *Lady Jane II* was crippled by her encounter with the 88 mm flak gun. She was forced to leave the safety of the formation due to the damage to the oxygen system as the bomber dropped to 13,500 feet. Hardtack and Willy were wounded but conscious and alert, mostly; Fred was having some problems and would phase in and out of consciousness. At around 12:20 p.m., after Dave demanded that the ship return to Deenethorpe, five P-51s appeared and escorted the bomber for a brief period. Then, as suddenly as they arrived, they jettisoned their drop tanks and disappeared. JJ couldn't understand why; Gene thought they might have run low on fuel and needed to return to base. There was no radio communication between the bomber and the Mustangs; they simply disappeared about 100 miles northwest of Berlin.

Almost immediately, cannon fire erupted from behind the battered bomber. Six jets of JG 7 had been following the *Lady Jane* since Berlin. The Stormbirds opened up as they raced toward her at speeds no bomber of the time, and certainly not a damaged one, could counter. The *LJ2* rocked and vibrated as all the gunners opened up on the new targets. The bomb bay door was still open as JJ was trying to crawl to the rear of the ship on his mission to check on the flak damage and hand out lunches to the crew. Uncomprehending the situation, given its suddenness, initially he thought Hal was shooting through the bomb bay doors, but that would have been impossible. He saw streaks of tracers from cannon fire flash under the bomber, just a few feet from his face. Without speaking over the interphone, Hal was trying to warn him back to the controls using quick hand signals as he operated the twin .50-cal. machine guns in the turret; he saw the threat and tried to push the co-pilot away. Then the reality suddenly struck home as Hal's spent casings bounced off JJ's head: someone was trying to kill them. JJ backed up and returned to his seat.

Streaking tracers appeared all around the *Lady Jane* like flaming hornets. The ship shuddered violently as the number 2 engine on the port side was struck. Fuel tanks in the wing ignited immediately. JG 7 had scored a successful hit. Just as the strikes came, Harold opened up from his position in the tail and apparently scored a successful blow. He could not have known it at the time, but he may have struck the jet piloted by Walter Nowotny's former wingman, Günther Wegmann.* Chunks flew off the Stormbird as it dove out of sight. Wegmann was leading *Staffel* 9./JG 7,the squadron equipped with the R4M rockets. Fortunately for the *Lady Jane*'s crew, no rocket was deployed from the Stormbird hit by Harold's fire.

The other jets careened closer to the now fatally wounded bomber, blazing past her, three per side. They had managed a single salvo and were peeling off to deliver another.

It was time to go. In the universal sign of surrender, Dave lowered the landing gear. Then he and JJ discussed bailing out; agreeing with his co-pilot, Dave switched on the bail-out bell and informed the crew over the interphone that they needed to jump. Hal dropped down from the top turret and strapped on his parachute; Harold crawled off the banana seat in the tail and joined the other gunners at the huge flak hole. No one bothered with the crew door on the starboard side; it wasn't needed. Gene had opened the forward escape hatch near the nose and had his feet dangling out as JJ made his way to the hatch. Jim Butlin was standing at his station adjusting his parachute as he waited for Gene and JJ to jump; Harold, Willy, and Bas helped Hardtack into his parachute and, while firmly grasping the D-ring, pushed him out the flak hole near the ball turret before dropping through the hole themselves and into space. They had sent Fred down with the chute cord pulled because he kept slipping in and out of consciousness. Hal had followed JJ out the front escape hatch after giving the co-pilot a coercive rump shove when the latter got hung-up in the hatch. Then Jim followed Hal. Everyone was out... except Dave. For reasons unknown to this day, he stayed onboard and died with the *Lady Jane II* when the portside fuel tanks finally exploded. The explosive concussion would have killed him instantly. When the wreckage was later searched by civilians on the ground, his body was found intact and still strapped to his seat. The civilians who found him removed his flight jacket as a souvenir before being burying him in the nearby Rosche cemetery.[1]

* Author Manfred Boehme stated in his book (p. 117) that 9./JG 7 pilot Günther Wegmann reported striking a B-17 in the left wing shortly before being hit with a salvo from the defending tail gunner. Harold Babcock stated that he was certain he hit a jet as he saw a chunk of metal fly off as a result of his fire. He stated that the jet dropped out of sight when the number 2 engine caught fire. Wegmann reported his right engine (number 2) was damaged and he was forced to bail out; he was severely wounded as well. The incident was over Glöwen, approximately 55 miles east of the location where the *LJ2* crashed. According to Heaton and Lewis, (p. 270), Wegmann claimed two B-17 kills on March 18, 1945. The evidence points to Wegmann as possibly being the pilot who took the *LJ2* down. However, another pilot would claim to be the victor when he met with JJ Thompson at the POW interrogation center. The actual Luftwaffe pilot who shot down the *LJ2* remains uncertain.

No one knows why Dave Vermeer didn't bail out. Indications are that the autopilot was still engaged and flying the ship at the time, as it was under control while the crew exited. He had plenty of time if he left with JJ and Hal. But he didn't. Interviews with his family completed for this book project have resulted in several theories: Dave's nephew Jeris suggested that his uncle may have been trying to fly the plane to the Channel, where it could be safely ditched and kept away from German hands; nephew Darrell suggested that Dave may have been flying the plane to make sure it crashed away from housing, thus avoiding civilian casualties. Dave was a deeply religious man; this may have been the reason for his decision. Either suggestion provides insight into a man conscious of his position with a profound understanding of his responsibilities. Perhaps he wanted to make sure the rest of the boys got off safely, but simply ran out of time before he could exit. No one will ever know. The *Lady Jane II* died in a wheat field in rural Uelzen, Germany. Dave had kept her from killing civilians in her death throes. No one on the ground was injured.

• • •

The six Luftwaffe jets patrolled the area to track the downed Americans and find more targets. JG 7 would destroy thirteen bombers that day.[2] It was a blessing that 9./JG 7 had already fired its rockets before the Stormbirds caught up with the *Lady Jane*. It is possible that Günther Wegmann's *Staffel* was among the jets that caught up with her, but by that point in the battle, they had most likely used their rockets and were shooting down bombers with cannon fire.[3] Had one of those terrible missiles struck Dave's ship, not one man would have survived and this story would not have been written.

Hardtack slipped in and out of consciousness as he glided down but remembered seeing the bomber blow up. He landed near a small village, waking up to find he had been helped by a young German boy. Upon arrival to the village, an adult civilian examined Fred's dog tags, kicking him when he saw his name, Gerhardt. How could a German be bombing other Germans? He was shortly loaded onto a pickup truck to be taken to a doctor to treat his numerous wounds. While riding in the back of the truck, he noticed his parachute was tossed in with him along with a second chute. They were bunched up curiously and Fred could tell there was something underneath. He gingerly lifted up one of the chutes to peer at the lump underneath and was shocked to see it was Milan Basara. Bas was dead. Hardtack didn't know if he had been shot or had died in the jump. The villagers did not say, and to this day, Milan Basara's death remains a mystery.

Gene Holley had dropped from the escape hatch and tumbled into the slip stream, end over end. He gained control by stretching out his arms and was able to slow his acrobatics so he could maneuver onto his back and safely pull the chute cord; the parachutes were mounted on the front so being on one's back was the safest position for deployment. He watched as the *Lady Jane* burned to death, exploded, and arched out of sight as she rained flaming debris onto farm fields below. Gene was unaware of who had made it off the ship and who had not. He saw only two other parachutes in his descent, JJ's and Hal's. Gene also saw something else; several jets were flying straight at him as he helplessly dangled in his parachute. A wave a terror briefly passed over him as he prepared to be blown apart by cannon fire from the Stormbirds. But they did not fire and shot past the defenseless navigator, causing his parachute to whip around in the violent air current. Gene hit the ground hard but landed safely. Unfortunately, he was within sight of angry farmers as they raced to catch him.

JJ hit the slip stream, spinning wildly. He remembered his training and spread-eagle to calm the rotations. It worked, but the mad gyrations had caused one of his electric booties to fly off. He couldn't watch the bomber, as his immediate concern was the scary descent into thick clouds. Should he pull the D-ring now, or wait? He looked down and saw more heavy clouds below him in between clear sky. What if that was not cloud cover, but fog? Fear shot through him as he grabbed the D ring of his rip cord, jerking the piece of metal so hard, he inadvertently flung it out into space. The canopy blossomed above him; his concern about not having a reserve chute proved unwarranted. He briefly lamented the loss of his D ring. Didn't tradition state that one was supposed to keep that as a souvenir? The question flew away as quickly as the piece of metal; he had more pressing concerns.

JJ watched as Gene landed and ran off into a copse of trees. The jets that harried the navigator did the same to the co-pilot. JJ too was terrified of being murdered in in his parachute, but, like Gene, was left alone by the jets. JJ landed in a small tree as numerous irate civilians ran to collect the downed Americans. Their initial target, Gene, had given them the slip as JJ conveniently landed a hundred or more yards directly in front of them. Several of the jets also continued to circle around the airmen, presumably reporting their positions to local troops. JJ ran into some woods to try to avoid the gathering farmers but was ordered to stop and was fired upon when he did not immediately respond to a shouted chorus of "HALT!" Dirt clods spit up from the ground as bullets spattered about him. JJ halted, throwing his hands up. The farmers raised their shotguns and .22s at him but stopped firing as soon as he stopped running. A single German soldier was with this crowd as he took the co-pilot into custody. For 2Lt. John J. Thompson, the war was over.

Willy, Hal, Harold, Jim, and Bas all apparently landed safely, but three of them would not survive the day. Jim was injured in the foot, most likely scraping it on the hatch as he exited the burning bomber; he landed safely and was treated by a German civilian who had kindly wrapped his bleeding foot in a bandage before turning him over to local authorities. Shortly afterward an officer of the Reich Labor Service took delivery of the captured togglier. For reasons unknown to this day, the German officer apparently put Jim on his knees and shot him in the back of the head at point-blank range.

A shroud of secrecy quickly passed over the village when Bas was found dead. Hal Churchill would suffer a similar fate and was gunned down shortly after he struggled out of his parachute harness and ran for the safety of thick woods. Milan Basara's killer(s) are unknown to us today, as the apparent crime went uninvestigated and unpunished. Fortunately, Hal's executioner was found and prosecuted by a war crimes tribunal, as will be discussed in greater detail later. But there is little information on the fate of Bas. It is possible he did not survive the jump, but this seems unlikely, since his deployed parachute was found intact by Hardtack. Unless a German villager who witnessed or had knowledge of what occurred ever comes forward, we will never know; that too seems unlikely, given the passage of decades.

After being detained by the angry farmers, JJ found himself at the local bürgermeister's house, where he was thoroughly searched. They handed his cigarettes, lighter, and a roll of Lifesavers back to him. The bürgermeister also handed JJ his handkerchief and rosary back to him, asking if JJ was a "*Catholich*"; he responded in the affirmative.

Present in the farm house were two little girls, perhaps sisters, around five and six years old. They were intensely curious about the American bomber pilot and stood next to JJ as he sat in an overstuffed chair in the farmhouse. JJ was popping one of his Lifesavers into his mouth and stuffing the remainder back in his pocket when he noticed the sad look on the girls' faces. Using his thumbnail, he cut the roll of candy in half, handing one section to the six-year-old to share with her sister. The joy expressed by the little girls at this precious gift triggered broad smiles from the adults all around the room; a small measure of peace arrived in a tiny German village on March 18, 1945. In return for American's kindness, he was given a tall glass of cool water, something he was desperately needing, and an old pair of shoes to cover his stocking feet. JJ was deeply moved by the show of compassion.[4]

While JJ was sharing his candy with the little girls, Eugene Holley was running to freedom, at least this was his plan, to dash all the way to Belgium. Upon landing near the town of Rosche, and snatching up his spent parachute, he ran hard for the woods, seeking to hide during the day and travel at night. He had heard several shots that were probably fired by the farmers demanding that JJ end his bid for freedom. They had lost sight of Gene as he practiced his Olympic style sprinting, still clad in his bulky electric flight suit, no doubt cumbersome in the extreme. But adrenaline ruled and Gene ran onward. German civilians were swarming the crew's landing area, searching for the "*terrorfliegers.*" Unknown to Gene or JJ at the time, several of their crewmates were in the process of being captured and executed.

Dave Vermeer, Hal Churchill, Milan Basara, and Jim Butlin did not survive that horrible Sunday afternoon. They were all buried hastily in the Rosche cemetery. The original crosses that once adorned their graves have remained stored in a nearby shed for more than seventy-five years. The four of them would all later be reburied at the Ardennes American Cemetery in Belgium. Hal's body was later disinterred and sent home to his family in Wisconsin. To this day, Dave, Bas, and Jim remain in Belgium, buried alongside hundreds of those heroes who never made it home.

• • •

Gene had reasoned that the civilians would not expect him to remain near the town, so he found a thick stand of bushes, buried his chute in leaf litter, and waited for nightfall within full sight of Rosche. He inspected his escape kit, finding a map, a tiny compass, and inedible concentrate powder with a bag of halazone pills to purify drinking water. He had no food. JJ had never completed his trip to the crew with their cookies and chocolate bars before the abandon ship order was issued. Gene looked down and noticed his hands were torn and bloody, probably from releasing the escape hatch and the subsequent launch through the small hole. He had left some of his blood on the parachute when he buried it under a pile of leaves. He waited for darkness, then headed northwest, toward Belgium, in a soaking rain. As with the other crewmembers, he had no shoes. The electric flying suits had booties that fit over the flier's socks; they removed their shoes while on a mission. Everyone who bailed out did so without their shoes.

Gene raced to Belgium in his electric booties, which he knew would not last long, especially in wet conditions, but onward he ran. His nighttime trek took him through farmers' fields and multiple strands of barbed wire fencing, seemingly everywhere. As dawn broke, he found a hiding place and lay down to sleep the day away. In late afternoon, he resumed his journey, careful to avoid civilians working their fields, at one point narrowly avoiding detection by an elderly farmer as he inadvertently walked right up to him. Fortunately, the man was preoccupied, probably hard of hearing, and had his back turned to the American. The second night of Gene's great escape was arduous. He was tired and terribly hungry, having had nothing to eat since breakfast the day before. Still he traveled on, reaching the outskirts of a small town. He had not yet secured a safe place to spend the daylight hours when he was suddenly surrounded by several dozen German civilians, some elderly and some Hitler Youth. Gene Holley's bid for freedom came to an abrupt end; throwing his hands in the air, he surrendered. Fortunately, he was not harmed by the civilians and was turned over to local authorities. This was fortuitous, as toward the end of the war it was Hitler Youth and other thoroughly Nazi-indoctrinated youngsters who often committed terrible crimes as the Führer insisted on carrying on the fight even in the face of obvious defeat. Gene may not have been aware at the time just how lucky he was to have been spared the fate several of his friends had suffered. Of course, he knew nothing of this at the time.

Gene was transported to a tiny jail in Uelzen, where he would sit alone in a cramped cell. The soldier who had collected him ground salt into Gene's emotional wounds as the German ate a delicious lunch of bread, cheese, and fruit right in front of his prisoner, devouring what Gene was certain was food meant for the POW, not the guard.

JJ was picked up from the bürgermeister's home later by a single German soldier riding a bicycle and was escorted to Uelzen where he was incarcerated in the local jail. The gift of shoes was declared *Verboten* by the escort and remained at the mayor's house. JJ was forced to walk to the Uelzen jail in his stocking feet, some 4 miles away. The kind treatment he had received at the bürgermeister's house was decidedly not extended at the jail where a German officer verbally and sometimes physically abused his prisoner. JJ spoke no German, and when he couldn't answer the officer's questions, he was yelled at, punched in the chest, and thrown against a wall. Fortunately, the treatment was meant to terrify, not injure, the flier so he wasn't seriously hurt. He was tossed into a tiny cell with a heavy steel door to await whatever the fates had in store. Fear crept over nineteen-year-old 2Lt. John J. Thompson in that dark cell.

While JJ waited, he could hear a radio. He could not understand most of the words, but he could discern that it was meant to relay information about Allied aircraft activity. It was dark outside as the co-pilot sat in silence, he speculated that the words "*Achtung, Luftwaffe*…" was a warning that bombers were active in the area. Since it was dark, this meant the RAF, as the Americans undertook their missions in daylight. The war was continuing without the *Lady Jane II*.

Later that night, JJ was hauled out of the Uelzen jail and loaded onto a horse-driven carriage. As he sat in the front seat next to the driver, his guard was seated behind him on one of the rear benches, no doubt with a rifle pointed at his charge. JJ then experienced another small act of kindness by a German civilian as the driver shared a blanket he had over his knees with the teenaged captive. It was chilly that mid-March night, and JJ greatly appreciated the gesture. The driver then pushed his team on, as they clopped through the darkness to deliver the young American to another prison.

The new structure looked like a barn and had cells on the second floor. JJ was stuffed into a tiny 8-by-4-or-5-foot cell. There was no furniture, just a narrow wooden bench meant to serve as a bed; there was no mattress, no blanket, nothing. In the cell next to him was a Dutch prisoner and in the cell beyond that were two RAF men. Shortly after entering his new abode, a guard brought JJ a nasty foul-smelling, mildew-infested quilt; it rotted to his touch and tore easily, but it brought a little warmth and was therefore appreciated.

Some of the guards apparently enjoyed terrorizing their prisoners, as one pulled JJ out of his cell to threaten him. At around 9:00 p.m., the American was treated to the sight of a guard loading his rifle, who then held it in front of his prisoner and drew a finger across his own throat before pointing to the twelve on his wristwatch. The meaning wasn't lost on JJ; he would be shot at midnight. He had admitted in his memoirs to having been a "card-carrying coward."

The guard's act had the desired effect on his prisoner; JJ was thoroughly terrorized as he was shoved back into his cell to await his execution. JJ laid down on the bench and pulled the fragile stinky quilt over him as best he could, but then the trauma of that terrible day took its toll and he passed out from sheer exhaustion. The fact that this self-proclaimed "coward" had boarded a thin metal tube for mission after mission, knowing his odds of survival were not good, reflected his true nature as no "coward" at all. He was as courageous and dedicated as anyone willing to step aboard a huge flying target to place his very survival in doubt day after day. John J. Thompson was no coward.

Still in possession of his GI watch, JJ woke the next morning full of astonishment. It was 4:00 a.m.; the guards had apparently forgotten to shoot him at midnight. It quickly dawned on him that they were playing a "joke" on him and probably thought it pretty funny to scare him. They had succeeded. JJ was taken to what passed for the mess hall where he received a breakfast of German black bread and a water glass full of ersatz "*kaffee*," a caffeine-free concoction of chicory, barley, acorns, and other available items, none of which taste very good but helped ease the now-persistent hunger pangs. When the guard stepped from the room, the cook quickly spooned some sugar into the "coffee." In broken English, the man explained he was a Frenchman imprisoned for five years.

Shortly after breakfast, JJ was collected by an armed guard and marched to the local railway station, amassing a small crowd of curious on-lookers. On the way there, they passed what was obviously a heavily bomb-damaged building. The guard smacked the co-pilot in the back of the head with the butt of his rifle, angrily declaring, "*Amerikaner bomb fraulein und kinder*!" JJ wasn't hurt when he was sent sprawling into the dirt by the sucker punch, but he was deeply embarrassed by the episode and quickly hopped to his feet. He was also afraid the curious civilians following the tiny entourage might become emboldened, work themselves into a frenzy, and attack the American bomber pilot. Fortunately, he and his guard made it to the train station in one piece, free of further incidents.

The destination of the train was Lüneburg, where JJ was conveyed to the local jail. After he had been there a day, something odd happened. A guard entered his cell and in broken English stated that the American had been shot down by an Me 262 jet. The guard then said, "Here is the pilot." A Luftwaffe officer then walked into the small cell and extended his hand in greeting. JJ took the older man's hand and they shook. The nineteen-year-old co-pilot thought the man looked "old," but he was probably in his thirties. It could have been Theo Weissenberger, or any of his pilots; JJ didn't recall the name. He was, however, impressed with the chivalry of the moment.

Unknown to the co-pilot at that time, the *Lady Jane*'s navigator would also be delivered to the same facility. Once he arrived, Gene was finally able to get some sustenance in the form of the ubiquitous black bread with margarine. It wasn't much food but helped ease his hunger pain, now more than forty-eight hours in the making. Several days after JJ arrived, he was delighted to find Gene there as well. They found each other when a guard came to JJ's cell and indicated that he follow him to the latrine. The co-pilot stated that he did not need to go at that moment, but the guard insisted, so JJ followed. His joy was apparent as he found Gene waiting in the latrine. JJ, surprised, told Gene that the Germans had shown him the latter's bloodied parachute. He thought his friend was dead or wounded. But there was Gene, alive and well. The guards did not allow them much time to catch up, but it seemed the nightmare was starting to wind down a little, and the three-day stay at Lüneburg wasn't too bad. But the feeling of relief would not last.

On March 23, the two Americans were sent separately from Lüneburg to the interrogation center at Pinneburg, near Hamburg. JJ was sent with a single guard and no one else. They had to pass through Hamburg to get to the POW processing facility. Exiting the train, the pilot was deeply shocked at the terrible damage wrought by the bombing campaign. Both British and American bombs had completely wrecked the city, including the train station. The catastrophe caused by the relentless bombings had devastated the city; the skeletal remains of the buildings, culture, and life were appalling to witness. JJ suddenly wanted to vanish, afraid the civilians around him would blame him for the destruction and attack him and his single guard. As they walked through the crowds, JJ followed his guard but in the press of people temporarily lost sight of him. Frightened, JJ stopped and looked frantically for his escort; they caught sight of each other, and the young pilot rushed over to the guard, relieved. Who knew what the civilians would have done to the American had they realized he was a bomber pilot? The thought was terrifying.

At that point in the war, all of Germany's large cities had been severely damaged by round-the-clock Allied bombing. Hamburg itself had been incinerated in July 1943 by the Allies in Operation Gomorrah. JJ was shocked to see much of this devastation as he exited the train station. The death toll had been incomprehensible in that raid when American bombers had followed the RAF with more destruction the next day. The crew of the *Lady Jane II* did not participate, as they were not in-theater at the time, but in a twist of fate, an American airman would see, up close, the terrible consequences of his missions. This is what frightened JJ so much when he saw the faces of the men and women who lived in this obliterated city. Would they blame him for the deaths of their loved ones and the loss of their homes?

JJ was desperate to get away from Hamburg. He and his guard boarded a crowded street car and settled in for the ride across town. JJ kept his eyes down, not looking into the haunted faces of the residents, desperate to be invisible, unknown and unknowable, a ghost with no reflection and no form. When they exited the street car, a sign showed they were near Pinneburg. A walk of several miles was required to reach their destination, a large POW processing facility. Gene was sent to the same location and arrived at about the same time. Like JJ, he was thrown into solitary confinement to "soften" him up for interrogation.

Thus far, neither Gene nor JJ had seen any other crewmembers from the *Lady Jane* and had no word of their survival. But as JJ entered the large latrine there, he was surprised to see a familiar face washing dishes. The tail gunner, Harold Babcock, was scrubbing away. The friends happily greeted each other and Harold told JJ that Willy was there too. Four of the nine *Lady Jane* boys were together again. But no one had word of the others. In light of his terrible injuries, they were fairly certain that Hardtack didn't make it and was probably dead, but they were unaware if everyone had made it off the burning ship. No one saw Dave or Jim bail out, and until after the war it was assumed the latter had also stayed onboard as the *Lady Jane* perished. But Jim did indeed evacuate, immediately after Hal, and was shot shortly after he landed.

As they were tossed into single cells, the fear that each felt earlier crept back. For the past five days, the four boys had had little to eat, and starvation was starting to set in. The meals at Pinneburg consisted of small amounts of cabbage and potatoes. (The interrogation center was a large facility where many American POWs were sent and processed before being shipped out to various camps. Many captured Allied fliers found themselves here, a harsh place meant to illicit cooperation by withholding basic necessities and rewarding compliance with food and amenities.) Gene sat across a desk from a very young German officer with a perfect command of English. Temporarily reversing roles, Gene prodded his captor a little, wanting to know just why the man felt that a German victory was still possible. The officer stated, emphatically, that the war would end very soon in a stalemate. Gene knew better. The Allied armies had completely surrounded what little was left of the Third Reich. The idealistic young German insisted that the Allies would "never cross the Rhine"; apparently unknown to the officer, the Rhine had already been crossed, days earlier. In effect, the war was already over.

JJ "celebrated" his twentieth birthday on March 25 at Pinneburg Interrogation Center. His gift was a tiny morsel of meat he found in his soup, over which he sang "Happy Birthday" to himself.

The survivors of the *Lady Jane II* stayed at Pinneburg for a week before being placed on a train together, bound for the Baltic coast; there were eight or ten other airmen with them in their group. Their travel rations consisted of a thick slice of brown bread and a small piece of sausage. It would have to sustain them for a two-day trip. At the behest of an American officer incarcerated with them, they were all advised to sign a pledge not to attempt escape during the trip. Any escape attempts would mean the loss of one's shoes, assuming they had a pair; it is not known what the punishment would have been if the POW did not have shoes. With the end of the war so clearly in sight, staying put was an easy decision for some, but more difficult for others. They were watched over by very elderly guards, most likely Volkssturm members.[5] This trip was especially dangerous as American fighter units roamed the skies at will. The Luftwaffe still had some teeth but could not be everywhere at once with their scarce remaining aircraft.

Trains were a favorite target of Mustangs and Jugs. Many prayers were no doubt uttered during the long ride to the prison camp at Barth. For two days, the POWs huddled in the cars, not failing to notice strafing and bomb damage already in existence on the ceiling and walls. The captives shivered in the heavily perforated cars as they traveled east. One of the guards engaged Gene in conversation during the trip. Careful that no one could overhear his defeatist comments, the guard said, quietly, in heavily broken English, that if he were to shoot Stalin, Churchill, Roosevelt, and Hitler, the war and the "worries of the world" would end. Everyone could see the writing on the wall; the war was very nearly over. But such seditious talk could still earn a German soldier a bullet to the brain if he were not cautious.

The train trundled through Hamburg, Lubeck, and Rostock. Like JJ, Gene had been aghast at the sight of the damage to Hamburg when he first saw it on the way to Pinneburg. Now on the way to Barth, they were seeing it again. But Gene reminded himself that Hitler had committed far worse acts; he had started the war and murdered millions. Civilians always suffered the worst of war, forever in the path of murderous intent by warring factions. Because non-combatants are unable to defend themselves, they are invariably the recipients of the worst atrocities.

As the train rumbled through Hamburg, not a single building remained without some damage. The entire city was on the verge of extinction, yet masses of humanity converged here, desperate to flee the approaching British army and the inevitable bloody clashes. Masses of humanity were also coming from the east to escape the Russian juggernaut, but with few available services, many were simply passing through, desperate to find some measure of safety. Indeed, it was rumored that one homeless woman, perhaps a refugee, called "*Flieger Liesa*" by the locals, would occupy the tail section of the *Lady Jane*'s wrecked shell shortly after the German authorities were finished combing through the destroyed bomber looking for secrets. The tail section had been the only extant part of the ship after the fuel tanks erupted. Every other part of the bomber had been blasted to chunks.

Two days of cold air blowing through the many holes in the punctured rail cars created miserable travel conditions. The prisoners suffered from the damp as well. But the three guards were very friendly and tried to converse with their charges as best they could, though they could speak no English. No one in the group of captives could speak German. While stretching their legs on one portion of the journey, the guards let the prisoners exit the train. While they were loading back up, one of the guards handed his rifle to a nearby American and asked him to hand the weapon to another guard who had already boarded the train and was thus out of reach. The captive flier complied and handed the rifle to the designated German guard; shortly afterward, the travel resumed. None of the POWs had broken his pledge to not attempt escape.

On March 30, 1945, after two days of little sleep and even less food, they arrived at their destination in Barth, on the Baltic coast of Germany. Exiting the train, no doubt grateful to be out of the cold and wet, the Americans marched through town and entered what would be their home for the remainder of the war, Stalag Luft I.

Chapter 8
Kriegies

... the inexorable lesson of centuries: suffering must be borne; there is no way out.

—Aleksandr Solzhenitsyn

It was the Luftwaffe that was responsible for the control and incarceration of captured Allied fliers during the war. The "Stalag" system of POW camps was spread across the Third Reich, with the most famous of these being Stalag Luft III in Poland, where the "Great Escape" occurred in March 1944 (later memorialized in the famous 1963 Hollywood film). In March 1945, the four survivors of the *Lady Jane II* found themselves on the Baltic coast, staring at the compound of *Kriegsgefangenerlager Nummer 1 der Luftwaffe*, also known as Stalag Luft I. This camp had been built in 1940 first to house Hitler Youth, then RAF prisoners. It was much smaller at that time, and through the course of the war had to be expanded as the Germans found the need to incarcerate more and more captured airmen.

By this time JJ, Gene, Harold, and Willy may have received word about Hal, but they would spend the rest of the war with many questions. At home their families received tortuous letters from the Army notifying their loved ones that they were "missing in action" and there was no information. The wait was terrible. Joanna Churchill would not learn of Hal's fate until October 1945, five months after he was killed.[1] Many times, the wives and mothers of GIs killed in battle would receive this horrible news in the form of a telegram or cold letter from an Army bureaucrat. But many times, the letter was from a commanding officer offering his deepest sympathies for the terrible loss and, in Hal's case, the promise of justice.

• • •

Bohdan Arct was a thirty-one-year-old Polish national who volunteered for duty with several Allied air forces following the capitulation of his country in 1939; he recorded his stay at Stalag Luft I in great detail. Arct was a pilot with the Polish air force and defended his nation until he was captured in late September 1939 and sent to an internment camp in Romania, where he managed to escape. Disguised in civilian clothing, he slipped out of captivity and traveled to Marseilles, France. He trained with French pilots in mainland France, then North Africa, until June 1940, when they too collapsed under the Nazi war machine. This time Arct traveled north and arrived in England, desperate to continue his fight against Hitler.

Flying Officer Arct trained in a Supermarine Spitfire as a fighter pilot and was posted to the 303 Squadron in Exeter.[2] He was part of a group of Polish patriots who would not stop fighting the Nazis even after their homeland surrendered. They were formed into their own squadrons within the RAF. The 303rd Squadron greatly distinguished itself during the Battle of Britain and was highly decorated and deeply respected by their British counterparts. In 1943, the 303rd was sent to North Africa to serve alongside the RAF's 145th Squadron. Returning to England in 1944, Arct was promoted to Commander of B Flight, 303rd Squadron. It was around this time that he penned his first book, *Chasing Down the Luftwaffe*. Shortly afterward he was promoted again and placed in charge of the 316th Squadron. On September 6, 1944, Arct's long string of good fortune came to an abrupt end when his Spitfire developed engine trouble over Holland. He sent his squadron on ahead as he was forced to bail out. He was captured and, as with so many Allied POWs, was sent into the Stalag system. One of Bohdan Arct's accomplishments was to become a prolific author of some forty-three books (by 1971), including his *Log Book*, which he would pen while locked up at Stalag Luft I. Keeping journals was not permitted, so this effort required secrecy. Arct generously illustrated his *Log Book*, which gives an in-depth description of the hardships suffered by inmates of the camp system. One of his greatest complaints was the repetition of the strip searches he endured when transferred from one set of jailers to another. Stalag Luft I was at the end of his transfers and the horribly humiliating and invasive "bend-over-and-spread-your-cheeks" exams. One must wonder just what the Germans thought he'd be hiding "up there." A file? Wire cutters? How about an entrenching tool? All of the POWs suffered under this terrible indignity.

The *Lady Jane* boys were in-processed at the camp with the ubiquitous strip search, then deloused with caustic powder, photographed, and issued identification numbers. Gene Holley was *Kriegsgefangennummer* (Prisoner of War Number) 7,936. After receiving their ID numbers, they walked over to the supply hut. Incoming inmates were issued American and British-supplied necessities such as blankets, mattress covers, basic toiletries, and footwear. JJ finally had a pair of shoes! It is doubtful, by this time, that anything existed of his bootless sock. He would have been thrilled with the gift of shoes. The British and American Red Cross supplied nearly everything needed by the POWs as the Germans faced a scarcity of many goods at this juncture of the war. Food and toiletries were provided in the form of Red Cross packages, upon which the inmates were deeply dependent. Since civilian clothes were *verboten* in the camps, permissible clothing items were pieces of Allied uniforms such as shirts and trousers. An American POW might be clad in an RAF shirt with his GI slacks, depending on what was available in his size. However, the POWs were allowed some clothing items from home. Families might send socks, underwear, a scarf, or other items not normally associated with military uniforms.

After the invasive in-processing, the new "kriegies" were assigned "blocks and bunks." The first structures they would have noticed were the high double fences surrounding the camp. Arct described them as barbed wire affairs with watch towers every 100 feet; each tower featured a machine gun. Inmates were forbidden to go near the inner fence with the machine guns positioned to provide intersecting fields of fire. A "warning wire" was placed about knee-high in front of the inner fence. An inmate could be shot with no notice if he crossed or even lightly touched this wire.

The camp was enormous, with some ten different enclosures, and held approximately 9,000 prisoners by the time the *Lady Jane* survivors arrived. Most of the inmates were housed in North 1, North 2, North 3, and the West compounds, with the vast majority being USAAF men; there were some RAF and Russian POWs as well, primarily held in the West enclosure. After being assigned their barracks, the Yankee fliers were greeted by an American officer who gave them the "rundown," explaining the rules and schedules for daily activities.

Gene and JJ were sent to live in room 2, block 307, in North 3 compound. Willy and Harold didn't record their room assignment but were no doubt sent to an enlisted men's block, also in North 3. The new inmates might take their bedrolls and "welcome" supplies, drop them at their assigned bunks, and then mingle with the other POWs, seeking more information, perhaps such as whether there had been any successful escape attempts. The location of Stalag Luft I was probably selected due to a high water table that would have prevented tunneling, although tunneling was indeed attempted.[3] The new inmates may have asked how tough the guards were, what the chow was like, whether there were available jobs in the camp, and perhaps what the other POWs did for recreation. North 1 compound was large enough to host a baseball diamond and/or a football field. The POWs already inside the camp would *not* have needled the new arrivals with questions about the progress the Allies had made thus far, because they were well aware of the course of the war. Most of the camps had illegal radios squirreled away; Stalag Luft I was no exception.

Twice per day several kriegies would pull out the device from a secret hiding place, tune in, and take notes. The radio was normally adjusted to receive the BBC at 1300 and 2100 hours daily.[4] Two radios were hidden in the West Compound. One was in the camp theater, stashed within a wall panel above a shelf, behind magazine cut-outs pasted to boards; another was hidden in a loose board behind someone's bunk. The notes were carefully typed on the smallest possible sheet of paper, then handed to the compound's security office for distribution to the other enclosures. The security officer concealed the notes in the false bottom of an empty can of dried milk.[5] To deliver the scraps of paper to compounds that were closed behind locked gates, the paper was wrapped around a rock, and when the "goons" weren't looking, it was flung over the wire. A designated Allied officer in each compound would act as the news reader and keep all the kriegies apprised of the news, while a "goon guard" kept a sharp lookout. In the case of the Stalag Luft I, the Germans were apparently aware of the illegal radios but could never find them. As a result of the radios, the inmates were able to produce their own illicit newspaper, *POW-WOW.* After the newsreaders completed their presentations, the sheets were relegated to the local stove. But one time, the Germans found a copy of *POW-WOW* in North 1. They tore the compound to shreds looking for the radio that was apparently present. But they never found it; the radios were in the West compound.

The inmates were allowed access to German newspapers and radios, with the daily news translated and posted on a blackboard. The POWs were even allowed to produce their own camp newspaper with stories gleaned from the German sources. However, given the Nazis' affection for propaganda and misinformation regarding the status of the war effort, such sources were of obvious limited value to the incarcerated men. Actual news was paramount. By late March 1945, they knew that the Russians were fast approaching from the east.

Arct had reported in his memoir that he was blessed with a hot shower upon completion of in-processing, something to which the *Lady Jane* crew would not be treated. Indeed, all of the taps other than some in the West compound dispensed icy water, not something in which one would wish to bathe, and certainly not in March on the still frigid Baltic coast. But Arct was fortunate to find himself housed with other RAF officers in the most developed of the camp's compounds with access to hot water. He watched as soccer, rugby, and softball games were played. Outside the wire, German guards patrolled. Inside the wire, numerous searches for contraband were conducted. The "goons" were forever looking for weapons, civilian-looking clothing, and that damned elusive radio. They knew it was *somewhere*, but they just couldn't find it. Indeed, most of the inmates had no idea where the radios were located, nor did they realize there was more than one.

Despite the relative "comfort" of the West compound, Bohdan Arct suffered from bouts of depression, as undoubtedly did most POWs. From dusk to dawn the kriegies were confined to the barracks. It was cold with only a tiny stove and never enough coal to feed it; a scant seven coal pieces per day were issued.[6] The underdressed inmates suffered terribly from the freezing Baltic weather. Men would bunch together and double up their blankets, desperate to keep warm. Arct did not say if any of his mates froze to death, but such a thought was certainly on the men's minds.

Cigarettes and coffee were included with the Red Cross packages and were the main currency of the camp. Real coffee was a rarity in the Reich at this point in the war and people were tired of the "ersatz" version. The POWs actively traded with the guards with the valuable Red Cross resources. A bar of chocolate cost 200 smokes.[7] The kriegies were able to obtain extra food and amenities, perhaps even extra blankets and coal rations, through the illegal barter system.

Arct was present when the Red Cross packages suddenly stopped coming in February 1945; he recorded this terrible ordeal as the "Starvation Period." A clerical error would later prove the main culprit in nearly starving thousands of kriegies to death as the Stalag Luft I allotment was misdirected. The Germans did try to assuage the problem with daily rations including several thin slices of the ubiquitous black bread, one or two potatoes and one or two turnips; the unpalatable ersatz *kaffe* was also on the menu. Without the Red Cross food, starvation was a very real possibility. The men suffered horribly. Arct and his roommates would pool what little they had and split it all equally. The men not only lost a tremendous amount of weight; they grew weak. As winter slipped away to spring, many were simply too lethargic to even roll out of their bunks. Death was approaching for many unless something could be done—and soon.

The few inmates with some remaining energy passed the time by putting on theatrical presentations. Sitting in seats made of old Red Cross parcels, the starving masses needn't spend too much precious energy while watching plays or listening to the camp orchestra. Chopin, Grieg, Tchaikovsky, and

Beethoven wafted from instruments donated by the Red Cross. Plays included dramas and comedic productions to help the boys divert their attention from their empty stomachs. Many of the POWs were trained actors or producers in civilian life, including famed British actor Donald Pleasence, and the productions were quite good.[8] Set designers made convincing backdrops, and costumes were fabricated with materials on hand. Though with the German prohibition against civilian-looking attire, costumes would have been fairly simple and most likely ephemeral in nature.

At the end of March, around the same time the crew of the *Lady Jane* arrived, some 30,000 Red Cross packages finally arrived in Barth.[9] It is not recorded how many inmates may have died as a result of a simple clerical error, but the starvation ended and the men grew stronger. However, even with the resumption of the parcels, the daily allotment of calories was still not adequate. But the prospect of starving to death subsided.

• • •

The *Lady Jane* boys may or may not have been introduced right away to the camp's highest-ranking officer and famous P-47 fighter ace Col. Hubert ("Hub") Zemke. Shortly after the Germans kicked off "Operation Barbarossa," the invasion of the Soviet Union in June 1941, Lend-Lease equipment began flowing generously from the US to Russia via ship convoys through the North Atlantic. With the equipment were American aircraft, specifically the Curtiss P-40 Warhawk. The Russians didn't have much experience with American aircraft, so Hub Zemke was sent over to instruct their pilots. Prior to that, he was training RAF pilots to use the Lend-Lease warbirds. Hub learned to speak some Russian while stationed in the USSR, a skill that would become useful later in his military career. While still in the Soviet Union, he was reassigned to the 56th FG and sent home.

The 56th was first inaugurated as the 56th Pursuit Group in January 1941. As the Germans overran the western Soviet Union in June of that year, the 56th was issued a cluster of worn out P-36s and P-39s. In December, the group was placed on alert with its tired aircraft shortly after the Japanese attack at Pearl Harbor. Many of the pilots probably felt concerned that while they were ready to deploy, their obsolete, exhausted equipment wasn't; so, for the time being, they remained stateside.

In February 1942, the Lockheed P-38 Lightning was being issued to pursuit groups; the 56th was due to receive them. But when 1Lt. Hub

Zemke, the new Assistant Materiel Officer, arrived in March, he petitioned to move to the P-40 over logistical concerns; he was concerned about the availability of the new aircraft. For a while the 56th FG had a collection of new P-38s and older P-40s.[10] Shortly thereafter the P-47, the aircraft that would make the 56th famous, came rolling off the assembly lines in numbers great enough to equip and sustain the group.

Hub would enjoy a stellar rise in the ranks of the 56th FG through hard work and determination. In November 1942, the group finally received orders for overseas deployment. With the equipment issue sorted out, twenty-eight-year-old, newly minted Maj. Zemke was given command.

In August 1944, Hub transferred from the 56th to help a new fighter group, the 479th FG, come up to speed and provide it with exceptional leadership. In October 1944, he was reassigned to take up a desk job within the Eighth Fighter Command, undoubtedly not something he desired. Before reporting to his new duty station, he decided to lead one last mission with the 479th. The decision would prove fateful. Disaster struck when he hit severe turbulence in his P-51 and was forced to bail out as the wing on his aircraft detached and the aircraft began a deadly downward spin. The P-51 was equipped with an detachable seat that released him out of the cockpit when he pulled a lever. With only one wing, the Mustang had begun a violent twist, and Hub was smacked forcefully in the bail out process. It was October 30 when he landed in a bog in northern Germany. As he hit the ground, he noticed his right arm was swelling and was excessively painful; he assumed it was broken. In addition to the sore right arm, his right leg was swelling as well; the right side of his face hurt; it was swollen and he now sported a black eye. He looked terrible, as if Joe Louis and beaten the crap out of him. He had apparently smashed the entire right side of his body when when he bailed out of the aircraft.

Being of German ancestry, and fluent in the language, Hub had an advantage most other American GIs did not. Given his extensive injuries, he knew he wouldn't be able to walk much farther and decided to give himself up. He hobbled up to an elderly couple he found harvesting sugar beets and asked for their help. Unfortunately, they weren't in a position to offer the American pilot any assistance; they were apparently captive Polish forced laborers. The woman, somehow terrified by the limping, swollen, and bruised airman, ran off; the Polish man made it clear that he could not help, and Hub had no choice but to move on. He hobbled off but shortly thereafter was surrounded by a group of local villagers. The Polish woman had apparently run to a nearby village and alerted the authorities. Hub was too injured to offer any resistance and was taken into custody peacefully. Besides, he knew all along that being an POW would be unavoidable. Had he not been battered by the breakup of his Mustang, he would have been healthy enough to make it to friendly territory.

Hub didn't record in his memoirs whether he had been kicked or otherwise chastised by his captors, as Fred Gerhardt had been, when it was realized he was of German ancestry. After several nights of captivity in local jails, he was transported via train to the interrogation center at Auswertestelle-West. Here he was strip searched and required to fill out a form demanding far more information than is normally obligatory. Hub gave his name, rank, serial number, and nothing else, much to the annoyance of his captors. He made it clear he would not complete the form. Shortly thereafter, he was tossed into solitary confinement to reflect on his sin of not collaborating. A German private first class, *Gefreiter* Hanns Scharff, informed him that if he cooperated, he would receive much-needed medical attention. Again, Hub did not oblige his jailers, so no doctor was immediately dispatched for his care. He was treated to several more interrogation sessions, but he quickly realized they knew pretty much everything about him, most of it no doubt snatched from US newspapers. Hub was disturbed to find that the Germans were also aware of operational data that could have come only from other captured airmen.[11]

Scharff also knew Zemke was fluent in German, despite the American's act of pretending otherwise. Still, he was treated well, for the most part, and on the third day at the interrogation center, he was finally walked under guard to a local hospital for treatment. The doctor determined that the colonel had no broken bones but was severely bruised. When they asked him how he came to be so badly pummeled, he stated simply that he "hit something" while parachuting.

There was even an attempt to turn him into a collaborator by allowing him to attend a swanky dinner at a local hunting lodge with a gaggle of high-ranking German officers. They offered to give him command of an American/German fighter unit to attack the Russians. The pay offered was the equivalent of an astonishing $1,000 per month. The idea was ludicrous on its face, and Hub refused, but he did use this occasion to have his clothes laundered and grabbed a much-needed hot bath. After refusing their silly offer, he was sent east. Their attempt to turn the American officer had failed. Hub also assumed, most likely accurately, that the real reason for the event wasn't to turn an Allied commander to fight against a common enemy, but to provide useful propaganda newsreels for the German people. Hub saw through it immediately.

From Auswertestelle-West, Zemke was placed on a train with a Luftwaffe lieutenant as his escort. They took a night train to Hanover, arriving early one morning. Shortly after arriving they were greeted by an air raid, courtesy of his old comrades of the Mighty Eighth. Some three hundred bombers dropped their payload upon Hanover as Hub and his escort awaited a connecting train. The rail yard was the target, triggering the Luftwaffe man, his American charge, and numerous other travelers to dash for cover as bombs smashed down on their very location. The rail station was obliterated, but the bomb shelter had weathered the storm. Now, like JJ Thompson months in the future, Hub was probably worried about the reaction of the locals toward his presence, a lone *terrorflieger* in their midst with only a single man guarding him. Fortunately, no one attacked him. Once the thumping and vibrations ended, the Luftwaffe officer led his charge out of the city on foot. The rail station was gone and the tracks unusable. The 8th AF had performed beautifully. The pair of men walked along the rails until they came across an east-bound train and continued their journey to Stalag Luft I in Barth. It was December 16, 1944, when they arrived, the same day that the Germans began their Ardennes offensive.

Upon his arrival at the POW camp, Col. Zemke quickly realized that he was the highest-ranking Allied airman. He was placed in overall command of the inmates when the current, and ailing, American officer Col. Jean R. Byerly, of the 301st BG, relinquished his position due to a chronic liver problem. Hub was in charge within one hour of his arrival at Barth.[12] Additionally, as senior Allied officer, he was granted a special pass that allowed him to travel outside the fence so he could access all of the camp's compounds. The inmates thought it a strange sight indeed to see an American POW walking around outside the wire. Hub, initially concerned that some of the guards might not have gotten the memo that this was allowed, peered nervously at the guard towers on his early outings. But there were no incidents of trigger-happy Germans impeding his duties.

• • •

An important association at the camp was "Provisional Wing X" (PWX), the resident POW organization. As the highest-ranking American officer, Col. Zemke found himself the man on top, with his predecessor as his alternate, though in name only. Col. Byerly's ailment could have been rectified through a proper diet, but such a solution was simply not available in the POW camp, and the poor man was often confined to his bunk, jaundiced and terribly sick, with little to no energy. Lt. Col. Mark Hubbard stepped up and provided Col. Zemke with backup as assistant commander of PWX.

The original purpose of this organization, as stated to the Germans, was to maintain military discipline upon confined men with no mission to perform, and to work with the Red Cross and YMCA to affect coordination and cooperation as far as possible within the confines of captivity. PWX maintained all records of the POWs—medical, disciplinary, and other concerns. The organization was structured similar to an 8th AF command with a personnel management section, intelligence section, education and athletics, and finally supply, which handled the interface with the Red Cross. Each compound was organized as an Air Force group and each barrack's building as a squadron. PWX was also tasked with the orderly evacuation of the POWs upon camp liberation, when the time came. Indeed, the organization would deploy military police to maintain order upon the exit of the German guards when the Russians finally arrived in Barth. The German *Kommandants*, first *Oberst* (Colonel) Scherer (then in February 1945, *Oberst* von Warnstedt), acknowledged the organization and allowed its existence; every Wednesday Hub met them to air out the various concerns of the POWs. The main office for PWX contained a lone typewriter that was used to type up notices and directives issued by Col. Zemke to the POWs.

At that time the camp was well on its way to filling up. The West compound held the most POWs, with some 1,400 Americans and approximately 800 British and other nationalities, including Russians. In the North I enclosure, Hub's home for the duration of the war, around 1,500 Allied airmen were housed; North 2 contained approximately 1,400 Americans; and North 3 had only around 80 men at that time.[13] More POWs would come and more barracks built. North 3 would end up with seven barracks buildings by the time JJ, Gene, Harold, and Willy arrived.

The North 3 compound was under the command of Lt. Col. Francis S. ("Gabby") Gabreski. Gabreski was a close friend and associate of Hub Zemke, both having served together in the 56th FG, and like his friend Hub, he was a famous P-47 fighter ace. Gabreski had chalked up twenty-eight victories by the time he was captured in July 1944. Gabby, like Hub, was due for a diversion in his career path and decided to go on "one more mission" with his old unit. Like Hub, he never made it back to base. Gabby's plane hit the ground unintentionally while on a strafing run on a German airfield, and he was forced to crash-land.

Gene Holley was none too fond of Gabreski and considered him a tyrant. But what Gene may not have been aware of was that North 3 was having problems with dishonest kriegies stealing from their comrades. Gabby reported this problem to Hub in February 1945.[14] Gabreski had been fighting a rash of thefts in North 3 that were especially egregious, given that all of the kriegies were in want of necessities. For a man to steal from his friends was one thing; for a man to steal from others who had little to give was quite another. All were suffering and most would, and did, gladly share what little they had; so, any theft was unconscionable. The main culprits turned out to be two American air gunners, one of which had entered the Army Air Force with a criminal record, so stealing from his kriegie brothers was not too difficult for him. Gabby and Hub had the *Kommandant* toss the miscreants into the camp cooler when their identities were discovered.

The cooler was a cramped stone edifice with windows that had angled boards that permitted the incarcerated to view only the sky. If the window leaked, they could expect water to pour into their cell as a direct result of this design. The cooler was intended to be as uncomfortable, cold, and damp as possible. The most common meal for those stranded in this prison within a prison was the ubiquitous black bread and water.

Gabby was forced to tighten the screws to keep the inhabitants in line and discourage aberrant behavior. However, Gene complained that the North 3 commander had an abrasive manner and suffered from a deficiency of social skills. Gene was distraught after the war to find that Lt. Col. Gabreski had received a Bronze Star for ostensibly taking good care of his charges in North 3.

The morning after their arrival, JJ, Gene, Harold, and Willy were all introduced to a twice-daily ritual they would come to know well. At 0645 and 1630 hours, *Appell* ("roll call") was announced via blowing whistles. The ritual was to determine if there were any escapes overnight and during the day. Men on sick call were named as a list was read, apparently rather slowly. The biggest gripe the kriegies had about this formality was that it occurred in all weather and didn't seem to move with any alacrity; if it was raining, snowing, or blowing, the under dressed inmates suffered. Each barrack was under the command of an Allied officer who was responsible for all its personnel. His men would line up behind him, five ranks deep. Each barracks commander made sure his charges were present before reporting this to the Allied compound commander; this man then reported to the German compound commander that all the men were ready to be counted.[15]

Gene and JJ were roommates in the same barracks room, but each would find new friends among the inmates; shared misery forms strong bonds. Harold and Willy didn't record their experiences in the camp, but they no doubt made new friends among the confined enlisted men. Gene quickly realized how dreadfully dull life was as a POW. The two *Appell* roll calls were important dividers in a day full of boredom and non-activity. One shocking realization was the appearance of kriegies that had been in the camp for any amount of time: they were painfully thin. Many men also sported handlebar mustaches that were clearly not in line with accepted military dress standards. But the thinness was especially alarming. It was quite obvious the POWs had not been receiving enough calories, even though this was after the Red Cross packages had resumed delivery following the "Starvation Period."

It did not take long for the *Lady Jane* boys to understand just why their fellow prisoners were so skinny. The new arrivals in Barth had already had their brush with slow starvation while going through the post-capture interrogation. They were intentionally starved to elicit cooperation, a literal carrot-and-stick process. Now they were underfed as a result of a lack of resources, despite the resumption of the Red Cross parcels. Even in good times, the parcels were doled out only once per week. The hungry men were expected to make one package last seven days. To add insult to injury, the Germans limited how much food the POWs could reserve from their precious parcels. Extra rations were placed in the compound's reserve stores for everyone, but the Germans began confiscating it, causing yet more needless hunger. The POWs complained to the Swiss authorities by writing to their Representative of the Protecting Power. These officials performed semi-annual inspections of the camps, making sure there were no violations of the rights of POWs; they were all the protection the kriegies had against sadistic jailers. The Germans were signatory to the 1929 Geneva Convention and were required to pass on the letter, but not before laying it aside to collect dust for weeks on end. As a result of these and other caloric restrictions, food was a never-ending preoccupation; the POWs talked about it constantly, swapping Mom's recipes and reminiscing about the last Thanksgiving or Christmas dinner at home. They became obsessed with the topic.

Three men already assigned in Gene and JJ's barracks did the bulk of the cooking. Any packages the kriegies received from home went through a screening process first through German examiners to ensure no contraband, then through Allied inmates to be inspected and doled out as equally as possible. All packages were shared, and no one POW had more than the others, unless theft occurred. If Aunt Mary sent cookies, the recipient would not necessarily be her nephew. Nearly everything that arrived went into the communal soup pot, so to speak.

The Red Cross parcels were the main source of food for the inmates and contained the following, more or less, with variations: a 1 lb. can of Spam or corned beef; a 12 oz. can of vegetable soup concentrate; a 1 lb. can of Borden's powdered milk; a box of ten cookies; an 8 oz. box of Kraft cheese; a 1 lb. can of margarine; a box of raisins or prunes; one or two bars of Hershey's chocolate; a half-pound package of sugar; a 4 oz. can of coffee; a package of K ration crackers, and a container of jam preserves. The vast majority of these items were confiscated and given to the camp cooks. Several packs of cigarettes, a bar of soap, vitamin C tablets, toilet paper, paper towels, a sewing kit, and other basic toiletries were also included in the parcels. The kriegies were allowed to keep the non-food items, and these were often used for bartering.

The cooks in Gene's and JJ's barracks would try to save up a little extra each week by withholding a small amount so that a "special" Sunday dinner could be served. Even in good times, the topic of food was a constant concern. The Germans did not supply much of it, except in the form of odd over-cooked, squishy vegetables. If Red Cross parcels were held up or delayed, the inmates suffered, sometimes dreadfully. By this point in the war, the Germans too were short on food and did not eat very well themselves. Stealing care packages was certainly not a rare event. Men unable to tolerate the grinding hunger any longer took what they felt they were more entitled to than their fellow inmates.

• • •

To remedy the boredom, the kriegies made things and were an ingenious bunch. If basic necessities were in short supply, they crafted replacements. They would make candles by separating the wax from wax paper that came with the Red Cross parcels by boiling the paper. The melted wax would float to the top where it could be skimmed off with spoons and applied to rags. The rags were then tightly rolled up and burned as candles. The leftover (now wax-free) paper was used to stuff into the openings in drafty barrack walls. Candles were needed as the Germans cut the power at 1800 hours each night, leaving the inmates in darkness. No one wanted to go to sleep that early so instead stayed up playing cards and visiting with each other in long discussions about, what else, food.

Another favorite pastime was crushing parasites. The humid Baltic coast was perfect bug-breeding habitat, and the kriegies bled for it. Some inmates amused themselves by disrobing and having louse- and flea-smashing sessions. It is quite possible that they held contests to see which among the kriegies killed the most bugs.

The camp had been expanded in 1942, with the West compound being the oldest and more extensive; it had absorbed the South compound. Because these barracks were originally designed to house Germans, not POWs, they contained indoor plumbing with latrines and tap water. The North 1 barracks also had indoor plumbing, but as thousands of American fliers became guests of the Führer, the increased expansions began to forego the luxuries with the crush of new inhabitants. The last compound to be built was North 3, where the *Lady Jane* boys found themselves late in the war.

The West and North 1 compounds each had a large building that served as kitchen and mess halls. These structures also hosted religious services and theater productions by the inmates. The North 2 and 3 enclosures had outbuildings that contained the latrines and wash facilities. Since the kriegies were not allowed to travel between compounds (Col. Zemke excluded), they were stuck with whatever amenities that existed within their particular perimeter. The sparsest of all the compounds was North 3, where Gene, JJ, Harold, and Willy sat, twiddling their thumbs and awaiting rescue. Gene was terribly bored. There were no jobs for them to do, no sporting events, no theater productions for the men in North 3, no entertainment of any kind. The only constant was the omnipresent hunger.

Gene and JJ were also sleep-deprived. The camp beds were little more than narrow slats, spaced 4 inches apart, attached to the barrack's walls. The arrangement was extremely uncomfortable, with rest nearly impossible. The boys hunted around for a larger sheet of plyboard to be shared between both beds; finding it, they were able to improve their sleep experiences somewhat.

Hunger and lack of proper sleep can destroy a human being, and Gene watched helplessly as a roommate descended into madness. Gene last saw the young man sitting before the compound's medical building rubbing two sticks together and "playing a violin." Gene did not record whether the affected airman ever made it out of the camp when it was liberated. Witnessing such a sight would cause any POW to reflect inwardly, wondering if such a fate awaited him as well. The thought would be horrifying.

There were some escape attempts prior to the arrival of the *Lady Jane* crew. Around ninety attempts were made, primarily by RAF fliers. One man ran some 35 miles from camp before being recaptured and no doubt tossed into the cooler upon return. No one else would make it so far.[16] The Russian POWs would have wanted to escape more than any others, as they were treated with revulsion by their captors. Did not the Führer state that all Slavs were *untermenschen* (sub-humans)? They were given all the "shit duty" in camp, literally: cleaning latrines, hauling waste, and performing any and all tasks considered repugnant by their German jailers. They were treated horribly by their captors.[17] Gene remarked that the Russians' attitudes reflected their poor status, and they were nasty even to each other.

Next to the camp was an artillery school where civilians were trained to man anti-aircraft guns. It would have made a juicy target for the 8th Air Force if not for the presence of the POWs. Across the bay was an experimental facility for chemical warfare. At the Barth airfield, there existed an aircraft assembly plant manned by slave laborers. The 8th AF bombed Barth on May 31, 1944, and again on February 1, 1945.[18] The camp was not hit in either instance, and the local industries continued their work. The forced laborers quickly repaired any bomb damage.

Thanks to the illegal radios, the kriegies knew in April that the Russians were coming from the east, and the British army was advancing from the west. The war was nearly over, but the inmates were both excited and deeply worried. There were stories circulating of POW camps being emptied ahead of the approaching Soviet army. The inmates were either shot or forced into what amounted to death marches, as there were no more trains to carry them nor gasoline for trucks to transport them. Certainly, this crossed the mind of every man in Stalag Luft I. They were well aware of the rumors. In the meantime, the *Kommandant Oberst* von Warnstedt and his staff continued to act like nothing was wrong; there were no worries. They even allowed the camp to indulge in a little entertainment, besides the normal plays and concerts. Von Warnstedt was happy to permit a boxing match starring a very famous pilot.

Chapter 9
WAR CRIMES

Right is right, even if everyone is against it, and wrong is wrong, even if everyone is for it.

—William Penn

Harold E. Churchill was murdered; shot to death with an MP-40 machine pistol shortly after he landed in his parachute. Hal was born on November 25, 1923, and was barely into his twenties. He had an equally young wife at home, Joanna, who was pregnant with their daughter, a child who would grow up never to know her dad. He was one of many young American fliers to be executed by angry Germans waiting on the ground, furious with the ceaseless bombing campaign, perpetrated by *terrorfliegers.* But rather than direct their angst at the man who began the most destructive war in human history, and was directly responsible for their misery, they took it out on Allied airmen as they landed safely in their parachutes. Many fliers were told by their superiors upon the start of their combat tours that if they were shot down and could not evade capture to try to surrender to someone in uniform. Civilians were thought to be especially dangerous to downed airmen, particularly toward bomber crews. Fighter pilots, theoretically, killed other fighter pilots and military targets, but bombers killed everyone. It was "indiscriminate murder" in civilians' eyes, and many repaid in kind.

But the American daylight bombing campaign sought to avoid collateral damage, at least in the beginning of the war; such sentiment would change as the endless conflict ground onward and more innocents died under the bombs. Precision bombing was undertaken to directly affect the German war industry, not necessarily to slaughter civilians.

However, it could be argued that in such times, there are no non-combatants; civilians contribute to war production and defense by working in factories and manning flak guns. In total war there exists total participation as non-combatants contribute to the economic mobilization, in one form or another. Other than small children, there are no non-combatants. The RAF saw this, and their bombing strategy was to hit everything. The German Luftwaffe employed the same tactics as they too bombed at night, under cover of darkness, to avoid the terrible casualties with their crews inevitable in daytime bombing. Both the RAF and the Luftwaffe carpeted entire areas with death. For the Americans, sometimes this was unavoidable; sometimes it was not. The anger felt by those helpless on the ground is not assuaged by such arguments. Their fear and anger are real. Nor can the Germans be faulted for placing a madman at their helm. Hitler seized power in January 1933 by bullying Weimar Republic President Paul von Hindenburg into the chancellorship after the Nazis won some 37 percent of the seats in the July 1932 Reichstag election.[1] He was never elected into office. Indeed, he had lost the 1932 presidential election and had gained power not only by bullying the president but also by backroom wheeling and dealing with the current administration in an attempt to share power so he could get his foot in the door.

Field Marshal Hermann Göring had assured the Führer that no bombs would touch German soil and the Luftwaffe would destroy the Allied air forces; yet tens of thousands of civilians had died from those imaginary bombs. Hamburg, Dresden, and other cities suffered hideous retribution from the air in the form of fire storms. But still, the people did not blame Hitler; they blamed the Allied aircrews.

• • •

On August 24, 1944, the 8th AF was dispatched to the Hannover-Langenhagen area to destroy the local airfield. Nestled in the formation was a B-24 of the 491st BG, 854th BS, lovingly nicknamed "*Wham! Bam! Thank You Ma'm*" (42-110107). The aircraft was crewed by Norman J. Rogers (pilot), John N. Sekul (co-pilot), Haigus Tufenkjian (bombardier/navigator), Forrest W. Brininstool (flight engineer), Thomas D. Williams (radio operator), William M. Adams (gunner), William A. Dumont (gunner), Elmore J. Austin (gunner), and Sidney E. Brown (gunner).

As the 491st BG approached the target, the ubiquitous ack-ack roared up from batteries surrounding the airfield, and shortly after bombs away, *Wham! Bam!* was fatally struck. The burst knocked out the aircraft's hydraulic system, set the number 1 engine alight, and damaged two others; *Wham! Bam!* was as good as dead as she slowly made her way west. Steadily losing altitude, she finally slammed into the ground north of Münster. The entire crew was able to hit the silk and all came down safely, although Brininstool, Dumont, and Rogers all suffered injuries of varying severity from shrapnel during the flak explosion. Brininstool landed in a farmer's field and was immediately given first aid by the landowner and his wife for a stomach wound. The selfless care that he received would prove life-saving, in more ways than one. For their kindness, Brininstool handed the elderly couple his silk parachute, a valuable gift, as a number of useful items could be fashioned from it. He was later transferred to a hospital in Münster, where he received further treatment. The rest of the crew found themselves in the custody of Luftwaffe servicemen who, at the moment, showed interest in getting their charges off to a POW camp. But the relief of surviving the landings would not last. RAF bombings hours earlier had severely damaged the local tracks, and evacuation by rail was not possible. So, the boys were marched off to catch a train at an undamaged station farther up the line.

The crew was held in the town of Greven before being moved out on August 26.[2] During the night of August 25, in the nearby hamlet of Rüsselsheim, the RAF had flattened the Opel auto factory, destroyed surrounding homes, and killed numerous civilians. As the crew of *Wham! Bam!* was marched through Rüsselsheim, several women in the crowd howled for blood, thinking the downed crew was responsible for the nighttime RAF bombing. The civilians apparently did not know, or care to know, that the American fliers had been in custody when the bombing occurred.

The two women, Margarete Witzler and Käthe Reinhardt, shouted, "There are the *terrorfliegers*! Tear them to pieces! They destroyed our homes!"[3] A mob quickly formed. Shouting and cursing followed; then the weapons came out. Desperately, a member of the crew called out in German, "It wasn't us! We didn't bomb Rüsselsheim [last night]!"[4] One of the screeching women threw a brick. After that, it was a free-for-all. Whatever could be found quickly was employed, and the defenseless men were set upon and bludgeoned into unconsciousness and death.

Josef Hartgens, the local air raid warden, was one of those participating in the attack. Hours earlier he had mobilized the civilians into a fire brigade to mitigate the damage caused by the RAF Lancasters when the bombers dropped 2,000-lb. ordnance and numerous incendiaries. The Opel plant, rail station, and multiple civilian businesses and homes were destroyed. Hartgens had everyone who could pitch in and stop the fires. The damage was extensive, and the anger was uncontained. All of the citizen's pent-up fury rushed out in a single horrific event. The soldiers guarding the crewmembers stood back and let their charges be savagely beaten; they made no attempt to stop the assault. Hartgens didn't need a metal pipe, club, ax handle, or shovel to carry out his portion of the crime; he was armed with a pistol. He had the Americans, now unconscious or dead in the street, lined up, whereupon he carried out a "mercy shot" into each man's head until his six-shot pistol ran out of bullets. This left two of the eight men without being murdered via a coup-de-grace; though unconscious, they were still breathing.

The bodies were loaded onto a cart and taken to the local cemetery to be placed into a mass grave. Fortunately, another air raid sounded and the would-be grave diggers ran off to seek shelter, allowing the two survivors, William M. Adams and Sidney E. Brown, to crawl out of the cart holding the bloodied bodies of their friends. In terrible pain and no doubt traumatized beyond comprehension, they made their way to the Rhine River but were captured four days later. Fortunately, they were not executed but were taken to be in-processed as POWs at the Oberursel transit camp.

After the war, the town of Rüsselsheim was under the jurisdiction of the American occupation forces. In June 1945, the buried bodies of Norman J. Rogers, John N. Sekul, Haigus Tufenkjian, Thomas D. Williams, William A. Dumont, and Elmore J. Austin were located in the cemetery and exhumed. The townspeople started talking. The two women who instigated the massacre were arrested, as were numerous others, including Josef Hartgens. The trials commenced with alacrity by the following month. The main defense was predictable: The town was only doing what the propaganda minister Josef Goebbels told them to do—take revenge on *terrorfliegers*. Since terrorists were not soldiers, they were not protected by the Geneva Convention; therefore, by killing "terrorists," the townspeople were not guilty of any crimes.

The prosecutor, Lt. Col. Leonidas Jaworski, openly dismissed this argument saying, correctly, that the townspeople were adults and "If they are called upon to commit [a] murder and they do, they are just as responsible as any other murderers."[5] After a six-day trial, on August 2, 1945, ten of eleven defendants were found guilty; one was acquitted. Of the ten, seven were sentenced to death, including Margarete Witzler and Käthe Reinhardt. However, their sentences were commuted after Wittzer's husband Jean successfully argued that the only crime committed by the two women was "screaming." Inciting a riot may be reason enough for a murder conviction, but the judge showed leniency. Both women were sentenced to thirty years in prison.

On November 10, 1945, in a filmed execution, Josef Hartgens and four other convicted killers were hanged; a sixth man would follow suit in 1946. After the exhumation, three of the dead crewmen were repatriated home (Austin, Dumont, and Sekul) and three (Rogers, Williams, and

Tufenkjian) were buried at the Lorraine American Cemetery in France. Today, a memorial stands in the Rüsselsheim town square, honoring the six who were so brutally murdered.

• • •

On December 12, 1944, just east of Frankfurt, a young American crewman was captured by civilians in the town of Langenselbold, Germany, following a bombing raid on nearby Hanau. The 8th AF was dispatched to strike marshalling yards at Darmstadt, Hanau, and Aschaffenburg, as well as the synthetic oil production plants at Merseburg/Leuna, and other targets of opportunity. The 445th BG was part of the 2nd Division and flew B-24s; one of the bombers was 44-10493, flown as part of the 700th BS by 2Lt. William Thompson. His bomber crew was assigned on December 12th to hit the marshalling yard at Hanau. Despite some 193 fighter escorts, the bomber was shot down, crashing to the ground and killing everyone on board except the radio operator, Technical Sgt. Donald L. Hein, who managed to bail out and land safely on the ground. How he was able to bail out while his comrades perished may have been a testament to the sudden destruction of the B-24, most likely by flak, given the heavy fighter escort. Donald hailed from Marshall, West Virginia, the son of Reverend George Hein, a Lutheran pastor, and Luella, the daughter of German immigrants. Both George and Luella were from Ohio but had settled in West Virginia, where Donald and his older brother Robert were born.

Upon landing, Donald Hein was surrounded by angry civilians, but rather than lynching their captive, they did what they probably believed to be the right thing and turned him over to the Langenselbold police chief, Alfred Bury. Donald may have sighed a measure of relief when he was turned over to the uniformed officers of the police station; it would be a simple matter to in-process and be sent to a Stalag camp to await the end of the war, which by this time was no longer in doubt. The civilians had not harmed him, the greatest concern of any downed flier. But Donald did not know that the Langenselbold Police Station was full of angry, vindictive men who had no intention of turning the American over to the Luftwaffe as a POW.

According to documents presented at the "Dachau Trials" in July 1945 (Case No. 12-1397), Police Chief Alfred Bury was told by two of his superiors, Lt. Georg Kalte and Johann Loser, to get rid of the *terrorflieger*, per

SS chief Heinrich Himmler's dictate regarding captured bomber crews. This deed was then, ostensibly, delegated to three lower-level policemen, Wilhelm Häfner, Karl Henkel, and Wilhelm Plitt. No doubt bewildered and terrified, Donald was hauled out of the police station to some nearby woods and shot to death by Sergeant Häfner with the policeman's service pistol while Henkel and Plitt looked on.[6] Donald Hein was twenty-five years old.

Months after Germany's surrender, on July 15, 1945, the perpetrators of Donald's murder were placed on trial at the war crimes tribunal at Dachau. Bury testified that he had been following the orders of superiors. The "I was just following orders" defense was used in this case; such arguments were attempted repeatedly during the aftermath of the war to justify numerous crimes but were rarely, if ever, successful. Initially, Police Chief Bury claimed the orders were from Lt. Kalte, who, he stated, had said that bomber crewmembers were terrorists and were not to be treated as prisoners of war; therefore, *terrorfliegers* were not protected by the Geneva Convention. But in an apparent attempt to shift blame, Bury changed his story a number of times, including blaming the commander of the Security Police in Essen, Germany, Heinrich Himmler himself, and others.[7] The endless diversions from the facts and changes in his story lead prosecutors to conclude there were no direct orders and Bury had acted of his own accord due to extreme prejudice. Even if there had been orders, a moral man should always refuse to commit criminal actions if so required by a superior.

Sergeant Häfner testified he believed he would be severely punished if he failed to carry out Chief Bury's order to execute the prisoner. In his testimony, Häfner stated that he feared he would be sent to a concentration camp or sentenced to death if he didn't follow orders. This excuse was not bought by the tribunal. This line of reasoning has since been debunked. In his book *Ordinary Men*, Christopher R. Browning summarized various studies conducted over the years since the war ended. In the 1960s, German investigator Herbert Jäger and others found no cases during the course of war crimes trials wherein any German was punished by his superiors for failing to carry out an unlawful killing.[8] One of the overriding feelings of perpetrators appears to have been the desire to not seem "weak" in front of their comrades. Hence, "ordinary" people committed terrible crimes to avoid being looked down upon by their friends and peers, rather than the fear of being punished by their superiors. Sgt. Häfner did acknowledge, under scrutiny, that he was not aware of anyone being punished for *not* carrying out an extra-judicial killing. He also admitted that he had made no effort to protest or even prevent Hein's murder.

Sergeant Häfner's wife and children attempted to sway the tribunal by submitting a letter describing him as having been a victim of consequence rather than a cold-blooded killer seeking to appease his commander or to placate some deep inner lust for murdering defenseless fliers. Häfner's motive was, according to them, a sense of duty, so he should receive leniency. Again, the tribunal failed to be convinced with this argument and all of the men involved in the murder of Donald L. Hein were found guilty. On November 19, 1945, Alfred Bury and Wilhelm Häfner were hanged at Landsberg Prison.

In 1949, Donald's wife, Melva, located his body and returned him to the States. He was re-interred near her home in Baltimore, where he rests to this day.

• • •

On March 18, 1945, others in a long list of crimes were perpetrated when Hal Churchill, Jim Butlin, and Milan Basara all met their fates. Indications are that they all bailed out safely. Hal followed JJ Thompson after giving the co-pilot a friendly shove in the rump to push him through the small hatch. While there is still some confusion about Jim Butlin's escape, it appears he followed Hal and dropped or dove through the hatch, most likely injuring his foot in the process and scraping off several layers of skin. With Dave Vermeer still at the controls, Jim was the last one to exit the now furiously flaming wreckage of the *Lady Jane II* as she slipped from the heavens to meet the earth below. Milan Basara had dropped out of the huge flak hole after he, Harold Babcock, and Rodney Williams had stuffed Fred Gerhardt through the hole and held onto Hardtack's parachute D ring as gravity jerked him toward earth.

To this day we do not know exactly what happened as Bas and Jim landed near Uelzen, Germany. No inquiry was launched after the war, but hearsay information and at least one autopsy report have provided important clues. There is ample evidence that each survived the landing and was killed shortly thereafter. But confusion and uncertainty surrounded Jim's death, as none of the surviving crewmembers ever saw his body; nor did they see him bail out.[9] Even as late as the early 2000s, JJ still believed that Jim had stayed with the dying bomber.[10] The locals never came forward, and the bodies were quickly buried in the nearby cemetery. Hardtack had seen Bas's body in the back of the German pickup truck, so he knew the radioman's fate. Hushed testimony after the war revealed that one of the *Lady Jane* crewmen had run from furious weapons-wielding villagers and was "chased like a rabbit" through the underbrush and killed.[11] Evidence revealed during the trial of Hal's killer showed that Jim was brutally murdered, not by villagers, but by a German soldier. Additionally, Jim had been injured in the foot and it would have been difficult for him to run from anyone. This suggests than it may have been Bas who was chased around. We just don't know.

Hal's fate is known; a local Nazi leader was held accountable for his murder. On October 14, 1946, the docket of the Dachau war crimes tribunals included Case #12-1813, the *US vs. Siegfried Utermark*.[12] In a four-day trial, Mr. Utermark was charged with Violation of the Laws of War. Lt. Col. William Berman was appointed by the office of the deputy theater judge advocate general, Dachau War Crimes Group, as the prosecuting attorney. Nathan Racheal was assigned to represent the accused. Mr. Racheal was an American civilian working for the US War Crimes Group as a defense attorney to represent accused criminals in the absence or addition of German lawyers. The accused was granted access to interpreters, in this case a Mr. Herbert Rosenstock and a Ms. Lotte Heymann. According to extant court transcripts, Siegfried Utermark did have a German national as his representing attorney: Dr. Max Buerger was assigned by the appointing authorities to work for the post-war tribunals at Dachau.

According to his testimony, Siegfried Utermark was thirty-six years of age at the time of his 1946 trial and was a uniformed lieutenant colonel of the Reich Labor Service (*Reichsarbeitsdienst*, RAD) at the time of Hal's killing. As a member of the Labor Service, he was most likely a registered member of the Nazi party, but he did not testify to this possibility during his trial.

It was a young farmhand that testified first. Helmut Behn was working in a field near Göddenstedt, Germany, when he heard from a neighbor woman that a bomber had been shot down, and the crew were seen to be parachuting. The area was then, and remains today, a mixture of agricultural fields and forest. Seventeen-year-old Helmut ran out to one of the nearby fields and found a discarded parachute with tracks from the flier leading off to a wooded area. Helmut was none too keen on running into a possibly armed American, so he trotted off to a nearby village, Dallahm, where he informed the local police; it was here that the teen discovered that more downed airmen had landed close by and had been captured. Helmut then returned to the site of the tracks he had found earlier. Standing there was a policeman, also trying to locate the enemy flier. A small crowd was gathering, mostly teenaged kids. It was around this time that Siegfried Utermark arrived in his car. Pulling a machine pistol (an MP-40) from his vehicle, he began issuing orders to the assembling police and about a dozen boys. Utermark ordered those gathered to form a single line and move into the woods. The adults left the group to the sides of the woods to prevent the flier from exiting, while the boys lined up, some 10 meters apart from each other. Utermark posted himself in the center of the line. The woods were thick with ten- to-fifteen-year-old pine trees. They had been planted in neat rows, very near to each other. The searchers were close to each other, but the dense trees made it hard to see one another. The searchers moved with resolve, determined the find the enemy airman.

Shortly after their entrance into the woods, Helmut heard, but did not see, a short burst from a machine pistol; only Utermark was carrying an automatic pistol. Helmut heard Utermark speak after the first burst when he shouted, "Here he is!" as the search party converged on the sound of gunfire. Helmut testified that he ran toward the sound and saw the flier, later identified as Hal Churchill, lying on his left side and thrashing around on the ground, left to right, rolling on his back, wounded and crying out loudly. Helmut showed the court how Hal held up his hands and called out, but the young German couldn't understand the American flier's words. Standing some 15 to 20 meters away from Hal, Siegfried Utermark stood, watching impassively as the airman cried out; no one could understand his words, but it was undoubtedly a surrender plea; his hands were above his head at all times, showing he held no weapon.

The machine pistol erupted again, then a third time when the second burst didn't end the thrashing. Helmut testified that he had wanted to approach the flier after the initial bursts but was warned off by Utermark and was told, "Don't approach it yet." Helmut stopped and watched as a third burst tore into Hal's chest and ended his suffering.[13] Utermark approached; kneeling down, he felt for a pulse. There wasn't a lot of blood, Helmut observed, but the flier had been wearing a bulky flight suit. The thrashing had stopped as the flier's breathing slowed and then ceased.

Utermark's driver, a young man named Kurt Otte, arrived; he and Helmut picked up the body at the labor leader's request, and with the help of another young man, they hauled it out of the woods to the side of the road where Otte had parked Utermark's car. The dead man's pockets were turned out: a map, cigarettes, food rations, and some tablets were discovered, but no weapon. They also found the flier's dog tags, Utermark examined them and discovered his victim's name for the first time: "Harold Churchill." Once the body was searched, it was draped over the right fender of the car, head toward the lamps, to be transported.

Helmut was excused at this point in his testimony, and Count Victor Gröte, a local forester and farmer who had participated in the search for Sergeant Churchill, was called to the stand. Formerly a soldier in the Wehrmacht, Count Gröte owned a large farm very close to where Helmut found the parachute; as a licensed forester, he also tended the pine forests nearby. He was well acquainted with the area and may have participated in planting those forests. Due to his age, forty-four at the time of the killing, and a gall bladder condition, Gröte was no longer in the military, but was a member of the *Volkssturm*. (Older men filled its ranks while their sons fought at the front.) Count Gröte was directly involved in locating the downed American flier; he was also Helmut's employer as the young man worked on Gröte's farm, along with numerous French POWs. Like the young boys organized by Siegfried Utermark, Gröte joined the group scouring the woods. He had been phoned by the Göddenstedt mayor and notified of the downed airman. Like Helmut, he picked up the flier's footprints at the spent parachute. Others had gathered to search for the airman. Gröte recalled how Utermark had arrived with his driver, with the former taking charge of the search party. Gröte stated that as he was a *Volkssturm* member and Utermark was with the Labor Front as a local leader, he was hence not in the latter's chain of command, and Gröte was not obligated to report to him.[14] Fortunately, at the request of both the defense and the prosecutor, Count Gröte had produced a small map of the search area and labeled it to depict the locations of important factors, such as the places where the search was conducted and where Hal Churchill died.

But Gröte was not present and did not see the murder. He did testify as a witness for what transpired *following* the killing. By the time he rejoined the main group, Churchill's body had already been brought to the road by Otte, Helmut Behn, and one of the other boys. Gröte confronted Utermark asking him, "Why did you shoot him right away?" (i.e., why didn't you let him surrender?). Gröte did not witness the exchange with the flier and the labor leader, but he was close enough to hear voices; he testified that he had never heard Utermark demand that the fleeing airman halt. Siegfried Utermark had responded, "Because he tried to crawl away." That was that. Gröte decided to drop the matter, and no more questions were asked. He did state during his testimony that the reason Utermark checked for a pulse after the third volley was to ascertain whether a "mercy shot" was required. For whatever reason, the unarmed, prone, and defenseless enemy flier needed to die. No one attempted to stop the murder, though all must have known it was a crime.

It his testimony, Helmut Behn stated that he had heard of another flier being captured in Uelzen and another one that was shot in Rosche. A third witness for the prosecution, Aloys Gedig, also confirmed that he had heard news of *two* fliers that had been shot on March 18, 1945. One flier was shot "about 200 meters" from the Reich Labor Camp, according to Gedig. Given this testimony, it is apparent that another murder of the *Lady Jane*'s crew was known outside of Rosche.

Aloys Gedig was a sergeant with the RAD and employed in a local warehouse under Utermark's supervision. He testified on October 16, 1946, that Utermark ordered him to clean his machine pistol after Utermark had returned to the Labor Service office following the killing. While Utermark was at the RAD camp shortly after the shooting, he met with another officer in the mess hall, *Unterfeldmeister* Otto Kühner. Gedig, also in the mess hall, clearly overheard the men talking about the day's events. Kühner stated, "I shot a flier"; Utermark replied, "So did I."

Gedig left the mess hall to go clean the machine pistol; as he was leaving, he heard a little more of the conversation. He heard Utermark say, "I saw something in the bushes that was moving… and upon that I fired." Gedig heard no more and went out to clean Utermark's MP-40. As he walked across the camp yard, he saw a dead body lying across the labor leader's front right car fender.

Lt. Col. Utermark's driver, nineteen-year-old Kurt Otte, was called to the stand as a witness for the defense. Otte reported that he was in line with the other young men as they looked for the downed flier. He maintained that he was separated enough from Utermark, around 20 to 30 meters, that he could not see him but did hear him call out. Otte stated that he recognized Utermark's voice but could not make out what he was saying because it was "not in German." Then Otte stated that he heard shots after the words were spoken. Two of the other witnesses, Helmut Behn and Victor Gröte, both said they never heard Utermark challenge the flier and order him to halt. Both testified that they heard Utermark say, "Here he is," or similar words after the shots were fired. They never heard anything else before the bursts from the MP-40. Otte claimed he never heard the German words "Here he is," or anything similar; he also stated that he only heard two bursts of fire from the machine pistol, as opposed to three. So Otte's testimony conflicted with Behn's and Gröte's.

Another member of the Reich Labor Service, Karl Joachim, was called to the stand by the defense counsel. Joachim was a section officer with the RAD and served under Lt. Col. Utermark. When Utermark returned to the RAD compound, Joachim immediately noticed the body strung over the car's fender. Utermark spoke to him, ordering him to bury the body quickly so that there was "no occasion for the population to steal anything from that flier and besides that it was not necessary that the young workmen did see a corpse, they would see enough of corpses when they would get to the front."[15] Joachim then retired to the mess hall, where Utermark told him what happened.

Karl Joachim was also questioned by the defense counsel regarding Lt. Col. Utermark's orders concerning the treatment of enemy fliers. A meeting occurred on March 17, the day before the incident, in which this topic was addressed. Enemy fliers parachuting to the ground were to be treated as soldiers and arrested, not shot. A weapon was to be used only if the flier was shooting or not surrendering as ordered. This was counter to the propaganda minister Goebbels's instructions at the time and may be viewed with some suspicion. But according to Joachim, Utermark had commented that his brother was a POW in the United States and was concerned that if captive Americans were mistreated in Germany, Germans might be abused in the United States.

The next witness was Siegfried Utermark himself. He had surrendered to the British army on the day of Germany's defeat, May 8, 1945, and held until the twenty-ninth of that month. He was arrested at his home in Uelzen by the Americans several days later. He had not yet been discharged by the German Wehrmacht.[16] During his testimony on October 17, 1946, he stated that he was sitting at the dinner table on March 18, 1945, when he received a phone call from the RAD company office at Rosche. He was informed that several parachutists were observed to land in the Rosche/Göddenstedt area. Lt. Col. Utermark collected his driver Otte and headed to the area west of Dallahn where an enemy flier was seen to have landed. Utermark's intention was to lead the search party. He located a group of youths near Count Gröte's estate. Initially, he was to organize a detail from his RAD company, but they were apparently searching elsewhere. So the colonel organized the children and three or four adults into a search party line along the road. The adult men were armed with long rifles and would be hampered by the heavy brush, so he instructed them to wait just outside the thickest area to make sure the flier didn't double back. He then led the children, in a line, into the deep woods but they were quickly separated by the dense growth. The trees were planted in neat rows that were parallel to the search party.

Utermark then testified that he came upon the flier lying on the ground on his stomach. Utermark then stated he told the flier, in English, "Hands up, stand up." But the American just looked at him and started to crawl away, deeper into the brush. The labor leader then said he jumped a couple of quick steps to his right to stay in sight of the crawling man and fired a "warning shot" to compel the flier to surrender, but the American continued to crawl away, now on his hands and knees. Utermark stated that he thought the man would jump up and run off into the thick forest, so he pointed the machine pistol at him and squeezed the trigger, hitting him and causing him to collapse. Under testimony, during cross examination by the prosecuting attorney, Utermark was asked if he felt it was necessary to shoot the downed American flier dead after only one warning shot. Herr Utermark insisted he never discharged any "fatal shots"; he had killed the flier "unintentionally."

Much of this contradicts Helmut Behn's statement. Utermark claimed he rushed over to see if there was a pulse and did not find one. Otte, he claimed, was the first person he saw after the second burst; he made no mention of a third burst. Nor did he recall telling Helmut Behn, "Don't approach it yet" before firing a third round of bullets at the prone figure. He claims he saw Behn only after the body was carried out to the road, and that it was he, Utermark, not Behn, that carried the body with Otte. Utermark also testified that the flier made no sounds as he was being shot. This also directly contradicted what Behn had stated; he explained that the wounded airman was thrashing about and shouting loudly with his hands in front of him. Had Churchill been shot while on his hands and knees, one would suspect the body would collapse in a forward position and lie on the stomach. This is not what Helmut Behn relayed in his statement. Upon relating this discrepancy to Herr Utermark, he commented that the young man's testimony was false. The prosecution recalled Helmut Behn, who then reaffirmed all his earlier comments, changing nothing.

The prosecuting attorney then asked the defendant if he thought that he might have hit Churchill with his first shot and that the flier was attempting to get up to comply with the order to "Stand up" when the second blast was unleashed. Utermark stated, "No, I waited one more moment and when he continued to crawl, only then did I fire." The prosecutor asked the defendant again if it occurred to him that the man was trying to get to his feet to comply with the order. Utermark stated "No," it did not occur to him; whereupon the prosecutor commented, "As a matter of fact, you didn't give him a chance to say anything, did you, or do anything?"

Utermark had stated that they draped Hal Churchill's remains over the right fender to prevent an uncomfortable drive back to RAD with a corpse sitting upright in a seat with the labor leader and his driver. Utermark stated that he was anxious to bury the body quickly and in a "soldierly manner." Additionally, he stated that he did not want the locals to take revenge on the body for "low flying air attacks" committed on civilians. It was important to get the dead flier buried right away, so the colonel had Otte take the most direct route possible back to the RAD company compound. Upon return, Utermark and Kühner swapped experiences. The former insisted that the two fliers be buried next to each other. Initially, they were buried in the forest near the RAD camp, then the cemetery at Rosche on the orders of the local county administrator. The bodies remained buried in Rosche until they were exhumed by a war crimes investigation team months later and autopsies were performed. It remains a mystery why Milan Basara's body was not also examined and his death investigated.

• • •

On June 1, 1945, prior to his October 1946 trial, Herr Utermark had found himself in the custody of a British intelligence officer investigating the claims of war crimes committed in the area. The British officer granted him access to three attorneys, but he refused their offers of assistance. He was an officer, he declared, and would give his word of honor. He felt he had nothing to conceal and would testify truthfully. He wrote a statement accounting the incident that resulted in Hal Churchill's death, but oddly, he was not sworn to its validity. Utermark claimed the officer never required a sworn promise, as the German officer wrote the account in his native language.

The British officer also told Utermark that he was being suspected of having dragged one of the fliers to death. This was a rumor only at this point; Utermark quickly rebuffed the accusation, stating that he was "enraged" by the comment. The allegation then prompted him to produce a two-page written statement wherein he denied all charges and gave his version of the events that led to his being accused of a war crime. The document was translated into English by a British private first-class Erwin Birn.

Herr Utermark's written statement was not nearly as detailed as his courtroom questioning and so left much of the pertinent information in question. As with the verbal testimony, he stringently denied murdering his captive in cold blood. He further insisted that his orders to his men required that they treat downed enemy airmen per the Geneva Convention of 1929 and not kill them outright unless they saw a weapon or the subject attempted to flee. He blamed "wash women" for spreading false rumors about the treatment of enemy captives. In apparent contravention of Nazi dictates on the treatment of "*terrorfliegers*," Lt. Col. Utermark claimed he directed his charges with the mandate that all enemy prisoners of war be treated with respect.

As the defense and prosecution attorneys were wrapping up their cases, Herr Utermark requested that he be permitted to make a statement. He delivered this address to the court in fluent English. He asked that the court judge him as a soldier. He regretted having to go to war with England, France, and America; he felt the real enemy was in the East with the Soviets and their satellite states. He had instructed his men to follow the accepted rules of war even though the bombing of civilians made it difficult to do so. He stated that he was sorry that the flier "forced" him to use his gun; it was not his intention the kill the man. He went on to say that he would not beg for his life but requested that they remember that he was a soldier doing what he felt best for his country. He said, "Those who do wrong fear the light and don't come to the light, that they may not be punished for those deeds they did, but those who did the right comes to light that everybody may see what they did for they have acted in God."[17]

Regardless of whether Siegfried Utermark meant to kill Hal Churchill or not, the young man was dead. The most damning evidence in the case was the autopsy report.

Hal Churchill and Jim Butlin were both disinterred from the Rosche cemetery in June 1945. On August 11, a British Royal Army medical officer, Major William M. Davidson, performed an autopsy on each of them. Despite both of the bodies being badly decomposed, the pathologist was able to provide many important facts about their deaths. He published his report the following day.

On Ernest James Butlin, the togglier assigned to the *Lady Jane II*, Major Davidson reported that the body was one of a young male, of medium height and brown hair. He was dressed in a flight uniform similar to what Hal Churchill had been wearing. But Jim had no shoes on, no electric boots with which he was most likely equipped when he bailed out of the dying aircraft, and no socks. His feet were bare, but on his left foot was a field dressing. Before he died, Jim had apparently received medical care. (The pathologist was unable to discern an injury to the foot due to the advanced state of decomposition.) Jim would not have been barefoot on the *Lady Jane* due to the extreme cold of the aircraft. He most likely wearing the USAAF-issued electric boots and socks when he jumped. He may have lost a boot, as JJ Thompson had on the parachute ride down, or he may have lost both. We don't know. He may have injured his foot during the jump. While escaping from the forward hatch, he may have scraped his foot. Gene Holley had injured both of his hands to the point of bleeding while fumbling with that same hatch. JJ had mentioned he last saw Jim onboard the bomber as the crew was jumping out; he did not note that Jim was injured in any way, just that he was standing in the nose of the *Lady Jane*, apparently awaiting his turn to bail out.

Jim's limbs had no broken bones according to the pathologist, but he did have at least one fatal injury. Dr. Davidson reported that "the skin about the back of the neck was blackened over an area about four inches by three and, in addition to a circular or slightly oval entrance wound a third of an inch in diameter (situated in the upper part of the neck and to the left of the middle line) there were, on the right side, an oval tear and two deeper tears connected by a semi-circular superficial tear leading to the entrance wound." From there, the track of the bullet could be traced; the first cervical vertebra had been broken at the base of the skull, on the left side, and was shattered. The bullet then traveled through the foramen magnum, tearing through his brain, before exiting explosively through the left side of his forehead, blasting out bone, brain matter, and tissue in a large exit wound. The left temple, eye orbit, and forehead in this region were simply gone. Nineteen-year-old Jim Butlin would have died instantly.

While Dr. Davidson did not state so, it appeared that Jim was shot at point-blank range with a weapon pressed to the back of his neck. Powder burns would account for the blackened and damaged skin on the neck. His head appeared to have been pointed down at the moment he was shot, as the bullet traveled through the foramen magnum (the large opening at the base of the skull). He had most likely been on his knees at the time with his killer standing behind him. Otto Kühner had stated to Utermark that he fired at the airman's back while he was fleeing. That appears to have not been the case here. Jim's body had no injuries to the back.

Another curious set of evidence also arose with the pathologist's inquiry. Jim's body had been dragged; whether he was alive or not at the time, we don't know. According to the autopsy report, "There were no fractures about the limbs, but over both elbows the skin was absent. The skin over the regions of both anterior superior iliac spines and over the sacrum had been damaged in life and was dried and adherent to the underlying bone."[18] The doctor apparently believed that Jim was alive during the dragging.

Siegfried Utermark had been accused of dragging a body during his trial, but it would appear that it was Otto Kühner who was dragging Jim's body. Utermark commented during his testimony that they had strapped Hal Churchill to the fender to avoid having a corpse sitting in the car for the drive back to the RAD compound. It is very possible that whoever transported Jim's body back to the camp did not think of placing it on the hood or fender, but simply dragged it. The gaping and hideous damage to Jim's face would have been oozing and would not have been welcome either within or on top of a vehicle. The body was most likely dragged to transport it without leaving a gory mess on the car. This would account for the damage Dr. Davidson found. But after an apparent point-blank shot to the head, Jim would not have been alive, so the pathologist's findings are questionable.

The autopsy on Hal Churchill was a bit different in the conclusions made by Dr. Davidson. Both Jim's and Hal's bodies had been wrapped in "black-out paper" (heavy felt paper-like material used to cover widows to prevent light from escaping during air raids) when they were buried in the Rosche cemetery. Underneath the paper, Hal's body was fully clothed in an American airman's flight suit. The hair was brown and had been cut fairly short. The pathologist reported that the state of decomposition was too severe to discern any injuries to the face, but two penetration wounds were found on the torso. He stated in his report, "On the right side of the body, in the right intercostal space, just outside the costochondral junction of the eighth rib, there was a circular entrance hole a third of an inch in diameter." From here, the bullet's path went up from the eighth rib through the diaphragm; across the upper surface of the liver; through the diaphragm again on the other side; through the anterior part of the pericardium; through the tip of the right ventricle and tearing the heart open with an inch-long rend. Then the bullet smashed into the fifth rib, fracturing it before exiting the chest wall in a large tearing wound.

The other entrance wound discovered by Dr. Davidson was in the back in the left lumbar region. This bullet traveled through the left anterior edge of the liver to the outer part of the stomach, then through the dome of the diaphragm. It hit the seventh rib on the left side, fracturing it before exiting the chest wall on the left side. The pathologist also found, on the left side of Hal's chest, three oval-shaped wounds varying in length from one half to an inch in length. There was also a similar wound on the left collar bone. These were apparently non-penetrating bullet wounds from the MP-40 as Herr Utermark "shot badly," as he phrased it. There were corresponding tears in Hal's clothing that matched the wounds.

Dr. William Davidson provided a summation of his findings. Hal's body had a number of "superficial injuries to the skin, with corresponding damages to the clothes, including two entrance wounds—one on the right side of the chest and the other in the left side of the back in the lumbar region, from which tracks led through the body, in the former case through the tip of the heart." The pathologist further stated "that two bullets passed through the body in the region of the lower thorax while the skin in the region of the exit wound was being supported." This suggests that Hal was lying on the area where the bullet exited. Both bullets exited on Hal's left side.

Young Helmut Behn testified that Hal was thrashing about, rolling from his back to his left side. Herr Utermark stated that the flier was trying to flee from him on his hands and knees. Behn said that Hal's arms were above him as he rolled around. If his arms were next to his chest while he was crawling, it would seem logical that there would be damage to the left arm as the bullets exited the body. Additionally, how did Hal receive superficial non-penetrating bullet wounds to his upper chest if he were crawling away? These questions were not answered by the autopsy report. However, if Hal was laying as Behn described, presumably after receiving the non-fatal shot in the back, the other wounds could be explained. The non-penetrating bullet injuries could have been delivered while the flier was on his back, rolling around with his arms raised (hence, no damage to the arms). The fatal injury to his heart could have occurred while Utermark was standing to the right of Hal, firing down at him. *If* Behn's account was accurate, the following *may* have occurred: RAD commander Lt. Col. Siegfried Utermark heard some rustling in the undergrowth as he searched a particularly dense part of Count Gröte's forest. The foliage was so thick that the searchers to the left and right of him could not see him. As soon as he spotted the flier, he fired a short burst from his MP-40. Whether he intended to kill the man or not is not known and is unknowable; nor do we know for certain whether he challenged the fleeing man. One bullet from the burst struck the American in the small of his back, causing him to collapse immediately, perhaps landing first on his backside and then onto his back. The pathologist's report suggests he may have been bent over at the time the shot was fired, given the trajectory of the round through his body; this may corroborate Utermark's account that the flier was on his hands and knees, preparing to rise to his feet.

After the flier collapsed, Utermark called out, "Here he is!" causing Helmut Behn to rush over. Just as he saw the downed American flier, a second burst erupted. But Utermark only grazed the flier in the chest; none of the bullets penetrated. Hal called out, desperately trying to surrender. The wound in his lower back would have been extremely painful; he wouldn't have been able to stand or walk. He thrashed around, left to right, hands in the air showing he was unarmed. Helmut moved closer to the thrashing man, but Utermark warned him off, "Don't go near it yet." Then the MP-40 erupted again. This time the strike was true. A bullet ripped into Hal's chest, tearing open the heart. It took him several minutes to die. Utermark walked over to the now-quiet figure and felt for a pulse; he wasn't sure if the American needed a "mercy shot." When Helmut and Otte carried the body to the road, Count Gröte thought he saw the dead man's jaw move.[19]

However we may interpret the evidence and courtroom testimony, including the pathologist's report, it is important to note that none of this disproves Utermark's testimony. Hal could have received the wounds had he been on his hands and knees; this author does not wish to dispute that point. In the end, the court did not find Utermark's recollection as credible, and he was found guilty of murder.

• • •

The prosecution and defense both rested in the Siegfried Utermark case on October 18, 1946. The defense counsel called the accused to the stand whereupon he gave a statement. He did not request mitigation but asked that, as a solider, he be shot. The US military tribunals were not shooting convicted war criminals; they were hanging them. This request, had Utermark received a death sentence, would have most likely been ignored. But he received a harsh sentence regardless. The president of the court announced Siegfried Utermark would serve a life sentence. Shortly thereafter Siegfried Utermark was marched off to prison.

However, in 1955, he was paroled with a ten-year probation. Why? The West German government was in flux; West Germany was in the throes of the Cold War, as the Soviet Union had slapped East Germany behind the Iron Curtain. Nearly an entire generation of young men had died for Germany, leaving gaping holes in manpower for many industries, including white collar professions. With the Soviets next door and the threat of nuclear war ever present, the Allied Powers were eager to buttress against the Soviet Bloc states by admitting West Germany to the North Atlantic Treaty Organization. In May 1955, the Federal Republic of Germany joined NATO. Professionals were needed to counter the West German "brain drain," and Siegfried Utermark was paroled from his life sentence to help rebuild his country.[20] He returned to his home in Uelzen and became a school teacher. Apparently, in the late 1960s, there was even an attempt to award him with the "*Bundesverdienstkreuz*" (Order of Civic Merit), until his past came back to haunt the effort; the award suggestion was subsequently dropped. His son Wieland also became a school teacher, successfully earning the *Bundesverdienstkreuz* following his tireless efforts as an environmentalist.[21]

What about Otto Kühner, the man who, ostensibly, executed Jim Butlin? We don't know what happened to him. He apparently left the Uelzen/Rosche area after the war, perhaps joining the flood of Nazis fleeing to South America to avoid criminal courts. Relatives in the county could not be located during this book project.[22] He never stood trial; he never paid for the alleged crime. Nor did Milan Basara's killer ever come to light; we still don't know what happened to him. Both Bas's and Jim's murders remain unanswered. Given the passage of many decades, it is doubtful that justice will ever be done for these boys. Their killers have gotten off free.

CHAPTER 10
THE ENDLESS END

Patience is bitter, but its fruit is sweet.
—Aristotle

By April 1945, the inmates of Stalag Luft I were thin and exhausted; they could feel their ribs. While the Red Cross packages had resumed in "normal" delivery by March 26, the calories were still insufficient. More and more captured airmen were stuffed into the overstuffed camp, so what little resources the kriegies had needed to be stretched even further. To assuage boredom, pastimes included any distraction they could manage, given the limited resources, during the painful wait for the end of the war. One particularly silly prank was pulled during afternoon *Appell* one day in North 1 that caused no small amount of hilarity. As the count proceeded, one headless inmate was discovered standing at attention in line as the Germans passed. A nasty raw slab of meat sat where the neck belonged, and two bug-eyed heads were positioned under each arm of the "headless" person. The Germans ground to a halt before the wild image as the joke became apparent. A kriegie had secured an oversized coat whereupon he scrunched his head down into the shoulder area, placed the foul-smelling chunk of meat on his head; then two of his friends standing behind him stuffed their heads under his armpits; he clutched them as if they were loose objects. The act had the desired effect and the group roared in laughter. However, the Germans were not amused; the three offending pranksters were marched off to the cooler.[1]

There was also a boxing match with YMCA-supplied gloves. Hub Zemke had talked the camp *Kommandant* von Warnstedt into allowing a sporting match. Hub issued a camp-wide challenge to anyone, regardless of size or experience. Multiple applicants forced a drawing with some fifty names written on slips of paper; one was selected from a hat. Hub faced off with a Maj. Cyrus Manierre, Gabby Gabreski's aide-de-camp from North 3. The *Lady Jane* boys would have known Manierre, but they apparently did not attend the match. At that time most inmates were not allowed to travel between the compounds. Major Manierre was no doubt escorted to North 1 for the boxing bout. Even though Hub was considerably shorter than Manierre by some 4 inches, he made quick work of the bigger man and bagged the match in three rounds; both men were undernourished and under strength.

In addition to the sequestered radios, the kriegies kept a camera. It was sent to them clandestinely by a British intelligence organization in 1944.[2] The camera was used to photograph stolen documents for the purpose of reproducing them. It was stored inside a chimney behind some bricks. The Germans apparently never found it and were unaware of its existence. Most items smuggled into the camp were cleverly hidden inside unremarkable containers such as Red Cross boxes, food cans, sporting equipment, and so forth.

Forged documents were kept in the library inside books. These reproductions were very well crafted. Ink for them came in the form of canned jelly from the Red Cross packages. Sympathetic guards sometimes slipped actual documents to the kriegies who would then photograph them.[3] They developed their own film, then artistically reproduced the forgeries. The quality of the forgeries was impressive. Less impressive was the ability of the POWs to reproduce German uniforms. There was an incident in which three US officers walked out of a gate in German uniforms made by the kriegies and carrying forged papers. The alert guards spotted the escape attempt, but they apparently thought the documents were stolen, such was the quality of the fakes. Once the forgery was established, the Germans designed new, more complex passes, but these too were very quickly, and expertly, replicated.[4]

The inmates were able to construct a single escape tunnel in the West compound despite the high water table. The end of the war was near, and Hub Zemke didn't want to risk any unnecessary casualties. The tunnel was kept as an insurance policy should the Germans plan to "liquidate" the camp either by mass murder or by forced march. The rumors were already apparent as advancing Russians were witness to the heaps of dead along evacuation routes leading from major concentration camps. Hub was deeply concerned, so the soggy tunnel was kept open, just in case. The Germans never found it.

Nor did the Germans find any number of illicit items sent in YMCA boxes and parcels from home. The kriegies had a Morse transmitter stashed away. Hub recalled some one hundred packages with contraband sent to Stalag Luft I while he was there. Being sneaky wasn't too difficult. Coded messages found their way into the camp, via letters from "home" (often from Military Intelligence, Section 9, a.k.a. MI9) or even the illicit radio, to notify certain kriegies of in-coming contraband, so the package sorting crew was tipped off in advance. A German guard would sit and watch as kriegies sorted in-coming mail. Boxes were opened under "watchful" eyes while contents were checked, then the box was placed in a stack of parcels already screened. A kriegie would then distract the guard with a question or comment and a package known or believed to contain illegal goodies was slipped into the pile of boxes already checked.[5] It was too easy and the guards too complacent.

MI9 was a huge help to the kriegies during the war. This was a division of the British Directorate of Military Intelligence, not to be confused with MI19, which dealt with enemy POW interrogation and intelligence. MI9 was instituted to assist British POWs and, by extension, aided all Allied POWs. Since Stalag Luft I housed numerous nationalities, from Polish, Russian, French, American, and British, as well as others, all benefited from this organization's ability to sneak in much-needed equipment and information. Many of the ingenious gadgets smuggled to the kriegies were invented by a brilliant English engineer named Christopher Clayton Hutton. He designed tiny escape equipment such as a compass disguised in a uniform button; intricate cloth maps (to open and close silently and to survive weather as well as concealment in tiny places); razors that when dangled from a string would always point north; blankets with printed clothing patterns on them via invisible ink that were sent as "normal" Red Cross blankets. The kriegies could submerge the blankets in cold water, enabling the patterns to be seen. The blankets were made with much-higher-quality wool than normally found in blankets and could serve as civilian clothing items once cut and sewn together. Maps were secreted away into the board of Monopoly games; real bank notes were stashed in the Monopoly funny money.[6] Real currency was also smuggled into camp via playing cards and books; any number of paper items could be slid behind book bindings. Other hiding places for in-coming goodies included double-walled or false-bottomed tins of food, hollow thread spools and tennis rackets; pretty much anything that could conceal items was employed. The camp guards would scrutinize all in-coming gifts but rarely found the concealed contraband.

MI9 also smuggled in information. Sometimes Allied airmen were trained ahead of time to read and distribute coded messages. If they were shot down and captured, their families were told to share letters from their kriegie sons and turn them over to the intelligence agencies. This method was also used with letters from "Mom" including instructions or intelligence for the POWs. This information would then be given to the compound's security officer.[7]

Spies were known to abound in the camp. "Ferrets" were German guards who were fluent in English and would stalk around the camp, fishing for plots and intrigue. It was also suspected that the Germans would sneak in an agent disguised as a POW. Each barrack building had a security officer who would screen every in-coming kriegie, carefully examining the answers to every question. But no intruders were ever found in Stalag Luft 1.[8]

One particularly nasty behavior of the Germans was their apparent enjoyment of knocking the kriegies out of bed in the wee hours of the morning, making them stand at attention in the cold night air, and turning over the barracks in harassing "searches." Hub believed these were done for simple intimidation and not for actually finding contraband. It was done primarily to humiliate and remind the kriegies of their place by slicing open mattresses and tearing up private property. If the guards found anything, such as an illicit tool or potential weapon, the offending inmate could expect to spend time in the cooler. Col. Zemke complained bitterly in his autobiography about Major von Miller zu Aichholz, head of camp security at Stalag Luft I. Von Miller was apparently quite thorough in his harassing search-and-destroy barracks raids.[9] He was deeply detested by the kriegies.

• • •

Gene Holley, JJ Thompson, Harold Babcock, and Rodney Williams waited for the end of the war in North 3. By April 1945 the sounds of battle could be heard in the form of artillery as the Russians smashed the German army in a relentless push west. In the early stages of the Nazi offensive Operation Barbarossa in June 1941, the Soviets were caught completely off-guard. Stalin was utterly incredulous that Hitler had shredded the non-aggression pact signed by Vyacheslav Molotov and Joachim von Ribbentrop in August 1939. This pact allowed Hitler a free hand to invade Poland without Soviet interference as long as Stalin received eastern Poland after the offensive was finished. As Hitler violated the Soviet Union and the pact, Russian soldiers, unprepared and poorly led, had surrendered in the hundreds of thousands. The German invaders subsequently murdered some twenty million Soviet citizens: soldiers, civilians, Jews, and ethnic minorities. This was a lesson the Russians learned with a deep loathing of the Germans and with an intensity few could comprehend. To break an agreement was one thing; to break it and commit mass slaughter on a scale not seen by modern man was a completely different concept. Simply stated, the Russians *hated* the Germans. The Germans, in return, knew to expect no mercy if the Soviets caught them. They were terrified of the Russians.

So as the *Lady Jane*'s crew waited for the seemingly endless end of the war, so too did their guards and camp administrators. The Russians were coming and every few days, the distant thump of artillery grew slowly, steadily. In the West compound the kriegies listened to their illicit radio; they knew where the Soviet army was located: close, but not close enough. More waiting. Endless waiting. Hub was anxious; with the closing distance of the Russians was a growing and terrible fear. What if the Germans decided to evacuate the camp? The stories were known by now. POW camps in the path of the raging Russians were hurriedly emptied. The Germans didn't want the inmates to fall into enemy hands and possibly be repatriated back to their own lines to re-enter the fight. Thanks to the 8th Air Force's bombing campaign, there were few trucks, no fuel to power them, no trains, and no means of getting the inmates deeper into German territory other than to trudge on foot and head west. Because there were no rations for these journeys, no water, no food, no resources, they became literal death marches.

Knowing of the mass killings by forced march, Lt. Col. Zemke organized elements in Provisional Wing X into a commando unit, armed with homemade knives and bludgeoning weapons. The one surviving tunnel was kept in readiness should a mass escape be necessary. On April 20, 1945, several days after Hub's boxing match, he was called into the camp *Kommandant*'s office. Hub's greatest fear was realized when *Oberst* von Warnstedt informed him that per orders from the *Oberkommando der Wehrmacht* (OKW), the camp would be evacuated. Horrified, Hub exited von Warnstedt's office and called an emergency meeting of PWX. A vote decided their position: the kriegies would stay put; no one would be subjected to a death march. Then Hub returned to the *Kommandant*'s office to report their decision. Hub Zemke told him that any deaths or injuries arising from a forced evacuation would be reported to American authorities by the survivors. Von Warnstedt relayed the inmates' communication with his superiors. In the meantime, Hub was preparing to mobilize the PWX commandos to resist. It would be a suicide mission to counter the German guards' Karabiner 98 rifles and MP-40s with knives and clubs, but resist they would if given no other choice, or they would mass escape via the tunnel. They waited for the *Kommandant*'s answer; von Warnstedt waited as well. He had told the OKW the truth; he simply did not have the staff to move 9,000 inmates on a forced march. But no one at the OKW responded to his message.

While they waited for answers, on April 29, Hub sent out two teams from the front gate, dressed as civilian workers, to try to locate the Allied lines. As they traveled west, the teams interspersed with thousands of civilians and soldiers fleeing the on-coming Red Army. The next morning, on April 30, the six men were found to be missing, but the Germans didn't seem to care.[10] The POWs also managed to get a radio message out to MI9 telling them what was transpiring. Responding BBC broadcasts told them to wait where they were; Allied forces were coming. Hub also experienced an odd incident wherein one of the Luftwaffe officers approached him, asking the American to join him for a walk outside the wire, out of earshot of everyone. *Hauptmann* (Captain) Rath had been nasty and rude to the kriegies in the past, harassing them during barracks shakedowns; now he asked Hub, rather sheepishly, if the American would consider escaping with him. He handed Hub his revolver as a token of his sincerity. Rath wanted the airman to take him as a captive to the west and allow him to surrender to US authorities. The Germans were desperate to flee from the Russians by any means possible. If Rath were in the custody of an American officer, he stood a better chance of survival if the Russians caught up with them. Rath would provide Hub with a Luftwaffe uniform and papers; they could escape right away.

Incredulous, Hub just stared at the unexpected gift, then smiled and handed it back. No, he would not escape with the end so near; he had 9,000 men who were depending on him. He told Rath to keep his side arm; he might need it. The Russians were less than 100 miles to the east. Then the senior Allied officer turned and went back into the camp.

Von Warnstedt again called Hub to his office. He had received no response to his communique to the OKW. He had no instructions, and he needed to get his men out immediately; the Russians were approaching Barth and were just hours away. He asked Lt. Col. Hubert Zemke to take command of the camp so that he could evacuate his staff. Hub agreed, but he stated that the Germans should only take a bare minimum of small arms and leave intact all of the camp's infrastructure. There were rumors of POW compounds being burned to the ground by fleeing camp guards. Hub didn't know how long they would be stuck there at Barth and didn't want their survival jeopardized in any way. The *Kommandant* agreed and stated they would leave by midnight.

Hub notified PWX with a cautionary warning: do not release this news until after the Germans had departed. He did not want anyone hurt during a parting attack on their former jailers. Let the Germans go peacefully. At 2300 hours on April 30, 1945, the former camp guards, many in civilian clothing, assembled on the road just outside the gate. Zemke deployed the commando unit as a precaution. Von Warnstedt approached Hub, saluted him, and said, "*Auf wiedersehen.*"[11] The former camp commander then turned away and walked over to an overloaded sedan. As he drove away into the night, the former camp guards followed, on foot, on bicycles, or in vehicles. The Americans just stood there, watching the moment unfold. They were free and no one was hurt or killed in the process.

• • •

When Gene, JJ, Harold, and Willy woke in the morning of May 1, 1945, the front gate of the camp was open; Zemke's commandos, now designated as military police, were manning the watch towers armed with Karabiner-98 rifles that had been seized from the camp armory. There was not a German in sight. An American flag, apparently squirreled away in someone's possessions for who knew how long, was run up the flag pole, waving in a lazy breeze. While many of the now former kriegies had witnessed the Germans leave and were aware of their departure, many in the far northern compounds were not. They rubbed sleep-befuddled eyes, trying to register what they were seeing. While the European war would not officially end for another week, for the former kriegies of Stalag Luft I, it was over. Their thoughts turned to home. How would they get there? How long would it take to be evacuated? Would they have enough to eat while they waited? Red Cross parcels would no longer be delivered. Would they need to send raiding parties into Barth to rob civilians? Would that terrible starvation period return?

Hub moved his administrative staff into the *Kommandant*'s office. No persons other than the former POWs would be allowed to stay in Stalag Luft I, despite the fearful residents of Barth rushing to the gate, begging entry. Everyone heard the rumors: The Red Army was made up of rapine savages, violently seizing property, and violating every woman they came across, young and old. True or not, the German civilians were immensely fearful. A group from Barth even asked the Americans if they would send an "occupation" force into the town to protect them from the Russians. But few former POWs were concerned with their plight. Zemke wanted to limit the instances of trouble between his men and the locals, so he temporarily placed Barth off-limits. He sent foraging parties into the countryside with strict orders to find food supplies now that the Red Cross parcels had ceased. They raided farmers' fields and brought back potatoes and various vegetables. They had no money so were forced to steal. Someone then remembered that there was a stash of Red Cross packages that had been stored at the nearby flak school. Hub mounted an expedition to recover them. But the residents of Barth had beaten them to it.

As Hub and his detachment of scroungers reached the flak school warehouse, they found the main door under attack by around fifty civilians. Zemke approached the apparent leader of the group of raiders and asked the man just what the hell they were doing. The man snapped back that there was food in there and they were going to get it. Hub reminded the raiders that the food in there belonged to the Stalag POWs. "To hell with those heathens! The food is now ours!"[12] Hub did not arm his men to go find the food parcels, so he was not able to halt the looting; instead, he sent a runner back to camp to round up some MPs. A few precious Red Cross parcels were taken before the armed group arrived to chase off the looters, firing over their heads. Most of the parcels were secured as many of the terrified civilians dropped their ill-gotten gains in their haste to flee. Hub later reflected that the ring leader was most likely a former guard at the camp and knew about the stash of food parcels. The senior Allied officer had teams of former kriegies carry the precious packages back to camp, where they were stored in a safe spot away from looters.

To add to the problems, the fleeing Wehrmacht had cut electrical lines to impede the Red Army, and now the camp was powerless. Groups of former POWs were sent out: one to Barth to try to figure out what had caused the issue and, if possible, correct it; the other group was sent to the flak school to locate a generator. Without power, the well pumps didn't work and they had no water. The flak school contingent was successful and lugged back a generator. They were also fortunate to find gasoline to keep it running.

Hub Zemke was afraid that on-coming Soviet troops might mistake Stalag Luft I as a German military compound and attack it. He didn't want to risk any misunderstandings, so he located a vehicle and placed a British German-speaking officer and a Russian-speaking American in the car. With a small US flag waving from one fender and a white flag was affixed to the other, the small task force was sent off to find the Russians. Neither of the two groups of escapees deployed the night of April 30 had yet returned; consequently, it was difficult to know exactly where the Red Army was located. In addition to the missing scouts, several hundred former kriegies disappeared during the first forty-eight hours after the Germans left, apparently looking to find Allied lines.

The men manning the vehicle were successful when they ran into the advance patrol of the Red Army some 11 miles south of Barth and brought them to the camp shortly before midnight on May 1, 1945. After the Red Army entered Barth, Gene Holley was surprised: much of their equipment was American. There were Jeeps and GM trucks, along with American-made artillery and heavy weapons. Lend-lease equipment had kept flowing through the Arctic convoys despite some of the worst U-boat activity and horrific ice storms in the North Atlantic and Baltic Sea. Courageous sailors had helped keep the Red Army rolling.

Finally, one of the groups of "escaped" kriegies that left the evening of the thirtieth returned with another Russian officer. Hub decided it wise to collect some of his own officers to reach out to the Red Army. Using the Kübelwagen they had secured earlier, with the US and white flags still attached to the front fenders, Hub and several of his officers set out with the Soviet major who had received a ride back to the camp to make contact with the main Russian advance party. It didn't take long to find them. As the vehicle halted, the Soviet major exited the car and walked up to the column; he told them about the camp full of American and Allied airmen. While the major spoke the army continued to move, marching past Zemke and his little contingent. Some smiled and waved at the Americans as they passed. The Red Army was now victorious; they had been beaten badly in the early stages of the invasion in June 1941. Many of their men surrendered to the Germans with little or no fight. Stalin was forced to issue horrific orders to stop the mass surrendering: fight or be shot by your officers. Fight they did. They found their courage, and they had beaten back the invasion. With American-made steel and conscripts from across the Soviet states, they smashed the German advance. The look they gave Hub and his officers as they passed by the Kübelwagen was one of pride.

A high-ranking Russian officer drove up to the Americans sitting in the open German vehicle. He was a Major (later colonel) Zhovanik, regimental commander of the Soviet 65th Army. He heartily greeted his American counterpart. (Hub spoke a few Russian words, a skill he picked up years ago when he was training Soviet pilots to fly P-40 aircraft.) The Russian officer told him, proudly, that Hub and his men were now "free"; the Red Army had liberated them. Diplomatically, Hub expressed his deep gratitude at having been liberated by the Russians. While this comment might have seemed histrionic, it was probably true to some extent. If not for the Soviet advance, the kriegies might still be in German custody at least a few weeks longer until the British Army arrived.

Fear of the Russians not only caused panicked retreats; it also caused a rash of suicides among the Germans. The mayor of Barth had killed his entire family before ending his administration in a poisonous last meal. And nearby the camp, JJ Thompson and several of his friends were out for a stroll when they came across five dead bodies, three woman and two children, each dead from a gunshot wound to the head. The family was known in Barth so were identified. There was a middle-aged woman, a young woman, and an older female; the children were a boy and an infant just a few months old. JJ expressed extreme sadness at this event, and it haunted him for many years afterward.[13]

Long after the war, JJ was able to track down the local Barth historian, via email, who gave him more information on the family. The middle-aged woman was married to a committed Nazi and was herself, apparently, a loyal supporter of the party. The older woman was her mother, and the younger woman, her cousin. The family had fled Pomerania ahead of the Soviet advance, losing all their possessions in the process. The younger woman was a war widow; she and her son fled west with her cousin and aunt to avoid the Russians, ending up in Barth, and staying at a local hotel. But the Red Army had caught up with the family again, this time in Barth. It must have seemed like the end of the road for the women. They were most likely well aware of the rumors about Soviet soldiers' treatment of German women. Stashing a pistol in the perambulator, the middle-aged woman announced she was going to kill her infant child and end it all. Her mother apparently tried to stop her, but the daughter snapped back, "If you want to live, stay in the hotel!" Her mother apparently responded, "How can I live without you?" So, they all headed out to die where JJ and his group found them.[14]

Tragedy also stalked the former kriegies as three of them found a car and several bottles of booze. Having survived the war and the wait for evacuation, they sped their stolen vehicle into a ditch, killing themselves in the process. Upset with the senseless deaths, Hub Zemke tried to limit the carnage, as well as potential conflicts with the occupying Russians by issuing some ninety daily passes into Barth. The Russian administration, led by Major Zhovanik, warned Hub to keep his men on a leash and not interfere with the Soviet authorities as they administered from Barth. Hub heartily agreed.

To make sure the camp residents didn't go hungry, the Russians performed a roundup and drove a herd of forty-two beef and dairy cows (twenty-one of each type) into the compound. The cattle were taken from local farms, no doubt to the outraged objections of their owners. The animals were placed on rich grassy areas within the compound in order to sustain themselves, but freshwater was sometimes hard to get for them.[15] In addition to the farm, the inmates set up a slaughterhouse and a butcher's shop. Gene Holley wrote to Elinor that while they hated the endless waiting, they had plenty to eat; the chronic lack of calories, so prevalent during the German administration of the camp, had ended. In exchange for the food, the Americans performed services for the Russians such as providing skilled mechanics who could repair the American-made Soviet-issued vehicles. Apparently, the Red Army did not think it necessary to include such talent with their troops. The former kriegies also counted among their number electrical engineers who competently repaired the Barth telephone system that retreating German forces disabled. The Russian general was thrilled.

On May 7, Gene reported his first shower in a month and a well-intentioned, but poorly executed, haircut by Willy. Since they were all in the same compound, the *Lady Jane* survivors saw each other daily. Gene wrote Elinor as much as he could, but there really wasn't a reliable way to get his letters out. Writing the letters sustained him and helped him through an emotional crisis he could barely endure; like every other former POW stuck in Germany, he was desperate to go home. He also wanted to chronicle his experiences. Perhaps his children, yet to be born, would learn about this time in his life.

The Americans had been told that they would be evacuated by air, so they needed to make the airfield serviceable. There were also a number of live bombs left by the Germans to discourage curious interlopers. All of those needed to be defused. Scattered about the runways were Heinkel He 111, Focke-Wulf Fw 190, Junkers Ju 88, and Arado Ar 234 jets. The buildings included three two-story barracks surrounded by barbed wire and electrically-charged fences wherein French and Greek slave-laborers were housed. They put the jets together in hangers. Placing the assembly plant so close to the prison camp was a strategic decision by the Germans to limit bombing of the airfield. They knew the Allies were loath to strike close to the camps for fear of injuring the prisoners.

When the former POWs opened the forced laborer's barracks, they were horrified at the sight they beheld. The prisoners were emaciated and starving, little more than skeletons, so weak, they had lain in their own waste for days. The former kriegies nearly wretched at the stench of rotting corpses and human excrement. British medical officer Lt. Col. George Hankey closed off the building. He then called in as many medical men as he could muster, including a group of local girls to act as nurses. The entire airport was quarantined to prevent an epidemic; the dying prisoners were suffering from a number of deadly diseases. The ex-POWs tried desperately to help the 2,000 inmates, but to no avail. Not one survived.[16] Hub stated in his memoirs that at this time, the residents of Stalag Luft I were not aware of the camps so prominent during the Holocaust. The discovery of this house of horrors was something they were unprepared to address or even witness. Human cruelty was beyond human comprehension.

• • •

Gene Holley, along with many other former POWs, was getting extremely anxious. In one of his letters to Ellie, he lamented the situation and was thinking of doing what hundreds of others had done and strike out on his own. The British army was supposed to be fairly close to the west.[17] But Hub was cautioning everyone to be patient. *Patience!* As the days dragged on, Gene wondered just what the hell was going on. It wouldn't take much effort to send a couple of B-17s out to pick them up. On May 8, the European war officially ended; the residents of Stalag Luft I thought they would be picked up any day now. In the meantime, Gene and three friends he had made in the camp decided to sneak out and find a diversion to while away some time. They wouldn't escape to find friendly troops; they would escape and find friendly civilians, maybe hunt for nice things to take home to their sweethearts. It was a souvenir hunt.

They would need a pass to exit the camp, something none of them had, and Col. Zemke was limiting their issuance; so, they inserted themselves into a group that was visiting the camp. As the party left, Gene and his buddies slipped out with them. The boys were curious. What did freedom feel like? What would it be like to just go where they wanted? Speak to whomever they wished? One of the "escapees," identified as "Tom" by Gene, spoke pretty good German. They went into Barth for the day. With the Russians occupying the town, the boys needed to keep away from them, and avoid contact if possible.

The first people they ran into were a bunch of German kids who excitedly invited the Americans to their home. By now Hitler was dead, and the hostilities had ended. The Germans trusted Americans far more than Russians, so the kids were overtly friendly to the former kriegies. The Americans trailed behind the children and met their parents, who claimed to have some German flight boots for sale.

Also at this time, the German economy had descended into chaos and collapse. Citizens across the country needed food and other staples not readily available. The Russians certainly weren't sharing, having problems of their own in keeping their forces fed and clothed. So a number of civilians resorted to the barter system with occupying troops. Gene didn't record what he and his friend paid for the boots (probably cigarettes and food articles from the Red Cross parcels), only that they were able to barter for them. As they were making the transaction, an inebriated Russian officer barged in through the garden gate. There were several women in the yard: one was elderly, perhaps the kids' grandma. The ladies stiffened in fear as the drunk weaved his way over to the group.

At first, the Soviet soldier just wanted to shake hands and slap the Americans on their backs while offering robust salutations. Then he made clear what he really came for: he wanted a woman with which to celebrate the evening. Providing a united front, the Americans stood firm, glaring at the drunk and firmly turning him down. No, they would not allow any woman to be kidnapped and raped. Apparently, this fate had been met by two other women from this same house that morning. Grandma begged Gene and his friends to stay a little longer to protect them. They did, leaving a while later when they were sure the drunk wouldn't return. They continued into Barth to see the sights and, hopefully, avoid more sloshed Russians. They ran into more cigarette-begging youngsters willing to barter goodies for smokes. Gene found some nice things to bring back to Ellie. He was shocked to see seven-year-olds light up upon receiving the smokes in trade.

Gene's group was reveling in their day out when an officer from the camp rode up to them on a motorcycle and spoiled everything: Col. McKenna ordered the AWOL airmen back to Stalag Luft I. Grudgingly, they ended their sightseeing tour and headed back to the barracks. It had been a good day, this first taste of freedom. Gene would reflect on it for many years later in his memoirs.

On May 9, as the endless waiting for extraction continued, Gene met up with JJ, and the two friends discussed their missing buddies. What exactly had happened to Bas? They had heard a rumor that Milan Basara was dead. They had heard what had befallen Hal. They still weren't sure about Fred Gerhardt. Hardtack had been severely wounded, but they hadn't received word yet if he had survived. Just how they learned about Hal and Bas is unclear. Nor did they know about Jim Butlin's gruesome murder. They weren't aware of Bas's final resting place; they wanted to find out for the sake of his folks. (He was most likely still buried in Rosche at this time, but they didn't know that.)

While Gene and JJ visited, some of their campmates went into Barth and raised a lot of hell. No doubt requisitioning some Russian vodka, they found themselves tossed into the town's jail. Gene also recorded that one of the German Luftwaffe guards that used to lord over the POWs was found and dragged back to the camp. Gene didn't relate who it was or his fate, only that Gene wanted to kick "the goose-stepping fool's teeth in." The anger felt by the former kriegies would not abate for years to come, if ever. As he fumed, someone put a couple of baseball teams together to pass the time. Gene joined in, eager for a distraction. On May 9, the game went off and Gene's team lost, but it was a terrific way to forget about the endless end and the terrible waiting. Despite the distractions, camp-wide, morale was crashing. Everyone desperately wanted to go home.

Hub Zemke worked tirelessly to make that happen. While he struggled to keep GIs out of trouble by making adherence to camp rules mandatory, he negotiated regularly with the Soviet administrator for the area, Colonel Zhovanik. Hub's working relationship with Zhovanik was very good; the latter would grant the Allied men what concessions he could, as long as Col. Zemke kept them out of trouble. A suggestion was raised by Zhovanik's commander, General Borisov, to remove the former POWs via rail. Unfortunately, this would have meant an outrageously long trip for 9,000 men to Odessa, Ukraine, some 1,250 miles away in the wrong direction.[18] Nope, Hub trashed that idea as soon as it was proposed. Wing X (Hub had dropped the "Provisional" moniker when the Germans departed) remained the administrative entity for the airmen trapped in Barth. Their decision was to use the now serviceable Barth Airfield to evacuate the former kriegies.

Desperate, Hub wrote letters to both Gen. Carl Spaatz and Russian Marshal Rokossovsky of the Red Army. A British commander residing with the main army at the Elbe River was also notified when an English officer in the camp, senior British Officer Group captain Cecil ("Ginger") Weir, wrote a similar missive. Hub then dispatched three officers from the camp to deliver the letters; one courier was an American pilot serving with the Canadian Air Force, Flight Lieutenant William Pickens; another was a British officer, Group Captain Hilton; and the third an American colonel, Byerly.[19] They were dispatched to the British lines using a Russian escort and a requisitioned German vehicle to reach the Elbe River. Flight Lieutenant William Pickens carried Hub's letters for the American authorities, and Captain Hilton carried Weir's. They were fortunate that a small contingent did arrive from the British Army the same day the letters went out. But the wait dragged on, and several more former kriegies wound up dead in a ditch, one with his skull crushed. The consensus, following investigations, was that angry Germans murdered them, unhappy that American *terrorfliegers* were roaming at will.

Amazingly, Field Marshal Montgomery *did* get the message. The letter sent by the British officer in camp somehow found its way to Monty's desk via the group of ex-kriegie couriers. Pickens returned on May 8 with two paratroopers of the Sixth Airborne Division. Pickens was then dispatched again, this time to find the Americans. He made his way back to the Elbe where he was put aboard an aircraft and flown to the US Army headquarters at Lüneburg; here he reported that thousands of Americans were anxiously awaiting rescue at a prison camp north of Barth. Pickens was told that the USAAF XVIII Corps was tasked with evacuating American ex-POWs. Unfortunately, the Russians were not allowing US aircraft to use airspace they controlled. JJ Thompson stated in his memoirs that he believed this was a political ploy with the former kriegies being used as bargaining chips. He mentioned that a former Soviet officer who had defected to the Germans had been captured by the Americans, and was wanted by the Russians; the airmen were supposedly being held hostage until the presumed traitor was turned over to the Red Army and justice was meted out.[20]

Regardless of the politics, the situation was evidently discussed between Monty and Rokossovsky. The latter promised that all 9,000 ex-POWs would be delivered to the British army within two days. But that didn't happen. It was an empty promise. So, Hub made another suggestion to Zhovanik: if accommodations could be made for the sick and injured, the men would walk to the Elbe. They could probably cover the 70 miles in three or four days; they had plenty to eat now and the men were stronger. Together, they approached Gen. Borisov. But that didn't go over too well. Zhovanik was vigorously chewed out. Perhaps he should have known better: such decisions could only come from Moscow! Dejected, angry, and disappointed, Hub returned to camp.

He was fed up and so were the men trapped in the camp. They had long ago torn down the gates and wire, but they remained imprisoned as surely as if von Warnstedt and the detested Abwehr officer Major von Miller were still in charge. The latter had turned up in Barth after the German surrender and was now taking up a job as a new administrator in the town. As soon as Hub heard this rumor, he charged into Barth to confirm it. Sure enough, the Nazi who had so tormented the kriegies with his midnight shakedowns and endless harassment was a big man in Barth. He had apparently met the arriving Red Army outside Barth while grasping a white flag and posing as a policeman for the town. Hub would have none of it. He went straight to Zhovanik's office and denounced the hated man. Von Miller soon disappeared; Hub didn't know where.[21]

Gene was helpless. He tried to occupy his time when the weather was bad and he was forced to stay in the barracks. He read a lot and wrote letters to Ellie. Homesickness was tearing him apart. His twentieth birthday was in a couple of weeks on May 27. He felt like an old man for all the trauma he'd been through. The camp had been liberated some ten days ago and *still* they waited and waited and waited. Gene made plans to do his laundry the next day.

Gene's laundry duties were needed; his stinky clothes hadn't been washed since March and were as unkept as his personal hygiene. Everyone there, except those in the North and West compounds, had lacked access to laundry facilities and showers. Now that the camp residents had the freedom to travel between compounds, the problems with access evaporated. JJ wrote home and told his folks about a Russian variety show that was put on May 7 for the ex-POWs. With freedom of movement, North 3 residents could travel to the theater in the West Compound. Several thousand camp residents attended, hooting, howling, and issuing deafening dog whistles to the Russian ladies who performed. The RAF and USAAF boys couldn't understand the singing, but they didn't need to; it was terrific entertainment, especially the female forms, as many a young man pined for his girl back home.

Despite the retrieval of British and American troops and the endless promises to *do something*, evacuation just wasn't happening. On May 11, a thoroughly disgusted Ginger Weir charged down to Colonel General Pavel Batov's office in Tribses, 25 miles south of Barth. Probably driving the previously requisitioned Kübelwagen, and no doubt with a Soviet escort, Weir went to see the commander of the 65th Soviet Army; Barth was within Batov's sphere of command. The Red Army commander made more promises, but this time they didn't seem hollow, as so many before. He assured Weir that he would contact Moscow himself and clear the way for Allied aircraft to land in Barth. An excited Ginger Weir called Hub to give him the good news before driving two hours west to Hagenau, where he arranged for air transport. Monty had gotten word too, possibly from Batov, and provided clearance for the evacuations to begin on May 12.

Passes for all the airmen to be evacuated were pounded out in both Russian and English on several typewriters in the camp; each man would receive two of these documents. A head count was needed to make sure enough travel passes were issued. Hub was shocked to find that there were 730 impatient American airmen missing (out of 7,725, about 9 percent), but only thirty-one RAF men (out of 1,458, about 2 percent) were already gone, apparently walking out.[22] For the air transports, the sick and wounded would be evacuated first.

There were also some Germans the ex-kriegies wanted to evacuate. During their captivity, PWX had relied on several secretaries in the *Kommandant*'s office for intelligence. When the German guards fled the approach of the Red Army, the Americans protected the women by having them dress as nurses and employing them within the camp. The women were also instrumental in trying to save the dying inmates when they were found at the airfield. In exchange for their help, PWX agreed to evacuate them to the west and away from the voracious Soviet soldiers. The ladies would fly out with the Allied airmen and would be deposited in a safe location.

At around 2:00 p.m., on the afternoon of May 12, 1945, a glorious sound was heard over Stalag Luft I, the thunderous rumble of B-17 radial engines. A howl of pure joy rose up from thousands of throats in the camp. The Mighty Eighth had arrived to begin their journey home.[23]

Chapter 11

A FIGHT FOR HONOR

I am not bound to win, but I am bound to be true. I am not bound to succeed, but I am bound to live up to what light I have.

—Abraham Lincoln

Gene Holley, JJ Thompson, Harold Babcock, and Rodney Williams couldn't look out of any windows as they sat on the floor of the big, beautiful B-17G.[1] The ammo boxes were gone, removed; the machine guns had been taken out; the whole inside if the ship was devoid of everything that might interfere with room to cram more former kriegies into the limited space. It took two days to get all the men and women out of the camp. Some thirty-seven B-17s were flown out of England and pressed into service in what was called "Operation Revival." One bomber after another landed, loaded up twenty-five to thirty personnel, and took off, headed for France or England. Tommies were taken home to England; the Yanks went to Camp Lucky Strike on the French northern coast at Janville.

In September 1944, after northern France was liberated following D-Day, the Allies captured the big port at Le Havre. It had been badly damaged in the effort, but the American engineers swiftly brought the quays back into service, and the port would handle an enormous amount of traffic for the remainder of the war and beyond. Clustered about the port were the "Cigarette Camps," most situated between Le Havre and Rouen. These camps began as transit centers for replacement troops, incoming supplies, new unit transfers to be posted in-theater, staging areas for German and Axis POWs to the States, and other purposes. There were a number of these camps, code-named after popular brands of smokes: Pall Mall, Philip Morris, Chesterfield, Twenty Grand, Old Gold, Lucky Strike, and others. These camps began as tent cities, but as the war moved on, they began to acquire a PX, theaters, and other amenities necessary for civilized living. Some tents grew into wooden barracks. But many of the repatriated former POWs, called "RAMPs" (Recovered Allied Military Personnel), lived in twenty-man canvas tents with primitive toilet facilities. These were made of boxes with holes cut in them that then straddled holes or slit trenches in the ground. The amenities were often sparser than at the various prison camps from which they were released. But at least they were free!

Camp Lucky Strike had been a German-occupied airfield before the D-Day invasion. It was part of the defensive bulwark for Erwin Rommel's "Atlantic Wall." Since it was so close to the Channel, it served as a good spot to launch V-1 rocket attacks on England. It was also a strategic location for surveillance on Allied shipping and troop deployments. The single runway could be used to send lone reconnaissance aircraft to monitor the channel. (That runway still exists today and is used primarily for crop dusting operations on the surrounding farms.) During the war, the RAF and the Mighty Eighth made sure to include this airfield on its bombing runs. The 8th AF was particularly interested in the rocket launching skids, but these were hidden in forests near the airfield and were notoriously difficult to hit and destroy. When the area fell to the Allies, the combat engineers moved in swiftly to dismantle any rocket skids, repair the runway, and begin construction of Camp Lucky Strike. At that point in the war, it was used to send troops *into* Europe. By May 1945, its *raison d'etre* was to evacuate troops *out* of Europe.

A serious problem for many of these boys was the transition from prison rations to real food, causing many of the box privies to be persistently occupied. Fortunately for the former occupants of Stalag Luft I, thanks to the Russians and their cattle drive into the POW camp, they had been on "real food" for nearly two weeks, so their digestive tracts weren't traumatically shocked. But many former kriegies were required to be under medical supervision as they moved into a new reality of good, plentiful food.

As the boys settled into their Cigarette Camp tents, an ugly rumor was spreading that the former kriegies waited nearly two weeks for their flight out because they were being held as hostages by the Russians. The Red Army was seeking to bring a "traitor" to justice. The turncoat was an anti-Stalin general that had been recruited by the Nazis, and the Soviets wanted him, badly.

• • •

Andrey Andreyevich Vlasov was a Russian general who was a strong figure in the defense of Moscow and Kiev, Ukraine. Born in 1900, he was conscripted into the Red Army during the Russian Revolution. He had planned to join an Orthodox seminary but was prevented from completing his studies by the outbreak of the Bolshevik Revolution. He joined the Communist Party in 1930. While party membership may not have been compulsory, it may have been difficult to advance one's career in the military unless one joined the Party. Such circumstances existed with the Nazi Party as well; few people could gain promotions and benefits unless they were a party member. Vlasov was dispatched by the Red Army to advise Chiang Kai-shek as the Japanese ravaged China in 1938, two years before the Tripartite Pact between Germany, Japan, and Italy on September 27, 1940. He had returned to Russia in 1939.

In 1940, Vlasov was promoted to major general and placed in command of the 99th Infantry Division.[2] His men attained distinction by advancing when the Red Army retreated, retaking the key city of Przemysl. This and other successes brought another promotion, and in 1941, Lieutenant General Vlasov was assigned to command the 37th Army at Kiev, where he was able to break out of the German encirclement. In December, he joined the defense of Moscow at the head of the 20th Army.[3] He had all the guts and vigor of a successful Red Army general; photos from this period show a proud warrior with a chest full of medals.

On January 7, 1942, at the head of the Second Shock Army, Lt. Gen. Gen. Vlasov fought against the Nazis in an attempt the break the siege at Leningrad. His troops charged across the frozen Volhov River to the northwest of the city. Several other armies were due to take part in what was planned to be a coordinated assault on the German lines. Unfortunately, snafus up and down the Russian lines caused delays, and Vlasov's push, while initially very successful, began to bog down. By February 1942, the Second Shock Army had penetrated some 46 miles into the German perimeter.[4] Supplies began to run out as the Germans closed the gap created by Vlasov's advance. His army had been denied retreat by Stalin, and as a result, suffered immeasurably and starved. Cut off and without resupply, Vlasov and his men were surrounded and captured. They were expected to die fighting. If they had, it might have been better for them in the long run.

In interviews with the Red Army general, the Nazi interrogators quickly realized they had on their hands a disgruntled army officer and a potential propaganda windfall.[5] Even though Vlasov was a Communist, he was deeply disturbed by Stalin's purges of military personnel and felt that the efficacy of the Red Army had been damaged beyond repair. Stalin's mania had resulted in the mass detention and slaughter of many Red Army officers who could have made the defense of Russian territory more effective in the battles to come. Fortunately, Vlasov had survived the purges of 1940–41. He fumed and vented his animosity to his German captors. Seizing an important opportunity, the Nazis asked, would General Vlasov be willing to lead a counter revolution and march an army against Stalin? Knowing that he was already considered a traitor simply for surrendering, he agreed. Had Vlasov and his men not been abandoned to their fate and instead had been resupplied, and had the Red Army units deployed according to plan, it is very possible the entire affair could have avoided.

The force would be named the "Russian Liberation Movement"; its new general was given the freedom to recruit 50,000 Soviet prisoners of war.[6] To understand why so many thousands of Russian POWs would turn traitor, one needs to be reminded of the fate of each Soviet soldier who was captured in battle. Stalin considered such men as traitors, whether or not they actually collaborated with the enemy. Each POW being held by the Germans, or even the Allies, was considered tainted by western propaganda and could not be trusted. Any Soviet soldier who allowed himself to be captured did not fight for the Motherland forcefully enough and was therefore a traitor. Since it mattered not whether a Russian soldier was actually a turncoat or sat out his imprisonment quietly in a POW camp, Vlasov apparently had no problems recruiting men for the new unit. The new troops now fought against their Red Army counterparts. They wore German uniforms with special unit insignia "POA" (a reference to "ROA," *Russkaya osvoboditel'naya armiya*, "Russian Liberation Army"), on the arms of their shirts.

In May 1945, shortly before the war ended, Vlasov had changed sides yet again and fought off SS units to keep them from destroying Prague, Czechoslovakia. His unit fought voraciously and defeated the Waffen-SS troops before the Red Army arrived. Should they fall into Russian hands, he and his men were hopeful this act would cleanse their earlier sin of defecting. But to be safe, they surrendered to an advance scouting party of Americans. They were rightly terrified of being captured by the Soviets. But fate had her own plans, and the anti-Bolshevik army didn't get what they wanted; they ended up paying dearly for their transgressions. As part of the agreements made between the Allies at the Yalta Conference in February 1945, the United States was required to turn over any and all Soviet troops found in their custody. Stalin especially wanted Vlasov's head on a platter. He didn't care about Vlasov's defense of Prague; once a traitor, forever a traitor.

In his memoirs, JJ Thompson stated he was convinced that the Red Army's initial refusal to allow the 8th AF to evacuate Stalag Luft I was tied to the transfer of Vlasov from American control back to the Soviets. This idea was addressed in a work a few years ago by American historian Patricia Wadley in her PhD dissertation. She felt that the release of the former kriegies from Russian control back to the Allies was indeed part of a complicated series of negotiations with the Barth inmates as currency. She stated, "Vlasov was handed over at 2:30 p.m. on May 12. US bombers, which had been circling the Barth airfield, were allowed to land at 3:30 p.m."[7]

Andrey Vlasov was given a three-day trial back in Moscow from July 30 to August 2, 1945, and along with some of his officers, was hanged on August 2, 1945. Many of his enlisted men vanished in the gulags. Every repatriated Soviet POW faced a similar threat. Entire shiploads of returning Red Army captives faced execution or Siberian imprisonment, as witnessed by the British captain of a ship when he delivered a load of former Russian POWs back to Soviet custody. A portion of these men was marched off to a portside building and machine-gunned immediately after being turned over to the Russian authorities. The ship's captain was able to investigate after several covered trucks left the building. He found blood on the floor and bullet holes in the walls.[8]

• • •

The *Lady Jane* boys had been sent together from Barth to Camp Lucky Strike, where they ran into a very familiar face. None of the boys recorded just how they ran into Hardtack, but there he was, apparently healthy and mostly recovered from the wounds he had received on March 18.

After his shock at finding Milan Basara dead in the back of a truck, Fred Gerhardt was taken to a local hospital where he was operated on to remove the shrapnel in his body. The Germans were not about to spend precious medicines on a POW, so he was operated on without the benefit of anesthesia. Relating his story after the war, Fred laughed; no anesthesia was perfectly fine because he quickly passed out on the operating table and didn't feel a thing. After a short hospital stay, he was transferred to a nearby camp occupied primarily by British POWs. He stayed at this camp until Patton arrived with his army. Apparently, Hardtack was able to speak to the famous general and told him he was an American among British soldiers, whereupon the *Lady Jane*'s waist gunner was taken into the control of the US Army.[9]

All of the survivors of the *Lady Jane II* were now together as they boarded a ship at Le Havre in June 1945 to head for home. They had been waiting at Camp Lucky Strike for about a month.

John Sites, the original bombardier assigned to Dave Vermeer's crew, had beaten them home. He ended the war as part of a lead crew so got to fly back to the States, as opposed to crossing the Atlantic via ship. They refueled with a stopover in Goose Bay, Labrador, then to an airfield in Massachusetts. After that, he boarded a troop train to Randolph Field in San Antonio, Texas.[10] John Sites was not released from the Army; he was to be posted as an instructor for new bomber crews headed for the Pacific; the war there was not yet concluded.

Also headed for the Pacific theater was the 8th Air Force itself, where it was stationed in the Mariana Islands, on Guam, Tinian, and Saipan. The Mighty Eighth was about to become mightier still as the returning B-17s and B-24s were flown to scrapyards and the new high-tech B-29 was issued in their stead. Had the *Lady Jane II* survived, she would most likely have been flown to the dismantling facility at Kingman, Arizona, and reduced to aluminum ingots in the on-site smelter. Only a precious handful of B-17Gs exist into the twenty-first century, most housed in museums; a tiny number are still capable of flight.[11]

The Mighty Eighth transferred with its new equipment, with the notoriously bellicose Gen. Curtis LeMay in charge. But John Sites ended up not sticking around. When Japan surrendered following the nuclear strikes on Hiroshima and Nagasaki on August 6 and 9, respectively, the world war finally concluded, and John was sent home on September 12, 1945. He had heard of his former crew's trouble by then and no doubt wondered if he would have survived; his replacement, Jim Butlin, had not.

In September 1945, while awaiting his mustering out paperwork, Gene Holley applied to the Case School of Applied Science in Cleveland. (The name of the school today is the Case Western Reserve University; its primary role is producing engineers.) Even though Gene was a grown and married man, his dad made his wishes known: Gene was to finish college. Period. In 1949, Gene graduated with a bachelor of science in civil engineering. He worked in the Ohio Department of Highways before moving into private industry. In 1982, he helped found a highway and heavy construction company, the Soda Construction Company. His son Mark took over the company when he retired; it has since been sold. Gene and Elinor had seven children and fourteen grandchildren; their grandchildren have had kids as well. In June 2014, Elinor was called home; she is buried in Rittman, Ohio. As of this writing, Gene is still with us, in his late-nineties, and is looked after by his children in Ohio.

John J. Thompson left the Army Air Force at the end of the war, seeking work in a factory; however, he stayed in the Air Force Reserves as a second lieutenant. In 1948 the air forces were separated from the Army and the

United States Air Force was born. Following the conclusion of the Korean War, "Jack," as he preferred to be called, left the reserves in February 1953 to be back in the Air Force full-time.[12] Promoted to first lieutenant, he was assigned to learn how to pilot a B-50 bomber, a souped-up version of the B-29D. The B-50 was one of the last radial engine heavy bombers before the advent of jet power. After so many hours of piloting the lower-tech, unpressurized B-17, Jack would have felt like he was flying a Cadillac. The aircraft had been ordered during the late stages of the Second World War but weren't actually delivered to the USAAF until 1947.[13]

In March 1954, assigned to Walker Air Force Base in New Mexico, Jack attended the Air Force Electronics School at Keesler Air Force Base in Biloxi, Mississippi. In 1955, he was sent to the Sidi Slimane Air Base in Morocco, where he served as an administrative officer for the 5th Aviation Depot Squadron. He was stationed there for several years and was present when the US Air Force very nearly blew up the base with a nuclear bomb.

The B-47 was a very high-tech, six-engine, swept-wing jet bomber. It was the offspring of the marriage between the World War II bombers and the jet age. Its engines could not provide enough thrust to take off and required rocket power assist from eighteen systems located in the aft fuselage. To land, it needed a rear parachute to slow it down. It was fast too! In 1949, a B-47 crossed the United Srates in four hours, averaging 608 mph.[14] The only armament was in the tail as no other jet during that time could catch it. Its payload could consist of thirteen 500-pound or eight 1,000-pound conventional bombs. It could also carry up to two nuclear bombs. It was a necessary asset in the beginning of the Cold War.

After World War II the entire globe was under threat of a nuclear holocaust as American and Soviet forces postured at each other from across the Iron Curtain. In the early 1950s, France had allowed the United States to set up bases in Morocco to keep the Soviets in check. But it had not been given explicit permission to store nuclear weapons there. In 1951, the United States had built the Sidi Slimane Air Base. While the French were still in possession of the country, the United States began secretly stockpiling nukes at the base to be deployed via the B-47 jets parked there. Morocco had gained its independence from France in March 1956, while Jack (now Maj. Thompson) was stationed there.

On January 31, 1958, three months before Jack was transferred back to the States, a B-47 was practicing a take-off maneuver when one of the rear tires blew out. The metal wheel hitting the tarmac generated sparks, setting the shredded rubber tire on fire. The fire spread at near preternatural speed and the main fuselage erupted in flames. The crew managed to stop the plane, jump out on the runway, and run for their lives. They knew what the bomb bay carried, but even if the payload had exploded, running would have accomplished nothing. Regardless, the base was quickly evacuated. Had the unthinkable happened, no one would have gotten far enough away and they would have been vaporized along with the base and surrounding environs. Jack was there; he would have been blown to atoms as well, had the nukes on board the plane cooked off in the fire. The blaze reached the bombs, but miraculously, they did not explode. It is a fair assumption that more than one airman reached the end of his sprinting endurance with soiled shorts.

Just why jets were "practicing" take-off procedures while nuclear bombs were onboard is anyone's guess. The whole affair was swiftly squelched by the Air Force and labeled "Top Secret." No one, including Jack, was allowed to speak about it. Even years later, after the topic was declassified, he suppressed much of his experience regarding the incident and spoke of it only sparingly.[15] After the Moroccans gained their independence from colonial rule, they had expressed a desire to kick out *all* foreigners, the United States included. All American bases in Morocco were closed by the early 1960s.

Jack was transferred to other duty stations, including air bases in New Mexico and Texas, during his Air Force career; he spent three years in Okinawa, Japan, in the early 1960s. He also served in Vietnam. Jack might have wondered if he was cursed when another air base he was serving at also suffered a near-fatal catastrophe. On May 16, 1965, Jack was on temporary duty at the Bien Hoa Air Base when it experienced a major incident. A Martin B-57B Canberra twin-engine jet bomber exploded, setting off a conflagration of epic proportions. Four of the bombers were loaded and waiting to take off for a "Barrel Roll" mission using conventional bombs. Operation Barrel Roll was a covert series of missions to Laos to discourage North Vietnamese use of the country as a highway for supplying the war in South Vietnam via the Ho Chi Minh Trail. Technically, Laos was neutral and should have been left alone in accordance with the Geneva Conference of 1954, but the United States bombed and sprayed the country relentlessly both with conventional bombs and with "Agent Orange" defoliant. The Barrel Roll operations were kept secret as the United States did not have the authority to operate in the neutral nation.

Jack was on duty that morning at the Bien Hoa base, tasked with supervising the loading of the bombers. He decided to go grab a bite to eat before starting his shift and was at the mess hall when the bombload on a taxiing Canberra was inadvertently armed by a mechanical malfunction. The bomber exploded, setting off a cataclysmic chain reaction. Jack ran out of the mess hall to render aid if possible, but there was little he could do. Fire control teams had leapt into action but the disaster was out of anyone's hands as the bombers caught fire, cooked off, and exploded, setting off more fires and explosions. All anyone could do was stand back and watch the disaster unfold. When it was all over, ten Canberras, fifteen A-1E Skyraiders, and an F-8 Crusader fighter jet were destroyed; twenty-seven Americans died and more than one hundred were wounded. Jack's grandson Tom believed that had "Papaw" been at his station when the catastrophic explosions began, it would have been the end of him. After his tour in Vietnam, Jack spent 1964 to 1965 at Hollman AFB in New Mexico. He retired from the Air Force as a lieutenant colonel.

On November 26, 2012, the love of Jack's life, Joan, died after fifty-seven years of marriage. He followed her six days later, on December 2, ostensibly of cancer, but the family knew better. Jack had died of a broken heart. The couple is buried in Manchaca, Texas.

Fred Gerhardt was the youngest member of the *Lady Jane* crew; he was nineteen years and one month of age when the ship met her end. After the war he went to work at the Merchandise Mart in Chicago where he stayed for his entire working career of forty years. The scars on his throat were prevalent and he was permanently lame from the wounds to his legs. "Hardtack" succumbed to Parkinson's disease and dementia in a VA hospital and passed away on December 30, 2001. He is buried in Elwood, Illinois.[16]

Upon discharge, Harold Loren Babcock went home to Wisconsin, where he married a lovely gal named Nancy in 1964. Nancy was far younger than her husband, by some twenty-five years. He told Gene in an email in 2002, Nancy kept him young. In 1966, they had a son, Curtis, who married and lived next door to them; he helped his folks where he could. Harold passed away on May 3, 2008; Nancy followed her husband in November 2011.

Rodney Alverson Williams returned to Long Beach, back to his job at the J.A. Campbell Company, where he remained for the rest of his working career. He never spoke to his family about his time in the service, but his lingering trauma was apparent. He fathered two children, Mark in 1947, and Lorraine in 1950. His marriage to Doris Daisy Brown suffered as post-traumatic stress disorder manifested and Rod descended into alcoholism. He separated from the family and fought his demons alone, leaving his children to speculate. Lorraine believed that her dad suffered from profound survivor's guilt for the remainder of his days. He had been the oldest member of the crew, and fate led him to a long life when four of his much-younger friends had died, several horribly. He wrote nothing down and his family was unable to decipher his past, other than what they could learn from other *Lady Jane* survivors.[17]

When the flak exploded next to the ball turret on March 18, 1945, Rod was wounded in his legs. His injuries were far less severe than Fred's, and he selflessly ignored his pain and bleeding to tend to Hardtack, who was hurt badly and in dire condition. Rod healed up in the prison camp and forgot about the whole thing. He ended his service in October 1945, uneasily clutching an American Campaign Medal. As with most of his fellow veterans of the war, he sought only to put the whole thing behind him and get on with his life. He wanted nothing to do with medals or other reminders of such a traumatic period.

On January 24, 1994, at the age of eighty-two, Rod passed away, never having pursued the medals to which he was entitled. But Lorraine did, and eighteen years after her dad's passing, she began a letter-writing campaign. One obstacle to her effort was the loss of thousands of veteran's records in a catastrophic fire at the National Personnel Records Center in St. Louis, Missouri, on July 12, 1973. Most of her dad's military records were lost as a result. When no one could locate Rod's records, Lorraine was referred to the Department of the Air Force. She would issue more letters.

On March 12, 2012, Lorraine sent a letter to the Board for Correction of Air Force Records, requesting that Rod's discharge papers, his DD-214, reflect the issuance of a Purple Heart and a POW Medal. President Reagan instituted the latter medal in 1985; it applied to all service men and women who found themselves in POW camps following the April 6, 1917, US entry into the Great War. She was not seeking monetary compensation of any kind, only that the error in her dad's record be addressed. An additional problem was that the Air Force needed witnesses to Rod's injuries. The crew was not aware of his wounding, as everyone had been focused on Hardtack. A German doctor treated Rod, but then he apparently concealed his injuries at the POW camp. The only surviving crewmember in 2013 was Gene, and he never saw Willy exit the plane, as most of the gunners left the burning wreckage through the flak hole and the crew at the front of the ship exited at the forward hatch. There was no way to track down the German doctor who treated Lorraine's dad for shrapnel wounds, and most of Rod's military records were destroyed in the 1973 fire. Lorraine seemed to be hitting a concrete wall.

On February 18, 2013, she compiled a list of eleven cases wherein petitioners were granted Purple Heart medals even though the original records were lost. She received a form letter in response from the Air Force Review Boards Agency telling her that the request had been received, and she needed to be patient. The concrete wall got a little thicker.

On February 19, 2013, in a missive apparently unrelated to the Review Board letter, Lorraine received a correspondence from the Department of the Air Force, Headquarters, Air Force Personnel Center in San Antonio. The letter stated that since there were no witnesses and no records of Rod's injuries, the Purple Heart could not be granted. It stated:

> Recommendation: Disapproval of the Purple Heart. The next of kin was unable to provide an exact date in which the applicant was wounded, medical documentation, or witness statements. It is noted in the applicant's record that the next of kin states, 'All witnesses are deceased'. Due to the applicant's records being destroyed, there is insufficient documentation available to substantiate award of the Purple Heart. To grant the applicant relief would be contrary to the eligibility criteria established by the DoDM 1348.33.

The concrete wall had just gotten 10 feet taller. But Lorraine had inherited her dad's stubborn determination that had served him so well during the war. She kept fighting.[18]

After more letters and arguments with the Air Force bureaucracy, on August 26, 2013, Lorraine prevailed, and her dad was finally awarded the Purple Heart. In their review of his case, the US Air Force found documentation that Rod had indeed been approved for a Purple Heart clear back in June 1945.[19] But for whatever reason, the Army discharge clerk did not forward the award, and no further mention was made of it; it was simply forgotten. Had Rod known about the award, he never spoke of it.

On Wednesday, March 18, 2015, exactly seventy years after the *Lady Jane II* was shot down, Lorraine accepted the Purple Heart on behalf of her dad at the Los Alamitos Air Base in California in a ceremony covered by the local ABC affiliate.[20] Air Force Maj. Gen. Robert D. McMurry Jr. presided over the event and handed the award to a very grateful daughter. She had also managed to add the POW and Air Medals to her dad's service record. President Roosevelt had established the Air Medal in 1942; it applied to any bomber crewmember who served in at least five missions. The *Lady Jane II* crew engaged in six missions total.

If Rod Williams were alive in 2015 when Lorraine received his medals, it would be hard to gauge his reaction. Like so many of his fellow veterans of that terrible conflict, he probably would have accepted the awards reluctantly, wanting only to forget. But the loved ones of these brave men could not forget, nor indeed should ever forget their service and sacrifice, watching their friends suffer and die. Indeed, no American should ever forget.

EPILOGUE

No greater love hath no man than to lay down his life for a friend.
—John 15:13

Why does one crew matter? There were thousands upon thousands of crews, many suffering as the boys on the *Lady Jane II.* This bomber was but one cog in an enormous machine of war, perhaps the greatest in human history. According to the *Army Air Forces Statistical Data Report* (December 1945), some 10,081 heavy-bomber crewmen were lost in the European theater of operations, either killed in aerial combat or accidents, murdered on the ground following bailout, or perishing in POW camps.[1] By May 1945, a total of about 10,587 B-17s and B-24s had been delivered to the ETO.[2] Approximately 105,870 crewmembers were needed to staff these bombers. Some 20,000 total airmen in the European theater lost their lives in the years 1942–1945.[3] Some of those lost were never found and remain missing to this day.[4] One must wonder how many still lay in the cold waters of the English Channel because their aircraft failed to bring them home.

Approximately sixteen million Americans served in World War II. More than 400,000 of them died, 2.5 percent of the total. With no desire to disparage the courage of the GI in a foxhole or a Marine storming a beach under hellfire in the Pacific, they actually stood a greater chance of survival than a crewman on a bomber in 1943. A member of the 29th Infantry Division might curse the aircrews as the bombers roared above his foxhole; he might spit and cuss, "Damn flyboys! At least they get to sleep in a warm bed tonight!" Maybe… maybe not.

The aircrews suffered about a 10 percent mortality rate for the entire conflict, which was as high as 25 percent in 1942 and 1943 before long-range fighter escorts were employed. The total casualty rate (including wounded and battled fatigued airmen) was much higher. Of the 10,587 heavy bombers delivered to the ETO, 6,008 were lost to battle damage, accidents, mechanical issues, and other reasons, many becoming "hangar queens" to be scrapped for parts.[5]

The attrition rate was so high in 1943, some 75 percent, that the chances of an airman completing his combat tour was statistically impossible; he knew he would be killed, wounded, or captured long before he and his crewmates reached twenty-five missions. The strain on these crews was terrible. Imagine, for one moment, perhaps in 1943, the worst year for the 8th Air Force, climbing aboard a thin-skinned aluminum tube with limited armor. The pilots sat in chairs with some extra protection, but not the gunners, not the bombardier, not the navigator. The ball turret gunner sat with his ass hanging suspended in mid-air, totally exposed beneath the belly of the plane, the earth sliding beneath him, 25,000 feet below. Duty in the ball turret had to have been terrifying and was one of the most dangerous places to be in a B-17. After the Luftwaffe developed the head-on assault tactic, the cockpit became the most dangerous location on a bomber. Even after the P-51 was deployed to escort the bomber streams, and the odds of the crews meeting their tour obligations improved, but too many, like the *Lady Jane II*, failed to return.

Day after day the pilots and flight engineer would meet with their crew chiefs on the ground for a pre-flight check of the aircraft. The gunners would check out their .50-cal. guns from the armory, inspect, and install them at their firing positions. The bombardier (or togglier) would work with the groundcrew to load the bombs onboard and arm them once they were winched aboard in the shackles. The navigator would make sure all his maps were current; he made sure he that had the latest flak map, and the navigator's briefing he had just attended was matched against his charts. The ball turret gunner climbed inside the tiny sphere and tested the electronics, making sure everything was turning and responding readily to the foot controls. The entire crew worked together to make sure their bird, their baby, was in tip-top shape and could bring them home again.

One thing the crewmen tried, desperately, not to do was to think about what *might* happen, what could happen during the mission. They wanted to think that the direct flak hit, the strike by 20 mm cannon rounds to the engines, the fireball of rending death from a rocket, the head-on clash with Luftwaffe fighters spewing deadly rounds into the cockpit would happen to someone else, some other plane… not to *their* bomber, not *their* crew… but to *someone else*. They occupied their time readying their flight and tried to push these terrible thoughts away. They had a job to do, each one of them. One man, part of a team, part of a whole. Each and every crewmember, regardless of the size of the bomb group, was an intricate piece of this entire construct that was the Mighty 8th Air Force.

Every bomber mattered. Every crewman mattered. If just *one man* failed to do his duty, more lives would be at risk. If one gunner froze up mentally as a Fw 190 screamed into his firing line and he failed to discharge his weapon to protect his bomber and the ones in formation next to him, he risked a much-greater consequence than just killing his friends. If his plane was shot down by inaction, and the bombers in the three-plane formation he was flying in were also lost by his lack of response, then it was the loss of at least 12,000 pounds of bombs not placed on the target. The lack of proper response by that one gunner could have resulted in the factory or refinery below not being destroyed or placed out of commission for many months while repairs were undertaken. The lack of response could have risked many GIs in foxholes because they were not able to advance with limited casualties. The 88 mm guns that were created in the factory that was supposed to be bombed were instead delivered to the battlefield and not delayed by a successful strike. That one gunner who froze up and didn't fire his weapon may have killed many of his countrymen just because he didn't pull the trigger, didn't do his duty. Fortunately, such occurrences were rare.

The *Lady Jane II* crew did their duty. They, like so many of their compatriots, fought and died to bring this terrible conflict to a successful conclusion. Dave Vermeer, Milan Basara, Hal Churchill, and Jim Butlin were still very young men. They, like so many of their fellow soldiers, gave everything they could give. They did not plan to give the last full measure; they did not plan to die; they wanted to go home to their mothers, their wives, their girlfriends, their children. Dave would never return to the family farm, smell the wonderful aroma of fresh-tilled soil, or relish the sight of crops waving in a lazy afternoon breeze. Bas would never go home to Chicago and embrace his folks, have a future, and raise a family. Hal's daughter would grow up never knowing her dad except from the recitation of her mother's treasured memories. Jim would never swing his tennis racket again, never go to college, never marry and have kids. They were four of more than 400,000 who never came home.

Their friends who did survive would struggle with what we today call post-traumatic stress disorder (PTSD) for the remainder of their lives. It was recognized many years earlier, and called "shell shock" in both world wars, but was not completely understood. Gen. George Patton was famously disciplined after slapping several combat-fatigued soldiers during the 1943 Sicily campaign to push out German resistance. PTSD was not a wide concern during the war, but Patton's action was considered extreme at a time when Americans were concerned about the daily casualty reports. The incident cost Patton political currency, and Gen. Eisenhower suspended him from leading combat commands for a year. Patton was "old school" and didn't believe in combat fatigue. Even though he had served in both world wars and must have seen its effects, he considered it simple cowardice.

But even the stoutest soldiers could crumble after having seen their closest friends decapitated, limbs blown off, or suffering gruesome wounds while being helpless to save them. Every human being has a limit as to what the mind can process. Every man in combat relies, heart and soul, on the buddy next to him. They grow to love their friends as family could never understand. They would willingly die for that friend, take a bullet for him, or throw himself on a grenade. They were terrified of making mistakes that could get their friends killed, so they concentrated on the tasks at hand, not considering their own safety. It's a love that cannot be explained except by those who have lived through the terror of combat and witnessed the loss of someone with that same shared experience. The PTSD that is suffered is often not the result of three or four years of dodging bullets or artillery shells, but of surviving this terrible loss.

After the war, 453rd Bomb Group squadron commander Col. James M. Stewart had suffered from nightmares while filming *It's a Wonderful Life* in 1946.[6] Anyone who flew the missions and survived the war was most likely to suffer from post-traumatic stress for the rest of their lives. They commonly told their families, loved ones who could not fully comprehend their torment, "I'm not a hero. The heroes are the ones who didn't come home."

TSgt. Robert J. Conley was a waist gunner with the 306th Bomb Group, 369th Squadron. The 306th, famously called "The Reich Wreckers," was dispatched with the 8th AF to hit the ball-bearing works at Schweinfurt for the second time on Thursday, October 14, 1943. The first raid on August 17 was nothing short of a disaster, with sixty USAAF bombers shot down. The crews were well aware of their peril when they were again tasked with mauling this target. The lead aircraft, B-17F number 782, was piloted by Capt. Charles T. Schoolfield. Conley was manning the left waist gun five minutes before the target and shortly after the IP was reached. His buddy SSgt. Bert Perlmutter was manning the right waist gun. All of a sudden, a 20 mm shell exploded from a Fw 190 and slammed into Conley's position, ripping his left hand clean off his arm. Conley collapsed to the deck, bleeding profusely and passing out. Perlmutter grabbed material to make a tourniquet and wrapped up Conley's forearm. Bob came to, looking through the waist window as Bert was tying off the tourniquet. Bob suddenly shoved his friend aside and jumped up to man his gun. Stunned and in pain, he grabbed the right handle of the .50-cal. just as a Fw 190 was closing in for the kill with a flurry of 20 mm cannon rounds slamming into the ship. Bob didn't hesitate as he squeezed the trigger at point-blank range. His bomber was on the line, his friends' lives were on the line. His fire stuck true and the threat exploded in a ball of flame as it passed under the B-17. Bob passed out cold, falling to the deck again. Moments later, Bert was amazed when his severely wounded buddy regained consciousness and pulled himself to his feet and once again manned his gun…until he collapsed once more. Robert J. Conley survived and would be awarded a Silver Star for his selfless act of courage.[7]

Twenty-four-year-old Charles W. Spencer was serving with the 358th Squadron. On November 26, 1943, they were sent with the 1st Division to attack Bremen for the 303rd Bomb Group's Mission Number 83. Second Lt. Spencer was the ship's bombardier; his partner in the nose of the B-17F *Star Dust* was the navigator, 2Lt. Harold J. Rocketto, a green-around-the-gills newbie on his first mission. The pilot was 2Lt. William ("Bill") C. Fort and the co-pilot was 2nd Lt. MacDonald Riddick. Manning the guns were SSgt. Grover C. Mullins (engineer/top turret), SSgt. James H. Pleasant (right waist), SSgt. John G. Viszneki (left waist), Sgt. Howard H. Zeitner (ball turret), and Sgt. Bernard J. Sutton (tail); TSgt. James C. Supple monitored the radio.

Spencer was an experienced flier; this would be his sixteenth mission. But something was different, somehow *off*, this time. The nose gun he manned was sluggish and not firing well; the newbie introduction had been awkward; he left his pocket knife in his barracks room, and with most crewmen being a bit superstitious, leaving the knife felt wrong, maybe unlucky; the P-47s were late in escorting them. *Nothing* was right about this mission. Then the Fw 190s showed up.

Spencer was firing his sluggish .50-cal. in the nose; Rocketto was engaged with the cheek gun as the 190s screamed in from the right. The escorts were miles away attacking something. Then Spencer heard a big "splat" sound as a 190 trained its 20 mm cannon right at the *Star Dust*'s nose. Spencer was knocked back, briefly unconscious; when he regained his senses, he was covered in blood. In the cockpit Bill looked down at the left side of the ship's nose and saw the gun Rocketto had been firing in the cheek go slack, its barrel pointing up; he immediately knew something had befallen his navigator. Rocketto would never do a second mission; he was dead. Bill also had the unpleasant sensation of extremely cold air rushing up into the cockpit. Mac passed out in the co-pilot's seat, and the gunners began dropping like flies as the oxygen ran out: the system had been shot up. Mullins grabbed a walkaround oxygen bottle for himself as well as spares and began reviving the crew while Bill considered dropping out of formation and down to below the 10,000-foot elevation where they didn't need the onboard oxygen system. But he knew the risk of leaving the safety of the formation and stayed with the bomb group at 26,000 feet, at least for the time being.

After Mullins revived everyone, he went down to check on the crewmen in the nose. It was a ghastly sight. Spencer was badly wounded and the newbie navigator had been shot to pieces; blood and gore were splattered around the nose of the ship. Mullins grabbed Spencer and dragged him up to the cockpit, where he tried to put an oxygen mask on him, but the man's face was so swollen by wounds and the frigid temperatures in the busted-out Plexiglas nose that the mask wouldn't fit. Fortunately, Mullin's effort did bring the bombardier back to his senses. Spencer quickly realized that no one was manning the guns in the front of the plane, while the Luftwaffe was desperately trying to kill them. He rushed back into the nose, knowing full well that the cold could, and probably would, kill him as air roared through the smashed nose of the plane at some minus 60 degrees Fahrenheit. He tried hooking up his heated suit but he didn't have a complete set and lacked the electric boots and gloves. He wore what he had, grabbing the .50-caliber in both hands to defend his ship, his friends, his life. (This was before the advent of the nose turret guns. The head-on attacks were the best way to take down the B-17s before the introduction of the G model, which came standard with the nose turret.) The Luftwaffe roared in from the front, trying to silence Spencer's gun and destroy the *Star Dust*.

Everyone in the crippled bomber was suffering from the cold: Bill had problems steering with nearly frozen fingers. Mullins was running around helping where he could. Meanwhile, Spencer was in the nose, freezing to death, but he took no notice as the air blasted in at fatal temperatures and with hurricane force. The bomber was still at 26,000 feet and the cold was lethal. But Spencer ignored it; he lined up his sights on one enemy fighter after another, somehow squeezing the trigger with flesh that had already died. He couldn't feel his face; necrotic tissue adhered to his bones as he fired volley after volley. The other gunners fired their weapons too; the ship vibrated and shuddered as the guns discharged. The ship made it to the English Channel, where Bill dropped down to 500 feet above the waves so that everyone could breathe easier; then they were over the beach and then a grassy field. They landed safely in the field just as the number four engine gave up the ghost. An hour later they were evacuated. They pulled Spencer out of the destroyed nose of the ship; stiff and frozen, they loaded him into an ambulance and took him to a hospital. He was still alive.

The *Star Dust* was severely damaged. That the ship survived the terrible beating she endured was a miracle. Bill Fort was treated for frostbite and lost the ends of some of his fingers, ending his career as a bomber pilot. Charles Spencer suffered far more. His head, fingers, and toes were badly swollen. He was blind in one eye, which was later removed; all of his digits, fingers, and toes were amputated. His face was severely scarred. He would lose his ears and nose as he suffered through numerous sessions of reconstructive surgery. In old age he eventually lost the sight in his remaining eye. He suffered as he did to defend his ship and his buddies. He knew the consequences and stated years later that he never expected to survive. As he prayed to God, he pleaded for life but accepted his death. He was awarded the Distinguished Service Cross; surely, his act warranted a Medal of Honor. But it was not to be.[8]

During Big Week, on February 20, 1945, twenty-three-year-old 2Lt. William R. Lawley was piloting a Fortress with the 305th Bomb Group, 364th Squadron on B-17G *Cabin in the Sky* (42-38109). Bill's co-pilot was Paul Murphy; Harry Mason manned the bombsight; Harry Seraphine served as the navigator. The gunners were Ralph Braswell (waist gunner), Thomas Dempsey (radio operator), Joe Kobierecki (ball turret gunner), Carroll Rowley (top turret gunner / flight engineer), and Alf Wendt (tail gunner). Their mission that day was to flatten the Messerschmitt plant at Leipzig. Before they could release their payload on the target, some twenty German defenders hit them hard. Everyone in Bill's ship was badly wounded as 20 mm cannon fire ripped through the thin skin of the aircraft. Paul Murphy was killed instantly. His body slumped forward onto the aircraft's controls, shoving the stick into the panel; the big bomber began a steep dive. One of the engines was in flames.

Like everyone else on board, Bill was wounded. His face and neck were torn up; he was bleeding profusely. While steering the aircraft with his left hand, he fought desperately to get Paul's body off the flight controls; once this was accomplished, he pulled back on the stick and brought the crippled bird out of its descent to earth and levelled her out. It was nearly impossible to look out the windscreen: carnage from the attack was clinging to the glass, with gore hanging over the gauges. Bill looked over at the side windows and saw that the engine was still burning despite the dive. Bill rang the bailout bell, signaling the crew to abandon ship. But most of the crew stayed put; only one person jumped before Bill came on the interphone and announced he would try to fly the bomber home. The bombardier, Harry Mason, climbed up to the cockpit and informed Bill that two other crewmembers were too badly injured to leave the ship. To leave his friends would have been unthinkable; Bill decided to either land the burning plane or die with them. He bore down, ignoring his pain and the pooling of his own blood beneath his chair. Bill wiped the windshield so he could see out, steering the dying ship west.

As soon as the decision was made to stay with the ship, *Cabin in the Sky* was stalked again; the Luftwaffe was determined to take the foundering giant down. But despite his injuries and the creeping shock from blood loss, Bill used skillful evasion and threw off the aim of the enemy fighters. He succeeded in losing them in cloud cover. Bill continued with the wild gyrations and managed to snuff out the engine fire. Then he passed out.

Mason stood between the two pilots' seats and took the controls while trying to rouse Bill. He shook Bill awake and indicated that he did not know how to land the plane. He needed Bill to do that, somehow, without passing out again. They made it back to England via no small miracle, despite losing another engine as fuel began pinching out. Bill had sincere doubts the dying bomber would make it back to her home base at Chelveston, so he steered her to RAF Redhill in Surrey, some 80 miles closer. RAF Surrey was a fighter base with short runways, but Bill successfully belly-landed *Cabin*, not losing any of the other crewmembers.[9]

Bill Lawley survived and was awarded the Medal of Honor for ignoring his wounds and bringing his boys home safely. His friend Harry Mason was given a Silver Star for his selfless acts to help his ship's captain keep the crew alive on what should have been a fatal mission given the tragic circumstances.

First Lt. Edward ("Ed") S. Michael was assigned as a pilot with the 305th Bomb Group, 364th Squadron, aboard the B-17 *Bertie Lee* (42-37931). On April 11, 1944, the 305th was tasked as part of a maximum effort to hit German aircraft manufacturing targets. Some 830 heavy bombers from all three air divisions were deployed. Included on the menu were targets of opportunity in Bernburg, Cottbuss, Oschersleben, Halberstadt, Sorau, Arnimswalde, Stettin, Pölitz, Gulzow, Zarnglaff, and Rostock. It was a hideous day for the 8th Air Force, as they lost sixty-four heavy bombers, one of the worst days of its history.

Flying with Ed on April 11th were 2Lt. Franklin Westberg (co-pilot), 2Lt. John Leiber (bombardier), 2Lt. Meredith Calvert (navigator), TSgt. Rynold Evens (radio operator), SSgt. Arthur Kosino (gunner), SSgt. Clarence Luce (gunner), TSgt. Jewel Phillips (gunner), SSgt. Raymond Ridge (engineer / top turret gunner), Sgt. Anthony Russo (gunner), and SSgt. Fred Wilkins (ball turret gunner). The *Bertie Lee* was assigned to bomb Stettin.

The mission began as any other, boring and routine until they entered enemy airspace. Then a mass of Luftwaffe fighters slammed into the formation, despite the presence of an Allied escort. The Germans laser-focused on the bombers, on the *Bertie Lee*. They hit her relentlessly with cannon fire, tearing chunks of metal from her frame and wounding the crew. Flak exploded among the bombers and the enemy fighters. *Bertie Lee* began losing altitude, her tormentors following her down, shooting and shooting again, determined to kill her and her crew. Then a cannon shell exploded in the cockpit, blowing out a window and severely wounding Frank Westberg. Ed was seriously injured on his right thigh as smoke filled the cockpit and hydraulic fluid splashed on the windshield. Seeing out was nearly impossible. The flight instruments were wrecked as a result of the cannon fire. *Bertie Lee* was in her death throes as she dropped some 3,000 feet in elevation. But that wasn't even the worst of it.

Rynold Evens, the radio operator, called Ed on the interphone: the incendiary bombs had been set alight; the bomb bay was engulfed in fire. The aircraft was carrying a full load of incendiaries. When the emergency release lever failed to discharge the bombs, Ed hit the bailout bell. All of the gunners hit the silk, as did the navigator, Meredith Calvert. The only ones left on board were Ed, Frank, and the bombardier John Leiber. Ed ordered Leiber to bail out, but John reported that he couldn't do so, as 20 mm cannon fire had shredded his parachute. He was screwed; he would have to ride her down and die with her.

Ed would have none of it.

Ed and Frank were both wounded. Neither one would be able to evade capture even if they did bail out. Ed would not see John abandoned to die alone. He was determined to bring *Bertie* home. He gritted his teeth against the pain in his torn thigh and managed to level out the bird. The fire was brought under control and extinguished, most likely by John. For some forty-five minutes Ed swerved, rolled, and kept the badly wounded bird in the air, throwing off the pursuit long enough to find cloud cover. The three men might have thought the nightmare was over, but it wasn't. As soon as they emerged from cloud cover, ground batteries on the border with France opened up. *Bertie Lee* lost more chunks from her badly mauled body but miraculously she stayed aloft. Ed brought her down to treetop level. Then he passed out from loss of blood; it had been steadily pooling under his seat.

Frank was awake and able to take over the controls as he flew the survivors over the Channel. The aircraft must have been rattling and shaking itself violently with all the holes and destroyed systems onboard. Just keeping her restrained must have been hellish, doubly so for the wounded men pulling on her controls. They needed to get her on the ground, fast, or no one would walk away.

Frank was spying an RAF field near the coast when Ed regained consciousness and insisted on landing *Bertie* himself. In addition to the severe damage to the bomber's frame, the landing gear was stuck and could not be lowered. The bomb bay doors were jammed open; the hydraulic system had been destroyed along with many of the instruments. The ball turret was jammed with the guns pointing downward; there were no flaps, no airspeed indicator, no altimeter. With hydraulic oil still covering the windshield and no possibility of landing via instruments, it would come down to the exceptional skill of the pilot to bring *Bertie* down without killing the remaining crewmembers. It would have to be a crash landing.

But Ed brought her down safely, on her belly, with no more injuries to his friends. He could not have known the outcome of his decision to stay with the dying ship. He could not have known that he would survive long enough to land her safely. He could only reflect that his life was ebbing away with the growing puddle of blood beneath him. Without medical treatment, he would die, but he needed to focus, to ignore his own pain, die if he must, but make the attempt and try to save his friends. As he saw it, there was simply no other choice.

The ship was so badly damaged, it was scrapped, riddled with holes and shot to pieces. The *Bertie Lee* was the very embodiment of the legendary ruggedness of the B-17 Flying Fortress, able to bring home her charges when no other aircraft could have survived such a terrible beating.

Ed Michael survived his wounds and was awarded the Medal of Honor. Frank Westberg also recovered; he and John Leiber were returned to duty.[10] The crewmembers that had bailed out found themselves as POWs, guests of the Luftwaffe until the end of the war. Despite the horrific damage sustained by *Bertie Lee*, no one had lost his life, though much blood was shed.

When the 303rd BG deployed to Bremen for Mission 84 on November 29, 1943, the 360th BS joined the flight. In the bomber stream was B-17F *Dark Horse* (42-29498), piloted by 1Lt. Carl J. Fyler. Flying with him was 2Lt. Robert C. Ward (co-pilot), 2Lt. George Molnar (navigator), 2Lt. James S. Petrolino (bombardier), TSgt. William J. Addison (engineer / top turret gunner), SSgt. George C. Fisher (waist gunner), Sgt. Raymond B. O'Connell (radio operator), SSgt. Ray D. Ford (ball turret gunner), Sgt. Martin G. Stachowiak (waist gunner), and SSgt. Joseph R. Sawicki (tail gunner). Sgt. Nellings P.S. Egge rode along as the squadron photographer.

The mission over Bremen was undertaken in 10/10 cloud cover up to 25,000 feet, requiring pathfinder aircraft. The conditions were terrible, and many of the bombers suffered from iced-over windshields. The bombers following the PFF aircraft found it challenging to see if the pathfinders had fired their flares; most of the ordnance landed miles from the target.[11] Then the German defenders opened up, both from the ground and in the air. An estimated seventy-five fighters assaulted the group. There were escorts: P-47s tried to chase the enemy fighters away, but many of the attackers found their targets, and B-17s began falling to earth. German fighters sent rockets and 20 mm cannon fire into the formations. American gunners had a terrible time seeing the fighters because the Germans had closed the gap by hiding in contrails; the frosted-over windows on the bombers added to the visibility problems. The Germans were able to close within fifty yards of the luckless Americans before shredding the bombers at essentially point-blank range. But at such close ranges, the American gunners were able to send many of the enemy aircraft down as well.

Adding to the mass of fire and confusion, two captured B-17s flown by Luftwaffe pilots tried to slip into the formation and began firing on the bombers.[12] Commandeered aircraft would have been easy to spot, as they would have lacked bomb group and squadron markings. They were apparently not with the formations for long; it is probable that they were shot down either by the escorts or by furious American gunners. The after-action report does not specify their fate.

During the firefight, just after the release of their payload, *Dark Horse* was struck violently by flak. Part of the right wing was destroyed and two engines were knocked out, a third was in flames. The rear right horizontal stabilizer was destroyed and much of the tail was missing. The strike savaged the crew. Bob Ward, in the co-pilot's chair, had his face torn open by shrapnel. Bill Addison was at his station firing the twin .50s in the top turret when 20 mm rounds hurled into the ship and tore his leg to shreds. He fell out of the turret and onto the flight deck, heavily bleeding. Carl Fyler and George Molnar were also wounded.

Joe Sawicki was sitting in the tail gunner's banana seat when the flak exploded, ripping his left arm off at the elbow and sending shards of burning shrapnel into his abdomen. He must have known he was dying. Nevertheless, he crawled out of his position and found both waist gunners collapsed in the narrow passage of the plane. Sergeants Marty Stachowiak and George Fisher were incoherent, bleeding, and each had a broken arm. There was no way they could save themselves. Using his one arm, Joe positioned each one so that he could strap parachutes to each of their harnesses. (They could not fire their weapons encumbered with parachutes so did not wear them in combat.) Then Joe dragged one, then the other, to the crew door and kicked them out into space, hoping they could pull the D-ring with their one good hand. After making sure his friends were safe, he collapsed from blood loss and shock. He had no more strength to strap on his own parachute. He died with *Dark Horse* when she plummeted to earth.

Raymond O'Connell, Ray Ford, and Nellings Egge died with him. The rest of the crew had been wounded but managed to bail out and found themselves POWs. After the war, Carl Fyler found some of his crewmates at Camp Lucky Strike, where he learned of Joe's sacrifice to save his friends. Carl spoke with Marty in a hospital and was deeply moved by Joe's actions. He wrote up a request for a Congressional Medal of Honor, but it wasn't reviewed with any seriousness and the award was not granted, despite its obvious qualification. Carl made another attempt in 1947, and finally in 1995. All attempts failed.[13]

On November 9, 1944, the 452nd Bomb Group lifted off their base at Deopham Green in Norfolk for Mission 162. The target was the marshaling yards at Saarbrücken, Germany. The *Lady Jeannette* (42-97904) was among the B-17Gs climbing skyward, piloted by 1Lt. Donald J. Gott and crewed by 2Lt. William E. Metzger (co-pilot), 2Lt. John A. Harland (navigator), 2Lt. Joseph F. Harms (bombardier), TSgt. Russell W. Gustafson (top turret / engineer), TSgt. Robert A. Dunlap (radio operator), SSgt. Herman B. Krimminger (tail gunner), SSgt. James O. Foss (ball turret gunner), and Sgt. William Robins (waist gunner).

Don Gott joined the Army in September 1942 as a private in the Enlisted Reserve Corps in Hartford, Connecticut. He worked hard and earned his wings, receiving a commission as a second lieutenant in January 1944. The Army then sent him to Hobbs Field in New Mexico to learn how to fly heavy bombers. In April 1944 he was transferred to the Mighty Eighth to fly with the 452nd BG. His first mission with the 729th Bombardment Squadron was on August 25, to hit Pölitz in northern Germany. He had flown twenty-six more missions by the time he lifted *Lady Jeannette* off the runway at Deopham Green. He was truly an experienced pilot and crew commander. His boys must have looked up to him and felt they were in capable hands.[14]

Twenty-two-year-old Ohio native Bill Metzger had joined the Army on October 5, 1942. He trained with Army ordnance units until transferring to the USAAF in March 1943. He wanted to fly. He too battled hard and earned his wings, becoming a flight officer a year later. In August 1944 he was commissioned a second lieutenant; two months later, he was assigned to the 452nd BG as a co-pilot.[15]

The mission went well enough, but when the squadron was beginning the bomb run, accurate flak batteries found the *Lady Jeannette*, ripping holes in her thin metal sides and shredding the crew. Three engines were knocked out; engine number four on the right wing was blazing furiously, with enormous flames reaching as far back as the horizontal stabilizer. Smoke filled the cockpit.

Russ was wounded as he was manning the top turret; with a shrapnel hole in his leg, he was bleeding heavily. A few of the other boys were peppered with shrapnel. But the worst injury was to Bob Dunlap, the radioman. His arm was torn off below the elbow, and he began bleeding to death. Despite a tourniquet being wrapped around the stump, Bob passed out from blood loss and shock. Joe Harms managed to salvo the bombs as Don and Bill discussed their options. First and foremost, they needed to get those that could move off the flaming wreckage that was miraculously still airborne. Don hit the bailout bell, and everyone except Bob, Don, and Bill hit the silk. Bob wasn't moving and was in dire condition. Don and Bill could have bailed out, leaving Bob to go down with the bomber, but abandoning a brother was unforgivable. Bill sat back down in the co-pilot's seat after Joe and the gunners jumped free of the ship.

They would get the *Lady Jeannette* home, or to friendly airspace, or they would perish in the attempt. Bill didn't need to stay; he could have left with the others. The ship was on fire and was obviously dying. There could be no way she would survive a trip all the way back to England. But Don was staying, so Bill would as well. Miraculously, they made it to Allied territory and Don decided to attempt a belly landing. No amount of skill or talent would have been sufficient to save the ship as fate stepped in and decided the outcome. Just as Don was mere feet from landing the crippled bomber, the fire had finally reached the wing tank and she exploded.[16]

Don, Bill, and Bob died instantly. They were only seconds from saving Bob's life. Both Don Gott and Bill Metzger were posthumously awarded the Medal of Honor for their sacrifices. Also succumbing to the incident was the tail gunner, SSgt. Herman B. Krimminger, who did not survive the jump. While attempting to evacuate with the other gunners, he deployed his parachute too early and was caught on the aircraft's tail. He never broke free and was dragged down with the ship.[17]

Dave Vermeer had apparently tried to land the flaming *Lady Jane II* even though there were no crewmembers on board, but he may not have known that. He did know that Hardtack had been wounded. He also probably knew that the boys helped get Fred off the ship. He certainly witnessed Hal Churchill and JJ Thompson climb down from the flight deck to access the forward hatch. But he might not have seen Gene Holley and Jim Butlin bail out. JJ was certain Jim never bailed out. Did Dave also think Jim was still on board? Did he think Jim was wounded?

Dave might not have known if there were more casualties. His number one task as the crew commander was to ensure the safety of his men. Dave's job was to make sure his boys had the best chances of survival by following his training and completing the mission to the best of his ability, thus contributing to the overall success of the bombing operation. Since the *Lady Jane II* was obviously doomed, his family's theory that he was trying to crash land her away from homes is a very plausible assumption. Dave was a man of faith and may have felt it wrong to inadvertently harm anyone on the ground. He may have waited to evacuate to be sure his boys were off the ship. We will never know.

It brings us back to the discussion of the importance of *one man* within a giant war machine that was the Mighty Eighth. If Dave had not kept the *Lady Jan*e steady and under control, he risked killing his friends as they evacuated, or if there were more wounded on board. Like those mentioned above who gave their lives for their friends, so did Dave. Whether or not this was his intention, it does not matter.

It does bring a measure of comfort to know that not one of the *Lady Jane*'s crew was killed or harmed by any action Dave Vermeer did or did not take. He took care of his boys to the very end. Fate would decide their course after his mission concluded.

ENDNOTES

Chapter 1

1. Maj. Gen. Frederick L. Anderson took over as the commanding general of VIII BC in January 1943; Ira Eaker then became CG of the 8th AF. A year later, in January 1944, the VIII BC would become the 8th Air Force as a whole and would disappear as an entity.
2. War Department, *Operations Plan, RAINBOW No. 5* (Washington, DC, 1941), 4.
3. Wesley F. Craven and James Lea Cate, eds., *The Army Air Forces in World War II, vol. 1* (Chicago: University of Chicago Press, 1948), 652.
4. Giulio Douhet, *Command of the Air*, translated by Dino Ferrari (New York: Coward-McCann, 1943).
5. https://www.lockheedmartin.com/en-us/news/features/history/mb-2.html
6. Alfred F. Hurley, *Billy Mitchell: Crusader for Air Power* (Bloomington: Indiana University Press, 1964), 19.
7. William Mitchell, *Our Air Force: The Keystone of National Defense* (New York: E.P. Dutton, 1921), xxii.
8. William Mitchell, *Notes on the Multi-Motored Bombardment Group Day and Night* (Mitchell Papers, Container Number 35. Library of Congress, Washington, DC).
9. https://www.maxwell.af.mil/News/Display/Article/420450/the-enigma-of-the-norden-bombsight/
10. https://www.fbi.gov/history/famous-cases/duquesne-spy-ring. Lang was convicted in December 1941, as part of the "Duquesne Spy Ring." It was the largest espionage case in US history, with thirty-three members of the German operation receiving prison terms.
11. http://www.vo-67.org. "The Last Combat Use of the Norden Bombsight."
12. Army Air Forces, *Statistical Digest, World War II* (Office of Statistical Control, Headquarters AAF. Washington, DC, December 1945), tables 3 and 83.
13. Army Air Forces, *Statistical Digest*, Table 83.
14. Craven and Cate, *The Army Air Forces in World War II*, 658.

15. Ibid., 319.
16. 16. http://www.482nd.org/radar, 482nd Bomb Group website.
17. Roger A. Freeman, *The Mighty Eighth War Manual* (London: Cassel, 1970), 146.
18. United States Army Air Force. *B-17 Bomber Pilot's Flight Operating Instructions* (Originally published by the USAAF on December 25, 1942. Re-published by Periscope Film).
19. Freeman, *War Manual*, 157.
20. Ibid., 159.
21. http://401bg.org/Main/History/Aircraft, 401st Bomb Group website.

Chapter 2

1. Wesley F. Craven and James Lea Cate, eds., *The Army Air Forces in World War II, vol. 2, Europe: Torch to Point Blank, August 1942 to December 1943*. (Chicago: University of Chicago Press, 1949), 59.
2. Kit C. Carter and Robert Mueller, eds., *US Army Air Forces in World War II, Combat Chronology* (Washington, DC: Center for Air Force History, 1991). This book is organized by date; hence, there are no page references.
3. Ibid.
4. Roger A. Freeman, *The Mighty Eighth: A History of the Units, Men and Machines of the US 8th Air Force.* (London: Cassel, 1970), 28.
5. Lt. Col. Roy R. Grinker and Maj. John P. Spiegel, *Men under Stress* (Kindle Version: Pickle Partners, 2015), location 1490.
6. Ibid., location 1010.
7. The RAF aircraft escorting the 97th BG on its August 17, 1942, mission were new Spitfire IX models.
8. Roger A. Freeman, *Wolfpack Warriors: The Story of WWII's Most Successful Fighter Outfit* (Mechanicsburg, PA: Stackpole Books, 2004), 183.
9. Carter and Mueller, *US Army Air Forces in World War II*, Combat Chronology.
10. The rocket-propelled "Disney" bombs were developed by the British during the war and were one of the first "bunker-buster" high-explosives. It saw service in the latter stages of the war.

11. Carter and Mueller, *US Army Air Forces in World War II*, Combat Chronology.
12. Craven and Cate, *The Army Air Forces in World War II*, 264.
13. Ibid., 265.
14. John F. Kreis, *Air Warfare and Air Base Air Defense* (Washington, DC: Office of Air Force History, United States Air Force, 1988), 62.
15. Craven and Cate, *The Army Air Forces in World War II*, 601.
16. https://www.americanairmuseum.com/aircraft/486

Chapter 3

1. Craven and Cate, *The Army Air Forces in World War II*, 309.
2. Carter and Mueller, *Combat Chronology.*
3. Craven and Cate, *The Army Air Forces in World War II*, 845.
4. Carter and Mueller, *Combat Chronology.*
5. Craven and Cate, *The Army Air Forces in World War II*, 338.
6. Ibid., 639.
7. Freeman, *The Mighty Eighth*, 31.
8. Richard Overy, *The Bombers and the Bombed* (New York: Penguin Books, 2013), 144; and Sir Charles Webster and Noble Frankland, *The Strategic Air Offensive Against Germany, 1939–1945, vol. 2, Endeavour*, Part 4 (London: HMSO, 1961), 260–261.
9. Craven and Cate, *The Army Air Forces in World War II*, 847.
10. https://www.501csw.usafe.af.mil/News/Article-Display/Article/2125363/pathfinder-history-raf-alconburys-medal-of-honor-recipient/.
11. Craven and Cate, *The Army Air Forces in World War II*, 847.
12. Ibid.
13. Ibid., 848.
14. Ibid.
15. Overy, *The Bombers and the Bombed*, 285.

Chapter 4

1. Wesley F. Craven and James Lea Cate, eds., *The Army Air Forces in World War II, vol. 6* (Chicago: University of Chicago Press, 1955), 545–546.
2. The San Antonio Aviation Cadet Center is now known as Lackland Air Force Base and is still a major aircrew training facility.
3. Eugene E. Holley, *World War II Remembered.* Unpublished memoir, 1998.
4. http://401bg.org. After-action reports are posted on the 401st Bombardment Group's website.
5. Ibid.
6. Ibid.
7. *Fly Past Magazine* 33 (April 1984), "Airfield Archaeology," "No. 14 Deenethorpe." This magazine article was included in Gene Holley's *World War II Remembered* memoir.
8. Wesley F. Craven and James Lea Cate, eds., *The Army Air Forces in World War II, vol. 3, Europe: Argument to VE-Day, January 1944 to May 1945* (Chicago: University of Chicago Press, 1951), 47.
9. Freeman, *Wolfpack Warriors*, 131.
10. Lt. James L. Meredith, *613th Bombardment Squadron (H), 401st Bombardment Group (H), USAAF, From 1st April 1943.* Located at http://401bg.org/Main/People/Maslen/613th.pdf.
11. http://401bg.org, after-action report, 401st Bombardment Group (H).
12. Craven and Cate, *The Army Air Forces in World War II*, 63.
13. Ibid., 57.
14. http://401bg.org/Archive/Document/Mission/Report/224.pdf.
15. John C. Sites, unpublished memoir included with Gene Holley's *World War II Remembered*, 1998.
16. https://www.americanairmuseum.com/aircraft/2407.

Chapter 5

1. John C. Sites, from Gene Holly's *World War II Remembered.*
2. John J. Thompson, from Gene Holly's *World War II Remembered.*

Chapter 6

1. Mano Ziegler, *Hitler's Jet Plane: The Me 262 Story*, 23.
2. Ibid., 55.
3. Ibid., 56.
4. Ibid., 93.
5. Ibid., 52.
6. Ibid., 75.
7. Ibid., 95.
8. Ibid., 95.
9. Robert Forsyth, *Jagdgeschwader 7 "Nowotny"* (Oxford: Osprey, 2008), 6.
10. Manfred Boehme, *JG 7: The World's First Jet Fighter Unit*, 44.
11. Ziegler, *Hitler's Jet Plane*, 49.
12. Ibid., 95.
13. Ibid., 94.
14. Boehme, *JG 7*, 49.
15. Ibid., 51.
16. Ziegler, *Hitler's Jet Plane*, 113.
17. Ibid., 116.
18. Ibid.
19. Ibid., 126.
20. Ibid.
21. Boehme, *JG 7*, 63.
22. Ibid.
23. Ibid., 66.
24. Ibid., 113.
25. Forsyth, *Jagdgeschwader 7*, 67.

Chapter 7

1. Combined information from Lorraine Williams following her visit to Uelzen in 2013 and her interviews with witnesses, as well as a post-war casualty report regarding Vermeer's death. The report was posted to the 401st BG's website.
2. Boehme, *JG 7*, 118.
3. Ibid., 117.
4. John J. Thompson, unpublished memoir included with Gene Holley's *World War II Remembered.*
5. The *Volksstrum* was a national militia set up on the orders of Adolf Hitler in 1944. It was a civilian corps made up of men too old or disabled to fight in frontline units. Many served as air raid wardens, prison guards, and other roles suitable for older men.

Chapter 8

1. Information per a letter from Maj. Gen. Edward F. Witsell, adjutant general of the Army, to Joanna J. Churchill, dated August 29, 1946. Until receiving confirmation on October 16, 1945, Hal was listed as missing in action and Joanna was unaware of her husband's fate.
2. Bohdan Arct, *Prisoner of War* (Exeter, UK: Webb and Bower, 1988).
3. Hubert Zemke and Roger A. Freeman, *Zemke's Stalag* (Washington, DC: Smithsonian Institution Press, 1991), 35.
4. Ibid., 31.
5. Ibid.
6. Arct, *Prisoner of War*, 61.
7. Ibid., 60
8. Donald Pleasance played a supporting role in the 1963 Hollywood epic film *The Great Escape*, which took place at Stalag Luft III in Poland. In actuality, he was an inmate at Stalag Luft I from 1944 to 1945. In August 1944, he was serving as a crewmember on a Lancaster bomber when it was shot down over northern France. His experiences in Barth no doubt came in handy for his dramatic role in the movie.
9. Arct, *Prisoner of War*, 66.
10. Freeman, *Wolfpack Warriors*, 15.

11. Zemke and Freeman, 7.
12. bid., 14.
13. Ibid., 19.
14. Ibid., 53.
15. Ibid., 17.
16. bid., 35.
17. Holley, *World War II Remembered*, 19.
18. Carter and Mueller, *Combat Chronology.*

Chapter 9

1. Ian Kershaw, *Hitler: 1889–1936*, 369–370.
2. Gregory A. Freeman, *The Last Mission of the Wham Bam Boys: Courage, Tragedy, and Justice in World War II* (New York: Palgrave Macmillan, 2011), 5.
3. Reinhold Billstein, Karola Fings, and Anita Kugler, *Working for the Enemy* (Berghahn Books, 2004; Google Books version), 79.
4. Ibid.
5. James J. Weingartner, *Americans, Germans, and War Crimes Justice: Law, Memory, and "The Good War"* (Santa Barbara, CA: Praeger, 2011), 23.
6. https://www.online.uni-marburg.de/icwc/dachau/000-012-1397.pdf. Original scan of war crimes tribunal documents.
7. Ibid., 5.
8. Christopher R. Browning, *Ordinary Men: Reserve Police Battalion 101 and the Final Solution in Poland* (New York: Harper Perennial, 1993, reissued 1998), 192.
9. Only one body was found with the wreckage, Dave's.
10. Email from John J. Thompson to grandson, Tom Johnson, dated May 1, 2006. JJ also stated in this same email that Dave Vermeer's body was found still in the pilot's seat of the wreckage. He does not state that Jim's body was ever found on the plane.

11. The local Uelzen historian, Heinrich Priesterjahn, provided this information during a private interview between him and Lorraine Williams in 2013. The victim may have been Milan Basara, but since no investigation was conducted following the incident, there are no further details. The crime remains shrouded in mystery.

12. All of the following courtroom testimony comes from the transcripts of the Dachau War Crimes Tribunal Case 12-1813; October 1946, US vs. Siegfried Utermark.

13. Helmut Behn did not specify where the bullets hit, but stated that after Churchill had died, he noticed bullet entry holes in the flier's chest.

14. Enrollment into the Reich Labor Service (*Reichsarbeitsdienst*, RAD) was a compulsory six-month duty required by men, aged eighteen to twenty-five, prior to military induction. During the war, women were also required to serve in the RAD. County regions (districts) were under the control of local labor leaders such as Utermark.

15. Case 12-1813, 149.

16. The Reich Labor Service was an arm of the German army and helped supply labor to the armed services.

17. Case 12-1813, 240–241.

18. The anterior superior iliac spines are the bony projections on the hip bones. Both hips in this region had the skin torn free. The doctor listed the clothes found on the body but trousers were not mentioned, only underwear and upper body garments.

19. Case 12-1813, 76–77.

20. Information obtained by the author from interviews with Uelzen's local historians Heinrich Priesterjahn and Dr. Dieter Zube based on their personal knowledge of the Utermark case. With the exception of the Dachau War Crimes Case 12-1813, post-war written accounts are sparse.

21. https://www.landkreis-uelzen.de/.

22. Local historian Heinrich Priesterjahn conducted a search of the family names in Uelzen.

Chapter 10

1. Zemke and Freeman, *Zemke's Stalag*, 71–72.
2. Zemke referred to this organization in his memoir as "I.S.9"; it is undoubtedly "Military Intelligence Section 9," or MI9.
3. Guards often became sympathetic to the inmates as the Russians and British armies grew closer. Knowing that the war would soon end, the guards were concerned that newly freed POWs could be helpful in preventing their former captors from receiving harsh penalties if the inmates had been well treated. Some guards even had the kriegies write favorable letters on their behalf should the German guard be captured by the Russians. It was called a "Safe Conduct Pass."
4. Zemke and Freeman, *Zemke's Stalag*, 38.
5. Ibid.
6. The British company John Waddington and Co. held the rights to Monopoly and was instrumental in printing escape maps that were hidden in the game boards.
7. Zemke and Freeman, *Zemke's Stalag*, 41.
8. Ibid.
9. Ibid., 27.
10. Ibid., 78.
11. Ibid., 82.
12. Ibid., 89.
13. Hub Zemke mentioned this incident in his memoirs. JJ confirmed in a June 20, 2002, email to Gene Holley that it was his (JJ's) party that came across the tragic scene.
14. This information came from a series of emails, dated June 2002, from John J. Thompson to Gene Holley. JJ identified the women in his emails to Gene, but their names are not shared here in an effort to protect their identities. It is unclear how the dialog between the women was known, unless someone in the Barth hotel overheard the exchange. The emails were included in Gene's unpublished memoir *World War II Remembered*.
15. Zemke and Freeman, *Zemke's Stalag*, 103.
16. Ibid., 102–103.

17. The British and Canadian armies were, in fact, encamped on the Elbe River, 70 miles west at this time. They had halted their advance to allow the Soviets a little more space to bring the Germans to heel. The Soviets, per General Eisenhower's orders, were also allowed the privilege of securing Berlin. Both decisions would be debated for years to come.
18. Zemke and Freeman, *Zemke's Stalag*, 106.
19. Jean Byerly, whom Hub Zemke had replaced as senior Allied officer, had recovered sufficiently from his illness to participate in the courier mission.
20. Curiously, Hub Zemke never mentioned this in his memoirs.
21. Zemke and Freeman, *Zemke's Stalag*, 109. Von Miller had probably been shipped east along with many thousands of other Germans who then disappeared in the gulags. Hub wasn't too concerned for the man's fate.
22. Zemke and Freeman, *Zemke's Stalag*, 110.
23. Both Gene Holley and Hub Zemke marked this date as the day they began the evacuation.

Chapter 11

1. The evacuation of Stalag Luft 1 was filmed and is available online.
2. Aleksandr I. Solzhenitsyn, *The Gulag Archipelago*, 252.
3. Ibid.
4. Ibid.
5. http://www.ww2inprague.com/general-vlasov-and-russian-liberation-army-hidden-true-about-the-prague-uprising.
6. John Nichols and Tony Rennell, *The Last Escape* (London: Penguin Books, 2003), 250.
7. Ibid.
8. Ibid.
9. Fred Gerhardt's story was included in Gene Holley's memoir. Gene had spoken to Fred's wife and daughter after he passed away in 2001 to add his story to Gene's *World War II Remembered.*

10. John Sites's memoirs were included in Gene Holley's unpublished *World War II Remembered.*
11. One of those precious few included a B-17G built just as the European war was ending; it was destroyed in a tragic accident on October 2, 2019, at the Bradley International Airport in Connecticut. Seven people, including the pilots, died. The aircraft (44-83575), owned by the Collings Foundation, was a post-war re-creation of the 91st Bomb Group's "909"; it never saw combat. Gene Holley had visited the "909" in September 2002 when it landed in Wooster, Ohio. He took photos and shared them in his scrapbook.
12. Most of John J. Thompson's post-war biography comes from his grandson Tom Johnson. Tom was very helpful in this project, with numerous emailed data transfers. He sent the author dozens of emails, including ones from his granddad to Gene Holley dating to the early 2000s. Tom also shared many stories Jack told him when Tom was a child.
13. http://www.boeing.com/history/products/b-50.page.
14. http://www.boeing.com/history/products/b-47-stratojet.page.
15. Email from Jack's grandson, Tom Johnson, to the author on January 15, 2020.
16. Fred Gerhardt's post-war biography was collected by Gene Holley and included with Gene's unpublished *World War II Remembered.*
17. In 2013, Rod's daughter Lorraine flew to Ohio and had extensive interviews with Gene Holley. The latter provided valuable information that Lorraine could not obtain otherwise. Gene also handed her a copy of his scrapbook, without which this book project could not have been completed. The author gained permission to use Gene's unpublished memoir in 2015.
18. Lorraine Williams contributed a large stack of Rod's papers and sat down with the author for multiple interviews to relate the struggle she endured to have her dad's service record corrected.
19. Letter from Air Force Board for Correction to Lorraine dated August 26, 2013.
20. ABC Channel 7, Glendale, California.

EPILOGUE

1. *Army Air Forces Statistical Digest, World War II.* Office of Statistical Control, Headquarters AAF (Washington, DC, December 1945), table 67.
2. Ibid., table 98.
3. Ibid., table 65. These figures include all task forces serving in the European theater, bombers, fighters, transports, etc.
4. In 2016, the bones of 1Lt. William Gray were found embedded in a tree in Germany. Gray had been piloting a P-47 when he was shot down near Lindau on April 16, 1945. A tree grew over his remains, trapping the bones in its roots. DNA tests with his family confirmed the identity of the remains. These were extricated and he was re-interred at the Tahoma National Cemetery in Washington State.
5. *Army Air Forces Statistical Digest*, table 102.
6. Robert Matzen, *Mission: Jimmy Stewart and the Fight for Europe* (Pittsburg: GoodKnight Books, 2016), 3.
7. https://www.americanairmuseum.com.
8. http://www.303rdbg.com/358fort.html.
9. https://www.mightyeighth.org/medal-of-honor-lt-william-lawley-jr/.
10. https://www.americanairmuseum.com.
11. http://www.303rdbg.com/missionreports/084.pdf.
12. http://www.303rdbg.com/missionreports/084.pdf.
13. http://www.303rdbg.com/sawicki.html.
14. https://www.mightyeighth.org/medal-of-honor-lt-donald-gott/.
15. https://www.mightyeighth.org/medal-of-honor-2lt-william-metzger/.
16. https://www.americanairmuseum.com/.
17. https://www.americanairmuseum.com/.

BIBLIOGRAPHY AND SOURCES

Arct, Bohdan. *Prisoner of War: My Secret Journal.* Exeter: Webb and Bower, 1988.

Army Air Forces, *Statistical Digest, World War II.* Office of Statistical Control, Headquarters AAF. Washington, DC, December 1945.

Astor, Gerald. *The Mighty Eighth: The Air War in Europe as Told by the Men Who Fought It.* New York: Berkley Caliber, 1997.

Atkinson, Rick. *The Guns at Last Light: The War in Western Europe, 1944–1945.* New York: Henry Holt, 2013.

Billstein, Reinhold, Karola Fings, and Anita Kugler. *Working for the Enemy: Ford, General Motors, and Forced Labor in Germany during the Second World War.* Berghahn Books, 2004; Google Books version.

Boehme, Manfred. *JG 7: The World's First Jet Fighter Unit 1944/1945.* Translated by David Johnston. Atglen, PA: Schiffer Military History, 1992.

Bowman, Martin W. *B-17 Flying Fortress Units of the 8th Air Force (Part 1).* Oxford: Osprey, 2000.

———. *B-17 Flying Fortress Units of the 8th Air Force (Part 2).* Oxford: Osprey, 2002.

———. *The Mighty Eighth at War: USAAF 8th Air Force Bombers versus the Luftwaffe 1943–1945.* South Yorkshire, UK: Pen and Sword, 2010.

Browning, Christopher R. *Ordinary Men: Reserve Police Battalion 101 and the Final Solution in Poland.* New York: Harper Perennial, 1993, reissued 1998.

Caidin, Martin. *Black Thursday: The Story of the Schweinfurt Raid.* Originally published by Dutton, 1960.

Carter, Kit C., and Robert Mueller, eds. *US Army Air Forces in World War II, Combat Chronology, 1941–1945.* Washington, DC: Center for Air Force History, 1991.

Craven, Wesley F., and James Lea Cate, eds. *The Army Air Forces in World War II. Vol. 1, Plans and Early Operations, January 1939 to August 1942.* Chicago: University of Chicago Press, 1948.

———. *Vol. 2, Europe: Torch to Pointblank, August 1942 to December 1943.* Chicago: University of Chicago Press, 1949.

———. *Vol. 3, Europe: Argument to V-E Day, January 1944 to May 1945.* Chicago: University of Chicago Press, 1951.

———. *Vol. 6, Men and Planes.* Chicago: University of Chicago Press, 1955.

Dachau War Crimes Tribunal transcript of Case 12-1813; October 1946, US vs. Siegfried Utermark.

Douhet, Giulio. *Command of the Air.* Translated by Dino Ferrari. New York: Coward-McCann, 1943.

Fly Past Magazine 33 April 1984. "Airfield Archaeology" column, "No. 14 Deenethorpe." This magazine article was included in Gene Holley's memoir *World War II Remembered.*

Forsyth, Robert. *Jagdgeschwader 7 'Nowotny'*. Oxford: Osprey, 2008.

Freeman, Roger A. *The Mighty Eighth: A History of the Units, Men and Machines of the US 8th Air Force.* London: Cassel, 1970.

———. *The Mighty Eighth War Manual.* London: Cassel, 1984.

———. *Wolfpack Warriors: The Story of WWII's Most Successful Fighter Outfit.* Mechanicsburg, PA: Stackpole Books, 2004.

Grinker, Roy R., and Maj. John P. Spiegel. *Men under Stress.* Kindle Version: Pickle Partners, 2015.

Hastings, Max. *Inferno: The World at War, 1939–1945.* New York: Alfred A. Knopf, 2011.

Heaton, Colin D., and Anne-Marie Lewis. *The Me 262 Stormbird: From the Pilots Who Flew, Fought, and Survived It.* Minneapolis: Zenith, 2012.

Holland, James. *Big Week: The Biggest Air Battle of World War II.* New York: Atlantic Monthly Press, 2018.

Holley, Eugene E. *World War II Remembered.* Unpublished memoir, 1998.

———. Video of Gene Holley being interviewed by Lorraine Williams in November 2013 as recorded by Craig Holley.

Hurley, Alfred F. *Billy Mitchell: Crusader for Air Power.* Bloomington: Indiana University Press, 1964.

Kershaw, Ian. *Hitler: 1889–1936 Hubris.* London: W.W. Norton, 1998.

Kreis, John F. *Air Warfare and Air Base Air Defense, 1914–1973.* Washington DC: Office of Air Force History, United States Air Force, 1988.

Matzen, Robert. *Mission: Jimmy Stewart and the Fight for Europe.* Pittsburg: GoodKnight Books, 2016.

Meredith, Lt. James L. *613th Bombardment Squadron (H), 401st Bombardment Group (H), USAAF, from 1st April 1943.*

Miller, Donald L. *Masters of the Air: America's Bomber Boys Who Fought the Air War against Nazi Germany.* New York: Simon and Schuster, 2006.

Mitchell, William. *Our Air Force: The Keystone of National Defense.* New York: E.P. Dutton, 1921.

———. *Notes on the Multi-motored Bombardment Group Day and Night.* Mitchell Papers, Container Number 35. Library of Congress, Washington, DC.

Nichols, John, and Tony Rennell. *The Last Escape.* London: Penguin Books, 2003.

Office of Air Force History. *Army Air Forces Statistical Digest, World War II.* Washington, DC: Office of Statistical Control, December, 1945.

O'Neill, Brian D. *Half a Wing, Three Engines and a Prayer.* New York: McGraw-Hill, 1998.

Overy, Richard. *The Bombers and the Bombed: Allied Air War over Europe, 1940–1945.* New York: Penguin Books, 2013.

Sites, Lt. John. Unpublished memoir; date compiled not recorded. This essay was included with Gene Holley's memoir *World War II Remembered.*

Solzhenitsyn, Aleksandr I., *The Gulag Archipelago: 1918–1956.* Harper and Row, 1973.

Statistical and Accounting Branch Office of the Adjutant General. Army Battle Casualties and Nonbattle Deaths in World War II, Final Report, 7 December 1941–31 December 1946. June 1, 1953.

Szlagor, Tomasz. *B-17 Flying Fortress in Combat over Europe.* Lublin, Poland: SMI Library, 2013.

Thompson, John J. Unpublished memoir, June 20, 1988. This essay was included with Gene Holley's *World War II Remembered.*

United States Army Air Force. *B-17 Bomber Pilot's Flight Operating Instructions.* Originally published by the USAAF on December 25, 1942. Re-published by Periscope Film, 2006.

Wadley, Patricia L. "Even One Is Too Many." PhD diss., Texas Christian University 1993.

War Department. *Operations Plan, RAINBOW No. 5.* Washington DC, 1941.

Webster, Sir Charles, and Noble Frankland. *The Strategic Air Offensive against Germany, 1939–1945. Vol. 2, Endeavour, Part 4.* London: HMSO, 1961.

Weingartner, James J. *Americans, Germans, and War Crimes Justice: Law, Memory, and "The Good War."* Santa Barbara, CA: Praeger, March 2011.

Wilson, Bradford P. *Everyday P.O.W.* Pollock Pines, CA: Storyteller, 2010.

Zemke, Hubert, and Roger A. Freeman. *Zemke's Stalag: The Final Days of World War II.* Washington, DC: Smithsonian Institution Press, 1991.

Ziegler, Mano. *Hitler's Jet Plane: The Me 262 Story.* Stuttgart: Motorbuch Verlag, 1978. Translated by Geoffrey Brooks for Greenhill Books in 2004.

WEBSITES

http://401bg.org

http://www.303rdbg.com

http://www.447bg.com

https://www.501csw.usafe.af.mil/

http://aircrewremembered.com

https://www.americanairmuseum.com

https://www.az-online.de

https://books.google.com

https://www.fbi.gov

http://www.capitalpunishmentuk.org

https://www.expostfacto.nl

https://forum.axishistory.com

https://www.mightyeighth.org

https://www.online.uni-marburg.de

https://phdn.org

http://www.skylighters.org

https://www.lockheedmartin.com

https://www.landkreis-uelzen.de/

INTERVIEWS

In-person, email, and/or telephone interviews, as well as emailed data transfers, were conducted between 2015 and 2020 by the author with the following:

Craig Holley (re: Gene Holley)

Sue Holley-Suarez (re: Gene Holley)

Robert Jacobs (re: *Lady Jane II*)

Tom Johnson (re: John J. Thompson)

Heinrich Priesterjahn (re: Uelzen, Germany, *Lady Jane II,* and war crimes tribunal)

Martha Stone (re: Jim Butlin)

Phillip Suarez (re: Gene Holley)

Wilma Vande Berg (re: David E. Vermeer)

David Vermeer (re: David E. Vermeer)

Darrell Vermeer (re: David E. Vermeer)

Jeris Vermeer (re: David E. Vermeer)

Lorraine Williams (re: Rodney Williams)

Dr. Dieter Zube (re: *Lady Jane II* and Uelzen, Germany)

INDEX

C

I

J

K

R

Z